New Perspectives and New Directions in Foreign Language Education

Edited by Diane W. Birckbichler

In Conjunction with the American Council
on the Teaching of
Foreign
Languages

National Textbook Company
NTC a division of *NTC Publishing Group* • Lincolnwood, Illinois USA

Contents

Foreword

This volume, *New Perspectives and New Directions in Foreign Language Education,* is a special one in the ACTFL Foreign Language Education Series. It is distinct in that it focuses on the more than twenty years that ACTFL and the series have been a leading force in foreign language education and it honors the many authors and editors that have contributed to this series since its beginnings in the early 1970s. Thus, the editor and the Advisory Committee decided that it would be fitting to ask previous editors and/or authors to contribute articles to this volume. It was felt that their insights would bring perspectives and points of view that reflect breadth of experience, depth of knowledge, and the ability to view our profession globally.

Special thanks are due to the ACTFL Advisory Committee (James Becker, Toby Tamarkin, and C. Edward Scebold) who, along with the editor, planned this ACTFL Foreign Language Education Series volume. The editor would also like to thank the Department of French and Italian at the Ohio State University and its Acting Chair, Charles Williams, for providing the funds for a research assistant; Michele Sawyer, whose research assistance was invaluable; and Kathryn A. Corl, who provided many valuable suggestions. Michael Ross at National Textbook Company is owed a debt of gratitude for his unfailing patience with those of us who edit these volumes, and NTC's continued support of the ACTFL Series should be recognized. Thanks also to Geoffrey Garvey of Link Book Development for his careful reading and copy editing of the book. And finally I want to thank my mother, Virginia Weaston, and my daughter Katie for their support and love.

DWB

Introduction:
New Perspectives,
New Directions

Like Ponce De Leon searching for the elusive fountain of youth or the early explorers looking for a western route to China, our profession seeks continually to find answers to difficult questions and to solve complex problems. Although at first glance our quest may seem futile, this perception is not necessarily a valid one. In the face of a constantly changing world, an increasingly large research base, and a new and different group of foreign language learners, each generation of foreign language professionals pursues paths that allow them to reject or modify the old and create the new.

Our professional literature documents our profession's search for answers. The ACTFL Foreign Language Education Series, a particularly important part of this process, has been both a repository for the history of the profession in the last two decades and a vehicle for suggesting and implementing change. The themes of past volumes bear testimony to this role. In her introduction to the first ACTFL Foreign Language Education Series volume (then the *Encyclopaedia Britannica Annual Review of Foreign Language Education*) in 1969, Emma Marie Birkmaier (1) points out the changes in the profession: the expansion of the curriculum beyond the teaching of literary classics, the role of business and government in suggesting language goals, and the growth of inquiry into the teaching and learning process. In the face of a changing profession, she underscores the need for an annual critical review of the field. The sources available at that time (several foreign language education bibliographic sources, occasional surveys of the field, and a chapter in *The Review of Educational Research*) did not appear regularly enough. In her view, the field needed an annual critical review of the field. The ACTFL Foreign Language Education Series was designed to fill the gap that Birkmaier describes.

In his introduction to the second volume in the series, *Individualization of Instruction,* Dale L. Lange (11) places the volume in the context of the war in Southeast Asia, racial unrest and urban decay at home, and the cancellation of

Diane W. Birckbichler (Ph.D., The Ohio State University) is Associate Professor of French at The Ohio State University. Currently President of ACTFL, she also serves on the Board of Directors of the Central States Conference on the Teaching of Foreign Languages. Her articles have appeared in the *Northeast Conference Reports,* the ACTFL Foreign Language Education Series, and *Foreign Language Annals* and she has coauthored high school and college-level textbooks and readers. A frequent conference keynoter, she has also presented workshops at many state, regional, and national conferences. She is currently Associate Editor and Book Review Editor of *The Modern Language Journal.* Professional affiliations include ACTFL, MLA, OFLA, and AATF.

almost all foreign language research programs. Against this backdrop, he emphasizes the importance of the individual student and the need for educational institutions to respond humanely and intelligently to individual student needs. Lange's next volume (12) continues to explore the necessity for multiple responses to foreign language curriculum in view of the focus on the individual student (*Pluralism in Foreign Language Education*). The subsequent volume (Lange and James, 13), *Foreign Language Education: A Reappraisal*—coedited with Charles J. James—provides a critical overview of the field and portends the crisis in foreign language education, a theme reprised by Lange in this volume. Thus, two strands: a focus on the individual and curricular unrest and uncertainty appear as major emphases early in this series.

The need to provide perspectives of the field have also characterized the ACTFL Foreign Language Education Series since its inception. Volume 7, *Perspective: A New Freedom,* edited by Gilbert A. Jarvis (9), provided a bicentennial perspective of the field. Other volumes edited by Jarvis (7, 8, and 10)—*Responding to New Realities; The Challenge of Communication;* and *Choosing among the Options*—reveal the profession's view of language as a communicative act and emphasize the responsibilities inherent in the increasing flexibility of methodologies and approaches.

Volumes 9–12 edited by June K. Phillips (14, 15, 16, and 17) in the late 1970s and early 1980s also focused on a variety of topics. *The Language Connection: From the Classroom to the World* investigated the role that languages play in a globally interdependent world. *Building on Experience—Building for Success* focused on planning, implementing, and evaluating language programs. Imperatives for the 1980s were outlined in *The New Imperative: Expanding the Horizons of Foreign Language Education. Action for the '80s: A Political, Professional, and Public Program for Foreign Language Education* foreshadows the profession's growing interest in policy issues, a topic treated by Phillips in this volume.

Titles through the 1980s demonstrate the importance of programmatic and curricular issues, in particular proficiency-oriented instruction: *Curriculum, Competence, and the Foreign Language Teacher* and *Teaching for Proficiency, the Organizing Principle* (Higgs, 3 and 4); *Practical Applications of Research in Foreign Language Teaching* and *Foreign Language Proficiency in the Classroom and Beyond* (James, 5 and 6); and *Defining and Developing Proficiency: Guidelines, Implementations, and Concepts* (Byrnes and Canale, 2). Topics in these volumes cover numerous areas (e.g., the ACTFL Proficiency Guidelines, proficiency testing and materials development, proficiency-oriented teacher training, research, curricular trends). With the growing emphasis on proficiency-oriented instruction, volumes tended to focus on the teacher and on how and what should be taught and how this material should be tested; the student's role in this process was not treated systematically in these volumes.

The last two volumes in the series, edited by Wm. Flint Smith (18 and 19), focus on the importance of media and technology in the foreign language curriculum. *Modern Media in Foreign Language Education* and *Modern Technology in Foreign Language Education* provide a much-needed overview of how the foreign language curriculum can begin to progress toward the technological world of the next century.

Clearly, the ACTFL Foreign Language Education Series has remained true to its mission described by Birkmaier (1) in 1969: "This Review is intended to serve educators, and especially classroom teachers and curriculum specialists in the field of foreign language education. Appearing regularly, and covering the field comprehensively, it attempts to describe and appraise all the important work of the year" (p. 2). The expansion of this original function is also evident: series volumes have not only presented an analysis and synthesis of information but also provided directions, perspectives, and points of view important to the profession.

In the introduction to her 1979 volume, Phillips (16) described the political and social context in which foreign language instruction was taking place:

> The present scene in foreign language education is often bleak. Enroll-ments, if not shrinking, are described euphemistically as "no longer showing an increase in the rate of decline." The lack of foreign language expertise in this country is evident in news items from international affairs to campus governments. (p. 2)

She also mentions the "splash of editorials for more and better foreign language study" (p. 2) that fill various journals and newspapers.

Fortunately, the profession ends the eighties with support from an increasing number of groups and agencies. Yet the differences between the beginning of the eighties and the beginning of the nineties are striking. Enrollments are generally on the upswing; business and corporate interest in languages is increasing; our public advocacy group, the Joint National Committee for Languages, regularly brings policy issues to the attention of politicians in Washington; the states are proactive in determining the course of language study; and even our teacher shortage crisis is indicative of growth in the profession.

This is not to say that all is well. We still need to protect ourselves against bandwagons and idiosyncratic approaches to language learning; we need to persevere in our attempts to have an effect on language policy and planning; we need to find out how to respond better to student affective and cognitive needs; we need better ways to organize and conceptualize the teaching of foreign languages and cultures; and we need new and better ways to educate teachers. These general areas (bandwagoneering, policy and planning, curriculum, learner styles and strategies, and teacher education) have not always been treated systematically in the series in recent years; thus it seemed appropriate that these topics be the focus of this volume.

Frank Grittner's opening chapter, "Bandwagons Revisited: A Perspective on Movements in Foreign Language Methodology," revisits the theme of his now-classic 1973 *Modern Language Journal* article. He reexplores the bandwagon phenomenon and once again expresses his concern about the danger of those "evangelistic movements that suddenly emerge, capture the attention of many teachers, cause upheaval in methods and materials, and then—just as suddenly—

fade from view." As Grittner notes wryly, new bandwagons have appeared to replace those discussed earlier. He suggests that these bandwagons flourish in part because of the lack of standardization in American education and as a result of our traditions of local control of education and decentralization of authority. Also partly to blame is a void in leadership and direction. In his clear descriptions of the many methods and movements that have served as bandwagons throughout the past century, Grittner delineates the characteristics of each, touching on topics such as the role of grammar, language skill development, classroom atmosphere, error correction, and culture. His excellent historical perspectives show how these movements and methods have changed the course of language teaching. He also demonstrates that today's concerns and techniques (grouping, error correction, total physical response) are not really unique or of our own invention. Instead, they are modifications and reconfigurations of earlier ideas and philosophies. As the profession moves into the 1990s, it is worthwhile to take a hard look at where we are and where we have been. Grittner's insightful review provides us that perspective and we would do well to follow his advice and avoid thoughtless adherence to bandwagons of any sort.

June Phillips's overview of planning and policy issues as they relate to language instruction is particularly appropriate and important as the profession moves into the 1990s. She begins by describing the opposing views and philosophies that differentiate those who seek to encourage language learning at all levels and those who attempt to mandate English as the only official U.S. language. In reviewing policy and planning issues, Phillips notes that languages in this country have not profited from deliberate and concentrated planning efforts; instead, "the changing tides of economic, social, and political pressures have influenced whether English has been actively or passively promoted, whether foreign language study has been advocated or ignored, and whether ethnic languages have been preserved, protected, or abolished." Phillips's description of these "shifting winds" bring to mind Grittner's observation about the relationship between leadership voids and bandwagons. Phillips goes on to examine present and past federal and state actions that relate to language policy (the National Defense Education Act, Title VII of th Elementary and Secondary Education Act), and she addresses the increasingly i nportant role of business and commerce in language education. She also discusses the importance of states, acting through their boards of education, in determining the amount and content of language instruction; of particular interest is table 2-3, in which Phillips outlines both elementary/ secondary and college requirements in more than forty states. Other important issues treated in her chapter are nontraditional majors and programs, language centers, enrollment trends, and the input of language professionals on policy issues, in particular the important role of the Joint National Committee for Languages. It is clear from Phillips's excellent article that language policy and planning issues have not been at the forefront of our thinking. Phillips also underlines the problems inherent in both implicit and explicit language policy and planning. Given our educational and political traditions, it would seem important that we strike a balance between the dangers of implicit or ad hoc policy decisions and the potential rigidity imposed by explicit policy and planning.

Dale L. Lange approaches the issue of curriculum building in his chapter, "Sketching the Crisis and Exploring Different Perspectives in Foreign Language Curriculum." Like Jarvis and Taylor, Lange believes that education in general and foreign language in particular are experiencing a crisis. The crisis in foreign language education, according to Lange, is more internal; and he relates our plight to Joseph J. Schwab's six flights, to which Lange adds a seventh. The use of Schwab's flights provides a provocative framework on which to build a convincing case to support his hypothesis. Lange's discussion of the current curricular crisis takes the reader through a careful examination of our relationship to psychology and linguistics; the simplistic way in which we often apply theory to practice; the role of metatheory; the tendency to observe, review the past, and critique others; the repetitive and cyclical nature of our field; the contentious debates that often mark our journals and conferences; and finally the plight of professionals so overwhelmed by the daily demands of their work that they have little time for professional growth. Lange also provides insightful suggestions about the nature and purpose of curriculum and describes a threefold categorization of the area (scientific-technical, also known as empirical-analytical; practical or hermeneutic inquiry; and finally emancipatory inquiry) and shows the relationship of these three areas to future directions in foreign language education.

Vicki Galloway and Angela Labarca, in their chapter "From Student to Learner: Style, Process, and Strategy," provide an important focus for this volume. They return us to our natural point of departure for professional discussions, debates, and dilemmas: the student and his or her relationship to the teaching-learning process. Like Lange, they focus on the importance of the student as a person. For Galloway and Labarca, the "new perspectives" of the title of this volume refers to a renewed emphasis on the learner and learning and less concentration on the teacher and the act of teaching. The first portion of their chapter deals with learning styles, that "set of biological or developmental characteristics, preferences, and tendencies that affect *how*—not how well—one learns. The second section focuses on the teaching-learning process and examines the contributions of learning theory and cognitive and educational psychology to our understanding of language teaching and learning. They do not simply review this literature but find new directions that can "facilitate learning through teaching and materials that are first and foremost 'learner friendly.'" In the final section, Galloway and Labarca examine the complex area of learner strategies and their relationship to the student's ability to learn another language.

In their provocative chapter "Reforming Foreign and Second Language Teacher Education," Gilbert A. Jarvis and Sheryl V. Taylor discuss why teacher education should be accorded special status as we examine curricular issues in the 1990s. The authors note that a new conceptualization of teacher education is emerging, and for that reason their chapter focuses on the future and the definition of new roles and major revisions in teacher-education programs. Of particular note are the commission and panel reports that have influenced teacher-education reform in recent years (e.g., the Holmes and Carnegie reports).

Jarvis and Taylor juxtapose the challenging goals of these reports with the realities faced by the practicing teacher (e.g., low salaries, low standards, teacher shortages) and criticize the minimal knowledge base in foreign language education, one that is far too dependent on "craft knowledge and proposed conceptualizations." A large portion of the chapter is devoted to "modern conceptions of teaching," with a particular focus on the contributions of Lee S. Shulman, whose conceptualization of teaching focuses on comprehension and reasoning, transformation, and reflection. New roles for teachers, both inservice and preservice, are discussed, and ideas for the reform of foreign language teacher education and a relevant knowledge base for such reforms are presented by the authors.

The analyses and insights provided by the authors of the articles in this volume will provide an impetus and point of departure for working through what ACTFL has called the "Priorities Process" in the 1990s. This volume and subsequent ones, along with the results of discussions of priorities and publications on the topic, will enable us to move into the next century with new perspectives and new directions that capitalize on the best of the past and establish challenging goals for the twenty-first century.

References, Introduction

1. Birkmaier, Emma M., ed. *Foreign Language Education: An Overview.* The ACTFL Foreign Language Education Series, vol. 1. Lincolnwood, IL: National Textbook Company, 1969.
2. Byrnes, Heidi, and Michael Canale, eds. *Defining and Developing Proficiency: Guidelines, Implementations, and Concepts.* The ACTFL Foreign Language Education Series, vol. 17. Lincolnwood, IL: National Textbook Company, 1986.
3. Higgs, Theodore V., ed. *Curriculum, Competence, and the Foreign Language Teacher.* The ACTFL Foreign Language Education Series, vol. 13. Lincolnwood, IL: National Textbook Company, 1981.
4. _____, ed. *Teaching for Proficiency, the Organizing Principle.* The ACTFL Foreign Language Education Series, vol. 15. Lincolnwood, IL: National Textbook Company, 1983.
5. James, Charles J., ed. *Practical Applications of Research in Foreign Language Teaching.* The ACTFL Foreign Language Education Series, vol. 14. Lincolnwood, IL: National Textbook Company, 1982.
6. _____, ed. *Foreign Language Proficiency in the Classroom and Beyond.* The ACTFL Foreign Language Education Series, vol. 16. Lincolnwood, IL: National Textbook Company, 1984.
7. Jarvis, Gilbert A., ed. *Responding to New Realities.* The ACTFL Foreign Language Education Series, vol. 5. Lincolnwood, IL: National Textbook Company, 1973.
8. _____, ed. *The Challenge of Communication.* The ACTFL Foreign Language Education Series, vol. 6. Lincolnwood, IL: National Textbook Company, 1974.
9. _____, ed. *Perspective: A New Freedom.* The ACTFL Foreign Language Education Series, vol. 7. Lincolnwood, IL: National Textbook Company, 1975.
10. _____, and Alice C. Omaggio, eds. *An Integrative Approach to Foreign Language Teaching: Choosing among the Options.* The ACTFL Foreign Language Education Series, vol. 8. Lincolnwood, IL: National Textbook Company, 1976.
11. Lange, Dale L., ed. *Individualization of Instruction.* The ACTFL Foreign Language Education Series, vol. 2. Lincolnwood, IL: National Textbook Company, 1970.
12. _____, ed. *Pluralism in Foreign Language Education.* The ACTFL Foreign Language Education Series, vol. 3. Lincolnwood, IL: National Textbook Company, 1971.

13. _____, and Charles J. James, eds. *Foreign Language Education: A Reappraisal.* The ACTFL Foreign Language Education Series, vol. 4. Lincolnwood, IL: National Textbook Company, 1972.
14. Phillips, June K., ed. *The Language Connection: From the Classroom to the World.* The ACTFL Foreign Language Education Series, vol. 9. Lincolnwood, IL: National Textbook Company, 1977.
15. _____, ed. *Building on Experience—Building for Success.* The ACTFL Foreign Language Education Series, vol. 10. Lincolnwood, IL: National Textbook Company, 1978.
16. _____, ed. *The New Imperative: Expanding the Horizons of Foreign Language Education.* The ACTFL Foreign Language Education Series, vol. 11. Lincolnwood, IL: National Textbook Company, 1979.
17. _____, ed. *Action for the '80s: A Political, Professional, and Public Program for Foreign Language Education.* The ACTFL Foreign Language Education Series, vol. 12. Lincolnwood, IL: National Textbook Company, 1980.
18. Smith, Wm. Flint, ed. *Modern Media in Foreign Language Education: Theory and Implementation.* The ACTFL Foreign Language Education Series, vol. 18. Lincolnwood, IL: National Textbook Company, 1987.
19. _____, ed. *Modern Technology in Foreign Language Education: Applications and Projects.* The ACTFL Foreign Language Education Series, vol. 19. Lincolnwood, IL: National TextbookCompany, 1988.

1

Bandwagons Revisited: A Perspective on Movements in Foreign Language Education

Frank M. Grittner
Wisconsin Department of Public Instruction

Introduction

Through most of the history of foreign language teaching in America there has been concern in the profession about evangelistic movements that suddenly emerge, capture the attention of many teachers, cause an upheaval in methods and materials, and then—just as suddenly—fade from view. In the 1970s language teachers had to cope with bandwagons from outside the profession that aimed at completely changing the content, purpose, values, and evaluation of the teaching of foreign languages. In fact, in 1973 the author wrote an editorial on the limitations of the then current bandwagons, which appeared under such labels as "accountability," "career education," and "modern humanism" (21). At this time language enrollments were declining, the language laboratory had been called "education's Edsel," and educators were pressuring teachers to be "accountable" by stating their goals in terms of measurable, observable student behaviors. Since the 1970s, the ill-defined career education bandwagon was been largely absorbed into movements identified by titles such as "global education" and "international education." In addition, more holistic approaches to testing and goal setting have largely supplanted behavioral objectives.

Frank Grittner (Ph.D., University of Wisconsin) has served as State Supervisor of Foreign Languages in Wisconsin for the past twenty-nine years. Before that he taught high school German, Spanish, and English for eight years; he has also given graduate courses in foreign language pedagogy at the University of Wisconsin during summer programs in the 1970s and 1980s. He has authored two books on foreign language methodology and has written a number of articles and chapters on foreign language teaching. In 1975 he served as President of ACTFL and was elected President of AATG in 1984.

Currently, most languages are experiencing enrollment upswings, and outside attitudes toward foreign languages range from favorable to benign. Perhaps, therefore, it is a good time to look at what we are doing (and have done) to ourselves *within* the field of foreign language pedagogy rather than focus on *external* influences on the profession. Accordingly, the main focus of this chapter will be upon methodological movements within the field of foreign language teaching. First, however, a brief examination of the whole phenomenon of bandwagons would seem to be in order. One probable reason for their existence is the lack of any centralized national or state educational agency with the authority to prescribe purposes, goals, objectives, and methods of instruction. Instead, we have more than 16,000 school boards across the country, each with the legal authority to determine the curriculum and the instructional program in local elementary and secondary schools. Some limitations may be imposed, in the form of state guidelines and required textbooks, but by and large each school district (if not each school building within the district) makes the key decisions about how each subject will be taught.

Similarly, higher education is a loose confederation consisting of hundreds of colleges and universities, each largely autonomous. Many of these institutions house a teacher-preparation unit, which hovers somewhere between subject-area disciplines and the school of education. Where foreign languages are concerned, the level of communication between those who teach language and literature on any given campus and those who are concerned with pedagogy varies greatly from one institution to the other. For example, the instructional methods employed by staff members in language departments may vary substantially from what is being advocated in foreign language methods courses for future teachers. At the same time, the state educational agency may have guidelines for teacher preparation that differ sharply from what the universities are doing. Situations such as these create serious articulation problems between school and college and between teacher educators and their cooperating schools.

Bandwagons, then, are a means of filling the leadership void created by the American traditions of local control of education and decentralization of authority. Bandwagoneering is a means of establishing a degree of uniformity in the philosophy, content, and methods of instruction for any given discipline. When bandwagons gain momentum, their principles are quickly reflected in national journals, books on methodology, national workshops, and—ultimately—in the textbooks that are used for classroom instruction. The extent to which classroom practice is affected by any given bandwagon is difficult, if not impossible, to document.

The Nature of Bandwagons

In foreign languages, a bandwagon might be defined as a movement that evokes a fervent commitment to a single, unified theory of teaching. It is usually stated or implied that the new method has demonstrated results that are far superior to those of any previous approach. For example, a brochure advertising a workshop for the Lozanov Method (43) stated that, with this approach, "language learning is accelerated by 50 times more than through conventional methods," and that "memory retention is 80 percent over long periods as compared to traditional methods in which long-term retention is minimal." As in the quotations above, bandwagoneers tend to lump together all existing methods and to regard them as being outmoded, "conventional," or "traditional." Obviously, these outworn methods must be rejected out of hand and replaced in toto with the new, true bandwagon. Advocates of a given bandwagon often claim to have discovered some heretofore unrevealed truths about how one learns or acquires a second language. These truths, it is claimed, have been codified into a system of instruction which—if implemented properly—will lead inexorably to the mastery of any given language.

The main bandwagons of the past century in the United States have generally been labeled "methods," and "approaches," or "ways." Disciples of the method in vogue sometimes assume a cult-follower stance. Advocates are able to recite the commandments of the bandwagon as a series of do's and don'ts: "Do provide a period of prereading instruction," or "Don't allow the students to hear a word of English in the foreign language classroom." The theoretical basis for bandwagons has varied. Sometimes the new method generates its own research, or it may draw upon principles extrapolated from theories and research from outside the foreign language field (e.g., from linguistics, psychology, or the social sciences). Some bandwagons are assigned the lesser status of "movement" in that they are only peripherally related to a comprehensive theory of how to teach.

Concepts such as career education, behavioral objectives, immersion programs, language laboratories, and FLES are examples of movements that are not primarily focused on foreign language method.

Foreign Languages for Children and Other Movements _____

Many FLES enthusiasts of the 1960s reduced language learning to a single notion—that age was the only significant factor in foreign language learning. Thus, programs were set up on the apparent assumption that exposing small children to any kind of foreign language teaching for short periods a few times a week would produce fluent speakers of the foreign language and avoid all the drudgery usually associated with learning a second language. The naiveté of those associated with the FLES movement of the 1960s led to its rapid demise. Many programs were started with great enthusiasm, but without regard for such variables as number of contact hours, methods of instruction, teacher qualifications, teaching materials, and program continuity. Furthermore, the age-old argument emerged once more that adolescents and adults can, after all, learn a foreign language more rapidly and efficiently than can elementary school children, simply because of their more extensive experience and knowledge.

Foreign language in the elementary school has been a problem area through much of the history of American education because of the general tendency to regard childhood as the best time to teach foreign languages. Conversely, educators have often failed to take into account the many other factors that are essential if early language learning is to prove worthwhile. A report on the failure of a FLES program in Buffalo, New York, in 1914 is typical of what later happened during the 1950s and 1960s across the nation. As the evaluator of the Buffalo program expressed it:

> Instruction in the elementary schools was poorly administered and badly given. It consisted mainly of reading a given pensum, without regard to control or teaching of vocabulary. Drill in pronunciation and speaking was haphazard, and a syllabus nonexistent. After six years of this type of hit-or-miss instruction, the children took a uniform examination covering as much as might be achieved in an ordinary one-year high school course. . . . Of the 10,000 enrolled . . . fewer than 400 took an examination for advanced credit. As the report points out: "Measured by these results, nearly 10,000 pupils are taught by 67 teachers in 43 schools in order that approximately 400 may get what they would have been able to obtain under two or three teachers in one year of the high school course." (Zeydel, 60, p. 298).

The apparent belief that young children can profit from a haphazard program taught by indifferently prepared teachers with no clearly specified curriculum was naive in the extreme. Yet it is precisely this kind of faulty implementation that continued to derail the FLES movement through the 1960s. It should be pointed out that the Buffalo evaluation cited above was somewhat unfair in that it judged the local FLES program almost solely on the basis of pupil continuation into the high school level, an approach that would seldom be used with other subject areas. For example, the success of elementary school children in art, music, physical education, and English programs is not measured on the basis of how they compare with high school students or by continuation of such study into high school. Instead, experiences in these subjects are viewed as important to the educational and cultural development of the children. The fact that the elementary school foreign language program was singled out to be measured against achievement at the high school level reveals an important bias against foreign language in the elementary school. There is evidence that well-designed FLES programs can contribute much to the general education of all children. Curtain and Pesola (13) have summarized the rationale for FLES and have shown how it contributes to the learning of basic skills, career education, and cultural enrichment along with other positive outcomes (pp. 7–11).

During the 1980s there was a renewed interest in starting FLES programs. In fact, the State of North Carolina actually mandated such programs beginning in 1987. FLES programs also began to appear in many other states across the nation as "local option" programs. As Kennedy and DeLorenzo (37) have noted, exploratory or "FLEX" programs were implemented in many districts as an alternative to FLES. Immersion programs also appeared in a few schools around the nation.

In the hope of preventing the mistakes of past elementary school programs, the Johnson Wax Foundation convened a group of foreign language specialists and other educators from various parts of the nation at the Wingspread Conference Center in Racine, Wisconsin, in February 1988. The written proceedings of that group included the following hallmarks of a successful elementary school second language program:

1. Considers the makeup of the community and draws on the community's language resources
2. Has support from a strong community base as well as from the school board and administration (superintendent, principal)
3. Is the first stage of a carefully planned foreign language program that extends through grade 12
4. Is staffed by fully qualified teachers—persons who are prepared in the languages and in the cultures associated with the languages they teach and in elementary education
5. Provides its teachers with a range of in-service continuing education opportunities
6. Is accountable, that is, student progress is evaluated and reported to the community
7. Is serious. After-school work is expected, and there is a curriculum guide that is continually reviewed, updated, and improved
8. Has resource support, i.e., there is a wide choice of learning materials available to the program, including materials from the countries where the languages taught are spoken
9. Has a coordinator or supervisor who assists teachers and advocates the program within the school and community
10. Has high student involvement and interest
11. Has strong parent interest and involvement
12. Has contacts and relationships with the university community in terms of teacher training, research, materials production, and the collegiality of academic alliances of teachers at all levels who share a common interest in a foreign language and foreign language teaching (Halsted, 26, pp. 1–2)

Many new programs could avoid the errors of the past by conforming to these hallmarks as did one successful program called the "Cleveland Plan," which survived for decades in the Cleveland Public Schools (de Sauzé, 14).

The FLES experience of the past helps to illustrate a problem inherent in all bandwagon movements, namely the tendency to focus on one or two aspects of language learning and to base an entire instructional approach upon them. As Carroll (8) has reported, there is evidence to indicate that increased proficiency results from an increase in allocated time. Thus, the case for an earlier start in foreign language study could be made providing it includes program articulation and lengthening the sequence of study. To accomplish this would require close attention to other variables mentioned in the Wingspread Report, such as teacher competency, appropriate curricula, continuity of program, and many other factors. For very complex reasons, most school districts that experimented with FLES were unable to deal adequately with these variables, and the results were disastrous to the recurrent FLES movements of the past.

A similar scenario took place with high school language laboratories. Tens of millions of local and federal dollars were expended to place thousands of electronic classrooms and language laboratories in the nation's high schools. Often the hardware was ordered and installed before the schools had addressed such concerns as philosophy of use, availability of software, problems of scheduling and maintenance, staff development, and even quality of the equipment. With amazing regularity language consultants in the 1960s found that the equipment did not work, or, if it did, teachers did not know how to use it. Or, if they knew how to use it, they did not have tapes to go with their texts, and so forth. It was inevitable that a national study would show the high school laboratory movement to be a failure (Keating, 35). It was also predictable that other studies would show positive results when something other than the presence of hardware was taken into account (Lorge, 42).

And so it is with methodological bandwagons: The more popular ones have tended to follow a cycle in which they are initially perceived as the solution to all problems, only to end the cycle being discredited in the face of mounting evidence of failure. Sometimes two contending methods have claimed success on the basis of diametrically opposed principles. For example, the 1980s version of the "Natural Method" requires a period in which students are silent while they receive "comprehensible input." This approach to language acquisition is a basic hypothesis of the method described by Krashen and Terrell (39). However, the "Silent Way" by Gattegno (19) requires the teacher to be quiet while eliciting what might be called "comprehensible output" from the students. Both methods purport to be in tune with the psycholinguistic realities of language acquisition, and the proponents of both methods have made claims of remarkable success in second language teaching.

Content and Focus of Bandwagons

As Kelly (36) has reported in his extensive historical review, most of the methods that were being promoted in the 1980s have surfaced from time to time over the centuries. For example, Gouin (20) had devised a system for learning foreign languages in association with physical actions a hundred years prior to Asher's (2) "Total Physical Response Method" (Hagboldt, 25, p. 13). Handschin (29) has noted that the Natural Method, which enjoyed a period of popularity during the late 1800s, was then displaced by the Direct Method and grammatical methods in the early twentieth century (pp. 64–65). All these contending methodologies have tended to differentiate themselves on certain specific factors. The seven most common points of contention are listed below:

1. Grammar: What is its function in building curricula and in conducting classroom instruction?
2. Nativism: Is the second language acquired "naturally" like the first or is systematic drill and practice needed? Is cognitive understanding important?

3. Language skills: What is the order and priority for learning to speak, understand, read, and write the language?
4. Learning climate: Are affective factors more central to language mastery than cognitive and psychomotor factors?
5. Language used: What is the policy on use of the native versus the target language?
6. Error: How does the teacher deal with student mistakes?
7. Culture: How are the various aspects of culture treated?

Most bandwagons of the past have been built upon these issues. Current bandwagons tend to deal with the same topics, although the terminology may change to reflect the technological jargon of the times. Thus, "listening comprehension" may be relabeled as "comprehensible input," "grammatical forms" may be referred to as "language structures," and so forth. The discussion that follows will examine some of the major methodological bandwagons in terms of the seven categories listed above. For it is the shifting of emphasis on these seven factors that has largely shaped and defined methodological bandwagons.

The Grammar Bandwagon

A major problem with defining grammar bandwagons historically has been the variety of meanings attached to the word "grammar." Grammar, for example, can mean the memorization of forms, rules, and paradigms. Grammar can be taught inductively, deductively, or by drill and practice only. It can simply be ignored as in certain so-called "natural" methods. Whatever the method used, however, grammar—whether implicitly or explicitly taught—invariably appears as a prominent concern. As Bagster-Collins (3) wrote in 1904:

> One generation cultivates grammar as a precious thing in itself. The next generation says, "Away with grammar, we will have none of it." Still a third party says, "Grammar shall no longer be enthroned as a queen, but in the future shall serve as a handmaiden. We should no longer study grammar for itself alone but as a means to an end. (p. 105)

Although the emphasis may be cyclical, one central fact about grammar is clear: It is the most persistent and durable element in the history of American foreign language teaching. Over the past hundred years it has emerged under a variety of names such as the "Grammar Translation Method," "The Grammar Reading Method," "The Rationalistic Approach," and the "Cognitive Code Learning Method." By whatever name, however, grammar has held fast as the central content and organizing principle in both classical and modern language classrooms. In an 1886 speech, the German scholar Calvin Thomas (55) defended the Grammar Reading Method against the onslaught of the "Natural Method," which, according to Thomas, was in 1886 "really nothing new in the history of the world." He went on to describe the "traditional practice" of the day for learning German:

> A pupil . . . is first required to commit to memory the grammatical inflections of the language. For the purpose of aiding his memory in the retention of grammatical forms, and also for the purpose of giving him the beginning of a vocabulary, he reads as he goes along a certain number of easy . . . exercises in German, and likewise translates a number of early English exercises into German. All of this study is essentially grammatical. The learner then takes up some German reader, with which he works for a few weeks or months . . . the aim being to fix thoroughly in his mind the elementary principles of the language. . . . After this he takes up the study of literature, and his goal is henceforth to read German, as readily and as intelligently as possible. (p. 13)

During the first quarter of the century the Direct Method (also called the "Reform Method") was the main challenger of grammar-based teaching. In 1928 a methods text written by Buchanan and MacPhee (7) stated that "The Reform has fulfilled its mission" and "has laid to rest the ghosts of the Grammatical Method" (p. 19). This was merely one among the many challenges to the centrality of grammar as the basis for syllabus development, course content, and instructional approach.

However, another foreign language methods text published a few years later, in 1934, reported the following:

> Grammar still occupies a leading place in the minds of the majority of modern-language teachers in this country. . . . The American teacher continues to devote much of the classroom time and effort to drill in French irregular verbs and German adjective inflections. . . . The subjunctive of indirect discourse still invites to [sic] classroom analysis and discussion; the distinction between past descriptive and the preterit in Spanish still lies on the conscience of the teacher and becomes an active concern of the pupils. (Fife, 17, p. 30)

By 1953 it appeared that things had changed little in America and other parts of the world. As a UNESCO report (57) expressed it: "The teaching of grammar on roughly the old formal lines goes on. And so the children are set to learn the rules of grammar (so called), the parts of speech, the grammatical categories, parsing and analysis, instead of getting on with the learning of the language by using it." (pp. 73–74).

During the 1960s, 1970s, and 1980s an entire caravan of bandwagons in foreign language teaching emerged, each in opposition to the grammar approach to foreign language teaching. Yet, in his visits to schools and universities over the last thirty years, the author found that much of the grammar approach remains intact in our textbooks, syllabi, curriculum guides, and classroom procedures. In short, through the late 1980s, courses of instruction and textbooks were still mostly based on a sequence of grammar topics. In addition, a great deal of class time was still devoted to the discussion of grammar topics, usually in English, and textbook exercises were still heavily focused on manipulation of grammatical forms.

In her 1979 analysis of 864 French, German, and Spanish classes, Nerenz (46) found that "The largest portion of available time in foreign language courses is devoted to the teaching of grammar" (pp. 87–88). She also found that teachers tend to dominate class interactions when teaching grammar and to use English heavily (p. 89). In her 1985 study of interactions taking place in beginning Spanish classes, Long (41) found "that listening activities accounted for only two percent of total classroom time, while grammar activities constituted about 56 percent" (p. 29). Nearhoof (45) found similar results in his analysis of 54 French III classes in a study conducted in the early 1970s in Iowa, Wisconsin, and Minnesota. Grittner (24) found essentially the same pattern of student and teacher behaviors in the analysis of 90 German classes that were part of a three-year institute project funded by the National Endowment for the Humanities during the summers of 1984, 1985, and 1986. Pretest data submitted on audiotape by the teachers clearly showed a teacher-dominated classroom with instruction focused on discrete-point grammar items, mimic-memorization techniques, one-word student responses, and largely noncommunicative classroom interactions when the foreign language was used by students and teachers.

Language Skill Emphasis

The dominance of the various grammar-based methods early in the century was in large part due to the rejection of listening and speaking skills as course objectives by many influential people in the profession. The oral-aural emphasis of the Direct and Natural Methods was scornfully dismissed by traditional grammarians. As Thomas (55) expressed it, "The simple truth is that the attainable results . . . of teaching students in the classroom to speak a foreign language are so insignificant as to be utterly devoid of any practical value whatever, out in the world" (p. 23). Through the late 1800s and well into the twentieth century, disciplining the mind was seen as the main goal of foreign language study. During this time, modern languages were competing with Latin, which, for many decades, drew more students than French, German, and Spanish combined. In view of this, it was not surprising that modern language teachers were influenced by the goals and methods that had worked so well for classical languages. The methodological emphasis in classical languages was upon the reading of literature and the study of grammar. Thus, among a majority of modern language teachers, the reading skill became the dominant objective with the ability to read and translate literature as the ultimate purpose of the language course. Translation was mostly from the foreign language into English, although some translation exercises from English into the foreign language were also used as a means of mastering grammar. In reality, teachers often lost sight of reading and literature, in favor of grammar drill work. In such classes, literary selections were used only as a means of explicating grammar. In any case, conversational skill was not only considered impossible to do in the classroom; it was also considered to be of little importance. Calvin Thomas (55) stated the prevailing opinion when he wrote

The ability to speak a foreign language is a matter of practice, not of intellectual discipline. Proficiency in the accomplishment depends simply upon the opportunity one has had, and the use one has made of his opportunity for practice. It is a trick, a craft, a technique, quite comparable with the ability to telegraph, or to write shorthand. It has in itself only a very slight and a very low educational value. (p. 25)

Classroom Climate

The importance of a positive learning climate was not overlooked by the leaders of grammar-translation methods. In fact, in the opinion of many teachers the development of positive feelings for genuine literary material was inseparable from the final goal of language teaching. Translation and even grammar were merely tools; the real goal was to learn to read without translation. As Joynes (33) expressed it, "the student must learn to think and to feel, if not productively, at least receptively, in and through the foreign language. Then only can he truly know or feel its literature" (p. 41). Thus, in contrast to the affective movements of the 1970s and 1980s—in which enjoyment and personalization were seen as vehicles for learning language—the traditional grammar methods saw the challenge of dealing with the language as sufficient reward for months of drill and practice on grammar rules, translation activities, and vocabulary lists.

Classroom Use of the Target Language

With regard to use of the foreign language in the classroom, options varied widely among advocates of a grammatical approach. The overall feeling seemed to be that "it is nice, if you can do it." As Jagemann (32) stated near the turn of the century, "the extent to which the foreign idiom should be used in the classroom will depend on the varying conditions of time, teaching force, and general and special advancement of the pupil" (p. 175). In any case, the reason for using the foreign language in class "is not that it gives the student a speaking knowledge of it, but that it leads to a more thorough general acquaintance with the language, and a more intelligent appreciation of its literature" (p. 175). This idea was consistent with the goals of the method, which called for receptive mastery of grammar and recognition of vocabulary as vehicles that facilitated the direct reading and appreciation of literature.

Accordingly, speaking and reading the language in class were seen as techniques for reinforcing the learning of grammar because "every sentence . . . will be a drill in the noun and adjective declensions, in the conjugation, in the government of prepositions, and in the elementary rules for arrangement" (p. 179).

Error Correction

Jagemann (32) expressed the traditionalist view on error in the classroom when he wrote: "We suppose, of course, that the teacher is thorough, and that no faulty answer is ever allowed to pass"(p. 179). Similarly, the grammarian George Curme (11) saw error correction in terms of students' written productions and connected red ink on student papers with the pleasure that comes with a job well done:

> At regular periods under any system the teacher himself ought to correct the exercises of all his students and return them corrected in red ink. Many a good man, frightened at the shortness of life, has said: "I haven't time for this, I *must* reserve *some* time for my own development." The answer has always come to the author from the uplifted faces of his students, who look so confidingly at him, young men and women full of latent intellectual strength that is just awaiting a sympathetic touch, a word, to be aroused to a healthy activity for a whole life, which will go on when the teacher's life has stopped. The writer has on his shelf an array of empty red ink bottles that tell a story. As he looks at them he has no word of regret. Now and then a letter from an old student sends a warm glow throughout his whole body. It paid! (p. viii)

Culture

The teaching of culture in the various grammar and translation methods revolved mostly around literature. However, some attention to civilization and to historical events might be included in connection with the teaching of the vocabulary needed for reading and interpreting a given literary work. Although textbooks were sprinkled with pictures of famous people, churches, castles, and other "high culture" items, the people and items depicted usually had little or nothing to do with the ongoing business of learning, which was to memorize grammatical forms and lexical items and to get through the day's reading assignment.

The Direct Method Bandwagon

The Direct Method has periodically appeared as a reaction to the limitations of approaches based upon grammar, reading, and translation and in reaction to the lack of structure in the various versions of the Natural Method. The reported success of the Direct Method in France and Germany toward the turn of the century stirred interest in the method among American teachers who had become disenchanted with the single goal (reading) and the less-than-exciting procedures of grammar-based instruction. Because of numerous modifications in the European Direct Method model, the American version was sometimes called the "Direct-Eclectic Method." The main changes made by teachers in the United States were more tolerance of the use of the mother tongue and more emphasis on reading. Some American methodologist claimed that the "fourfold aim" was not inconsistent with the goal of direct reading of literature. In fact, Handschin (29) claimed that the Direct Method actually provided superior results in reading skill

(p. 74). In any case, an ever-growing number of teachers felt the need for a change of methods.

> Even if reading the foreign language is held to be the legitimate aim of teaching, the need was felt by progressive teachers for a more active control of the vocabulary and grammar than could ever be won through the mere learning of rules, paradigms and translation. The Direct Method suggested that this could be accomplished by developing language material, usually a connected passage, by means of questions and answers. This procedure had long been utilized in the elementary schools, but now began to grow important in high school classes (Zeydel, 60, p. 298).

Nativism

The Direct Method's almost exclusive use of the target language was not done in the belief that the learner will "naturally" acquire the language as does a small child; on the contrary, systematic practice and analysis are needed, as de Sauzé (14) indicates.

> The student of a foreign language learns to exercise discrimination in the choice of words. He senses the deeper meaning of words and becomes conscious of the fact that a language has no synonyms. Little by little, through close analysis of linguistic facts, certain brain cells that control language become trained, and in time the student becomes the owner of a most valuable possession, a language sense, that feeling for correct form, for the exact word, for an elegant style. (pp. 4–5)

The reason for the exclusive use of the foreign language in the Direct Method was to enable the student to discover the grammatical system and to develop a "feel" for how the new language works. Direct Method advocates believed that by interposing English the teacher undermines the entire process of language learning and ultimately destroys the student's ability to use the language directly for communicating and receiving real messages. Thus, the emphasis is upon conveying meaning from the outset. De Sauzé (14) believed that "fundamental vocabulary should be introduced not as detached words, but as a connected story. The unit in a language is the sentence" (p. 9). With respect to the traditional practice of learning vocabulary lists consisting of detached words, de Sauzé (14) commented that this "is about as thrilling and as successful as requiring them to learn a list of telephone numbers" (p. 9). Thus, acquiring vocabulary and even grammar was to be done with meaningful associations. Depending on the particular school of the Direct Method, these associations could be established by means of question-and-answer drills, drama, Gouin series (in which the material is learned in association with physical movement), through visuals, or a combination of such activities.

Approach to Grammar

Grammar is by no means taken for granted by most practitioners of the Direct Method. In contrast to the Grammar-Translation Method, however, lessons never start by having students learn grammar rules. Instead, grammar is learned inductively through listening and speaking activities. De Sauzé (14) notes: "Instead of presenting the student with a rule on a platter, we set up a few carefully chosen illustrations of that rule and we lead him to discover through skillful guidance the relationship of the new elements to others previously mastered and to formulate his observations into a law governing those cases" (p. 13). He also felt that the aural-oral practice "is a purposeful exercise aiming at the mastery through oral use of fundamental principles of grammar and of a connected topic" (p. 16). Thus, conscious understanding of the grammar system is needed.

Language Skill Emphasis

Despite the Direct Method belief that all human beings "have an atavistic aptitude for receiving linguistic facts more vividly, more satisfyingly through the ear," most Direct methodologists advocated the teaching of all four language skills. However, it was clear that "The eye constitutes merely an auxiliary organ, one that should be used only as a second and never as a first organ of reception" (de Sauzé, 14, p. 16). After the aural-oral introduction of material, students were to be systematically trained to receive messages directly from the printed page (without translation) and to express themselves directly in writing, drawing upon the material learned in the listening and speaking phases of study. Direct methodologists were forced by circumstances to compromise their commitment to teaching the four skills.

The near demise of German and the reduction in high school offerings in all other languages immediately after World War I temporarily silenced teachers who had advocated the Direct Method in the early 1900s. In the case of German—which had been the main modern foreign language in the United States up to 1918—all textbooks had gone out of print for several years after the war for want of students. Grammar-reading-oriented books in German began to reappear only in the 1920s.

By 1930, however, German studies had recovered to the extent that textbook author Prokosch (50) could state "Since 1909 when I wrote my *Introduction to German,* I have grown considerably more optimistic in my hopes for the ultimate general acceptance of the Direct Method in America" (p. iii). He also noted that the former compromises involving grammar and translation were no longer needed in the writing of German textbooks. According to Prokosch, "German has recovered to such an extent that consistent use of the Direct Method once more seems feasible" (p. 4). He then went on to outline the Direct Method principles that had succeeded so well in his earlier editions.

First of all, the method required that "speaking be treated as the one approach to all aspects of the study of the language—pronunciation, vocabulary and grammar" (p. iv). However, he still made concessions to the prevailing goal of the profession when he stated that "reading is admittedly the chief aim of our teaching; but even a reading knowledge is acquired by speaking more efficiently than in any other way" (p. iv). He then gave a concise summary of the basic elements of the Direct Method: "Each text is thoroughly practiced, by questions and answers, but *without translation*. Grammar is taught inductively and practiced by speaking, with occasional written exercises. Pronunciation is practiced systematically through the first third of the book" (p. iv).

Classroom Climate

As de Sauzé (14) had noted in his particular Direct Method approach, students "are very sensitive to this imponderable called the 'class atmosphere'"(p. 17). In the Direct Method, a favorable classroom climate is best established through the exclusive use of the foreign language for several reasons. First, students "take special pride in the fact that no English is allowed" (p. 17). Second, the art of teaching is "only the art of interesting, of arousing curiosity, and curiosity is only active in happy minds"(p. 7). However, this does not mean that the teacher should be an entertainer; instead, the interest and enjoyment should come from the challenge of the subject. As de Sauzé (14) stated: "Interest is maintained when the material to be taught is carefully organized along sound laws of learning, when students find in the subject a constant challenge to solve carefully graded difficulties and when the technique of introducing the new elements follows correct psychological and pedagogical practice" (p. 8).

Error Correction

Error correction is treated implicity in discussions of Direct Method philosophy and relates to two areas: accurate pronunciation and encouragement of self-expression. As noted by Omaggio (48), the development of accurate pronunciation was an important aspect of the Direct Method. Thus, training in pronunciation was provided from the beginning of instruction, and phonetics as well as phonetic transcription were important in Direct Method classroom practice. In addition, Rivers (52) notes that although the Direct Method provided an interesting way to learn a language, the focus on early self-expression in unstructured situations could lead to fluent but inaccurate speech.

Culture

In contrast to the Grammar Method, Direct Method teaching according to de Sauzé (14) focused on foreign customs and civilization by presenting readings that "touch upon the life of the people" (p. 6). Thus, early vocabulary tended to focus not upon the literary lexicon but upon the kind of concrete objects and actions that any child in the target culture would first encounter. Authentic materials from the country in which the target language is spoken were also recommended in connection with teaching culture (p. 67).

Attacks against the Direct Method

In 1940 Handschin (29) considered the Direct Method in America to be largely passé because the method erred "in laying too much stress on speaking ability, thereby failing to achieve real reading ability" (p. 68). He characterized the American "Direct-Eclectic Method" as requiring the following kinds of classroom work:

> (1) Great care in teaching pronunciation, especially the first days and even weeks of the course; (2) oral treatment of texts before they are presented to the eye, although reading later becomes important; (3) exclusion of the mother tongue from the classroom as far as possible; (4) grammar taught inductively in connection with oral work; (5) much free composition on matter that has previously been learned by hearing and speaking it; (6) translation reduced to a minimum; (7) use of realia and texts to teach foreign civilization. (p. 68)

Professional literature suggests that few programs fitting the above description, even in part, survived through the forties and fifties. The Cleveland Plan was a notable (and apparently successful) exception to the rule. Given the short, two-year sequence of study in high schools and colleges, most teachers were apparently willing to settle for the reading goal taught mostly in English and consisting of grammar drills and vocabulary lists. Curme (11), a grammarian who had once experimented with the Natural Method, foreshadowed the move away from the Direct and Natural Methods. In 1913 he reflected back on the 1890s noting that "live teachers were then talking about the 'Natural Method' just as many live teachers today are talking of the 'Direct Method.' In every generation we have a new name for our ideal" (p. iii). His years of using the Natural Method had kept him awake nights devising ways to teach German without using a word of English in the classroom. But little by little he decided that teaching through the target language was not efficient. As he expressed it, "Slowly, under the cooling effect of the written exercises of his pupils, the author realized that they knew very little German" (p. iv). He concluded that the advocates of Natural and Direct Methods "entertained their pupils more than they educated them," and that educators erred in putting so much emphasis upon teacher performance in the foreign language because "hard work on the part of the pupil alone can bring results" (p. iv).

The general consensus that the Direct Method had failed helped contribute to the continuing dominance of the Grammar Method. Another factor was the short sequence of study in the high schools and collages. As Handschin (29) stated in his 1940 methods book, "We know that 85 percent of the students beginning foreign language study take only two years or less of it. In these two years the only kind of positive achievement that can be attained is that in reading ability" (p. 145). Ham and Leonard (27) stated, "a thorough grounding of the essentials of . . . grammar" was seen as the best preparation for reading a foreign language (p. iii).

The Audiolingual Bandwagon

In fragmented segments, such techniques as mimic memorization, learning through grammatical patterns, and dialog memorization had been around since the latter part of the nineteenth century, as described by Berlitz (4). During World War II, language programs in the military adopted similar techniques and had added intensive language practice as a means of training military personnel to communicate in a number of then-critical foreign languages. Those who ran these Army Specialized Training Programs for foreign language learning had rejected the Grammar Method of the schools and colleges as being inappropriate to developing the oral-aural skills needed for military personnel. Instead, they drew upon theories and practices derived from structural linguistics and behaviorist psychology. Although there was some experimentation in higher education with this so-called "Army Method," the bandwagon effect was not widely visible until several years after the launching of Sputnik in 1957, an event that gave rise to the National Defense Education Act (NDEA). This federal program provided money to help the United States "catch up" with the Soviet Union in math and science education; foreign language education was added as a third component of the legislation. NDEA provided funds for language laboratories, for foreign language materials, for the creation of experimental textbooks, and for the retraining of foreign language teachers. Furthermore, it supported a doctrine that had many elements drawn from the "Army Method," such as dialog learning, contrastive linguistic analysis to determine learning "trouble spots," and a belief in intensive pattern practice.

Approach to Grammar

In his text, *Language Teaching: A Scientific Approach,* Lado (40) referred to three approaches that can be used in the teaching of grammar: "the older and discredited one of the grammar-translation methods, the newer one of the mimicry-memorization method, and the still newer one of pattern drills and pattern practice" (p. 92). He went on to state that the grammar-translation approach was not recommended, but that pattern practice is most effective. In the recommended approach, connected dialogs were to be memorized, in fact overlearned, and then grammatical items contained in the dialogs were selected for further intensive practice. In fact, the patterns were to be drilled to the point where a teacher's cue would produce an instant correct response. It was more important to "behave" grammatically than to be able to give rules about the language. As Twaddell (56) explained:

Our students have been learning the FL grammar since the first week of the first year of their FL study. The basic sentences were selected to exemplify the fundamental grammatical patterns, and every pattern practice has been part of the process of forming the basic grammatical habits. Throughout the first level of FL learning, the grammatical habit-formation was a progressive evolution through the aural-oral and reinforcing reading practices. Both grammar and pronunciation were learned as habits. (p. 21)

It was assumed in the Audiolingual Method that teachers could guide students through various stages of memorization: (1) recognition, (2) imitation, (3) repetition, and (4) variation. Through all of this memorization and drill work students would eventually reach the fifth stage, selection, at which point they would be able to communicate by pulling material out of their mental repertory of statements, questions, and requests that had been mastered through previous practice. That is, they would theoretically be able to select the appropriate structure, vocabulary, pronunciation, and word order from the vast pool of memorized material for use in the real world of communicative interchanges.

Nativism

As for nativism versus behaviorism, the Audiolingual Method was unabashedly behavioristic. In a bulletin on foreign language learning in 1960, O'Connor (47) stated that "Everyone now recognizes that a language, any language, consists of a set of habits. . . . If the foreign language is to be usable, it must consist of a set of habits which are as deep as the opportunities for practice allow" (p. 1). In addition, the method clearly rejected in the school setting "the slow, natural process" by which the native language is learned in childhood (p. 1).

Language Skill Emphasis

With regard to the four language skills, audiolingual advocates followed the opinions of structural linguists, that is, listening and speaking were seen to be primary skills and, as such, were to be learned first. The written word was considered to be a secondary representation of spoken language. Hence the teaching process should initially provide for teaching students to read and write only that which they have mastered audiolingually.

Classroom Climate

Classroom climate and other affective considerations were not emphasized in the writings of most audiolingual advocates. Language learning was to involve intensive practice and systematic learning of certain clearly prescribed behaviors. If motivation was mentioned, it was generally in the context of rewarding students verbally for giving correct responses to cues supplied by the teacher.

Error Correction

Error was another matter. According to the theory of operant conditioning as interpreted by audiolingualists, students would learn best by having correct responses reinforced positively. As for wrong responses, Nelson Brooks (6) stated that

> Like sin, error is to be avoided and its influence overcome, but its presence is to be expected. The principal method of avoiding error in language learning is to observe and practice the right model a sufficient number of times; the principal way of overcoming it is to shorten the time lapse between the incorrect response and the presentation once more of the correct model. (p. 58)

In some cases, the fear of errors approached the obsessive, as in the following statement by Quilter (51) on audiolingual techniques:

> Incorrect responses must be corrected at once. When a student misses a response or is unable to respond (wait no more than five seconds), it is your responsibility to get the correct response, either by calling on someone you know can respond or by giving the response yourself. Do not waste time going from one student to another looking for the correction: get to it immediately. (p. 7)

Culture

Culture in the Audiolingual Method was considered to be inseparable from the teaching of language. Textbooks for this method often contained cultural notes in English to make students familiar with similarities and differences between American culture and the target culture. The early levels involved mostly information about the everyday life of people in the target culture. As the authors of *Modern Spanish* (44) stated in 1960: "In order to liberate the student from his single-culture limitations, Spanish and Spanish American cultural values and patterns of behavior should form a significant part of the content of the linguistic material from the beginning and at every stage" (p. xii).

Attacks against Audiolingualism

The Audiolingual Method came under heavy fire toward the end of the 1960s. Part of the attack came from classroom teachers who, in increasing numbers, claimed that the method did not produce the promised results. In addition, competing theories that claimed audiolingualism was seriously flawed emerged at that time. Generative grammarians directly assaulted habit formation theory when they stated that language is a creative, stimulus-free process. Language, according to generative grammarians, is somehow "innate" to the human species. Each child comes into the world equipped with a "language acquisition device" or LAD. Therefore, a person does not learn a language through drill and practice in response to outside cues. On the contrary, language-acquisition potential is built into human beings in the same way that flying is genetically programmed into birds. Thus, according to modern advocates of the Natural Method, it would be as silly to drill language behavior into humans as it would be to run birds through flying drills. Instead, the teacher simply provides a meaningful linguistic environment in the target language, and productive skills (reading and writing) will, at some point, emerge. It is simply a matter of activating the LAD.

Criticisms of Habituation.   Reports from classroom teachers tended to give support to those who opposed habituation. According to teachers, students could give near-perfect responses to the specific cues supplied during pattern practice, but their fluency deteriorated badly when they were confronted with real communicative situations, that is, students could produce only what they were conditioned to say, not what they needed to say. In view of all this, many experts concluded that people do not learn to communicate ideas through the manipulation and selection of a repertory of prelearned behaviors. Another problem with the grammar-based curriculum was that native speakers often failed to use the patterns in the way that textbook writers had set them up. For example, students who had been drilled intensively on the future tense found, when they went abroad, that native speakers were perversely avoiding it. Instead, they used the present tense or the near future, such as the Spanish *ir a.*

The Functional-Notional Challenge.   Another challenge to the Audiolingual Method came from developers of notional-functional syllabi who claimed that both traditional and audiolingual approaches emphasized grammatical forms without regard for their meaning, register level, or frequency of use. The idea that learning a language means learning the grammatical patterns was said to be badly flawed. Therefore, according to van Ek (58), there was a need to convert "language teaching from structure-dominated scholastic sterility into a vital medium for the freer movement of people and ideas" (p. viii). This conversion meant that students should acquire everyday idiomatic speech rather than formal textbook language. For example, foreign students who had learned formal English grammar found that Americans had apparently not used the same textbooks. Their friends in the United States did not say things like: "Will you go with me to the cinema tonight?" or "Yes, I shall be delighted to go." They said instead: "Ya wanna go to a movie tonight?" or "Yeah, great idea!"

In short, where communication was concerned, grammatical form often had little to do with communicative functions performed by real people whose use of the language extended beyond the formal constraints of the grammar book. The emphasis on form over functional use of grammar also made it difficult to use class time efficiently. Teachers had no systematic way to prioritize the grammar so that structures used most frequently for oral production could be emphasized and those needed for recognition purposes only could be treated briefly.

Register Level.   A third problem identified by the new syllabus designers had to do with proper register level. For example, after having mastered the imperative forms of many regular and irregular verbs, American traveling abroad soon discovered that overuse of command forms was interpreted negatively by native speakers. In real speech acts, people in most countries use polite circumlocutions to influence other people's actions rather than commands. Thus, more important than imperative forms were foreign language equivalents of expressions such as "How would it be if . . .," "Would you please . . .," or "Could we perhaps . . ."

Such expressions typically are of much higher frequency in daily discourse than are the command forms. Yet the imperative is often taught early in the course while subjunctive and conditional forms are postponed to more advanced levels. This could well be questionable practice in view of the importance of using proper register level in communicative contexts. In fact, considerations of proper register level were to be used in the functional-notional syllabus to determine the use or nonuse of grammatical forms. In this approach to syllabus design, according to van Ek (58), "the grammar and the lexicon is not an end in itself, it is simply a tool for the performance of the communicative functions which are what really matter" (p. x). As Knop (38) has summarized it, "Language learning is organized around speech acts and communication, not around a series of grammatical points or vocabulary items" (pp. 119–20).

Grammar, Meaning, and Context

As criticism of the Audiolingual Method continued, the relationship of grammar, meaning, and context became a more important issue. Discussions centered not only on ALM classroom practices but also on the legacy of the Grammar-Translation and Direct Methods.

In the Grammar Method, grammar was generally taught without any regard whatever for meaningful context. The following translation exercises from Cochran's (10) German grammar book help to illustrate the approach:

1. Nobody was in that large room.
2. My dear friends had seen no one.
3. No one else understood the first sentence.
4. My little brother has little patience. (p. 178)

It is obvious that no one would say things in such a sequence. The only reason for having these particular items is to practice (or test) German adjective endings. The Direct and Audiolingual Methods provided a step that went somewhat beyond this traditional approach by presenting grammatical material in connected sentences. Audiolingualists used dialogs and pattern drills involving complete utterances; Direct Method teachers made use of questions about the material that had been presented in a sense-making context. However, both methods tended to be teacher-dominated. So, even though students were exposed to contextualized utterances, the actual use of language was only pseudo-communicative at best.

"What is the color of Mary's dress?" a typical Direct Method question, called for a response such as "Mary's dress is red." Although an improvement over the traditional noncontextualized examples given above (in that "real world" meaning is involved), the student may not care about clothing colors and, in any case, it would be obvious that Mary was wearing a red dress. So, very little information would be exchanged. In essence, the exercise is still mainly a drill that requires the student to manipulate the grammar in relation to material originated by the teacher, the text, or a set of visual materials. As for audiolingual dialogs and pattern drills, they were almost pure drill work involving grammar and phonology. Unlike the Direct Method approach, students could manipulate the pattern drill forms without attaching any meaning whatever to what they were mouthing. Thus, ALM and its predecessors, the Grammar-Translation and Direct Methods, did not encourage real communication—i.e., the exchange of new information among students.

The Affective Bandwagon

Advocates of the various affective approaches were strongly critical of this kind of depersonalized use of language. Therefore, they tended to focus heavily upon personalized messages as the key to learning a language. In fact, Curran's (12) Counseling-Learning approach is based upon the principle that eliminating emotional blocks to learning is a key factor in language acquisition. In this approach, students sit in supportive group circles and, with the help of the teacher as translator, they express what they want to say to each other. Similarly, the "Confluent Education Movement" calls for students to examine, explore, and express their feelings as a basis for learning a foreign language. As Wilson and Wattenmaker (59) expressed it,

> We've discovered a fascinating thing: That as foreign language teachers we have an exciting opportunity to satisfy the students' need to become more aware of themselves, interact with others, and develop more positive self-concepts. We believe in fact that we have a better chance to achieve this than any other discipline in the schools. (p. 3)

Affective or "confluent" approaches to language teaching added a wide range of personalized games and interview techniques in which students were not only active participants, but were also encouraged to express their own opinions, preferences, and feelings. Critics of such approaches felt that the releasing of emotions often overshadowed the need for some degree of precision in grammar and phonology. Rivers (52), for example, noted the positive values of personalized expression through the use of affective techniques. "Yet all of these activities," she said, "require the student to seek the most appropriate forms in the new language to express nuances of meaning" (p. 89). The fear that students will acquire substandard language forms has tended to limit the full-scale development of affective approaches to language teaching. According to Galyean (18) these fears are unfounded, because empirical studies "indicate that students taught via confluent methods tend to score significantly higher on tests of oral and written communicative competence" (p. 126).

The Natural Method Bandwagon

The new version of the Natural Method had a number of areas of theoretical and practical support that had been lacking in the nineteenth century versions. Its basically nativist approach was justified by positing the existence of an LAD. In this view, communication was not to be learned by drilling the anticipated difficulties (as identified by contrastive linguistic procedure). Instead, the communicative use of language could only be acquired through "comprehensible input," i.e., students are to hear and read material that is comprehensible, but slightly beyond them. As for choice of language, only the target language is to be heard as in the Direct Method.

Grammar

The attitude toward grammar is one of the most striking departures from traditional practice in the new Natural Method. In this regard, grammar is seen to have no value in the process of acquiring a language. Acquisition involves the activation of the LAD, which leads to *acquisition* of the language. This is entirely different from the *learning* of a language according to Natural Method doctrine. The claim is that "Language acquisition is the 'natural' way to develop linguistic ability, and is a subconscious process." Krashen and Terrell also believe that children—and, under proper conditions, adults too—can "acquire" a second language (39, p. 26). With proper comprehensible input and a supportive learning environment, correct spoken and written forms will emerge as a matter of course, as with one's native language. Acquisition is contrasted with "learning" a language, which involves formal knowledge of the language or "knowing about" it. Thus, in language acquisition "formal grammar instruction does not have a central place in the curriculum, but it does have an important role to play" (p. 45). This "role" involves conscious monitoring of one's language use, which is seen to be especially valuable for learning written material where the learner has time to use the monitor function. However, the monitor works too slowly to be of value in speaking.

Language Skill Emphasis

It is clear that listening and reading are basic skills in the Natural Method because they provide the necessary "comprehensible input" on which the method is built. By contrast, "Speaking fluency is . . . not taught directly; rather speaking ability 'emerges' after the acquirer has built up competence through comprehending input" (p. 32). The Natural Method presupposes a "natural" order of grammatical difficulty, which means that more difficult forms will be accquired later in the acquisition process as a matter of course.

Classroom Climate

The concept of positive classroom climate is an important one in the Natural Method. As with affective approaches, Natural Method students must never feel fearful or emotionally threatened. Natural Method terminology calls for the "affective filter" to be kept very low. Interesting material, relevant communicative situations, and accepting teacher behaviors are suggested as ways to lower anxiety levels. If anxiety levels get too high, the affective filter will rise and block the flow of "comprehensible input," thereby interfering with the language acquisition process.

Error Correction

Therefore, error correction should be avoided, particularly in oral work. Error correction is viewed as largely unnecessary because it is "natural" for students to err. To correct errors would raise the "affective filter," which would, in turn, inhibit the natural flow of comprehensible input. Presumably, aversive error correction would also interfere with the "natural" emergence of spoken and written language. Krashen and Terrell (39) indicate that they are concerned about accuracy but believe that "in the long run students will speak with more grammatical accuracy if the initial emphasis is on communication" (p. 58).

Culture

The question of the teaching of culture in its various forms does not seem to be addressed directly in discussions of the tenets of the Natural Approach. The focus is rather on language acquisition and the development of communicative skills. The teaching of culture seems to be more implicit than explicit. For example, the focus on functional skills would imply the use of culturally authentic situations, and the development of reading and listening skills include the use of authentic materials from the target culture.

A Critique of Bandwagons of the Past

This chapter has reviewed some of the bandwagons that have been prominent in the literature over the past 100 years. The prevalence of any given method in actual classroom settings is, however, more difficult to document. There are several problems inherent to all bandwagons both past and present. All appear to be subject either to a "single emphasis" distortion or a "theory-to-practice" dysfunction. The first problem involves taking one facet of "truth" in language teaching and building an entire learning system around it. In this regard, Diller (15) has described several "unconventional" methods (e.g., The Silent Way, Community Language Learning, TPR, and Gouin Series System) and he comments on them as follows: "The problem with these unconventional methods is that they each latch onto one key idea and follow it long and far—organizing things in series, teaching only through listening comprehension, minimizing the teacher's speaking, teaching through response to commands, or emphasizing interpersonal relations" (p. 150).

The problem of moving from theory to practice is the most common source of difficulty for the classroom teacher. Traditionalists, for example, built upon the obvious fact that languages exist in patterns and that they can be described in relation to classical grammars. However, the system became dysfunctional when grammarians extended themselves into the classroom and declared, in effect, that the best way to learn a language is to memorize prescriptive grammar rules and literary vocabulary from which the student constructs language forms. Essentially the same thing happened when structural linguists adapted Skinnerian behaviorism and then presumed to impose the system upon classroom teachers, declaring it to be some kind of "scientific method." When generative grammarians began to influence language-learning theory, the theory-to-practice problem assumed comedic proportions. For their interpretations of theory, various experts reached three different and conflicting pedagogical conclusions from a single body of psycholinguistic theory. One spinoff was the new Natural Method (described above), which focused on the LAD hypothesis. The nativistic idea that languages can best be "acquired" without conscious study of grammar and without drill and practice was the interpretation of one group of practitioners (Diller, 15, pp. 90–95).

A second spinoff focused on the Chomskyan (9) descriptions of grammar. This group of experts concluded that teachers should go in the other direction. That is, they decided that even *more* sophisticated dialog and drill materials were called for. In other words, they perceived the theory as supporting audiolingual techniques (Diller, 15, pp. 88–90).

A third spinoff from this same theory resulted in pedagogical recommendations that emphasized grammar. Diller referred to it as a "Rationalist Approach," which has these basic tenets: (1) a living language is characterized by rule-governed behavior; (2) the rules of grammar are psychologically real; (3) human beings are specially equipped to learn languages; and (4) a living language is a language in which we can think (p. 23). This, in effect, is an updated version of the historic grammar-based methods, which go back to the Middle Ages. From the psychological standpoint, the Rationalist Approach pushes the calendar back past behaviorist and Gestalt theory into introspectionist practices of the previous century, an approach that had historically fallen from favor due to its highly subjective process of exploring one's own thoughts.

One problem in discussing bandwagons is that the more prominent ones tend to overlap. In many instances the difference between methodological schools of thought lie more in the terminology than in the substantive content. Various versions of Direct and Natural Methods, for instance, have had much in common. For example, exclusive use of the target language, the emphasis upon aural work, and the importance of a supportive learning environment in the classroom were all commonly advocated by both Direct Methodologists and Natural Method advocates. Perhaps the main difference between the newer versions of the Natural Method and the mainstream Direct Methodologists lies in the attitude toward learning and acquisition. Those supporting the Natural Method posit a dichotomy between learning and acquisition. Krashen and Terrell (39), for example, hypothesize that "Language acquisition is the 'natural' way to develop linguistic ability and is a subconscious process." Language learning, on the other hand, "is 'knowing about' language or 'formal knowledge' of a language" (p. 26). The authors further state that "It is probable that the study of grammar rules in early stages of language acquisition contributes very little directly to the ability to comprehend the input from the instructor" (p. 92).

In the Direct Method (as in most other approaches), grammar rules and grammar drills are seen as instrumental to developing communicative skill. According to de Sauzé (14), "We recognize two stages of knowledge of a language: the 'conscious' one, during which we use the language slowly, applying rules of grammar and reasoning various relationships as we proceed. The second one, which I shall call the 'automatic' stage, occurs when we speak, read, and write the language substantially like our mother tongue" (p. 14). In summary, the Direct Methodologist acquires a language through grammar drill work; the Natural Methodologist by avoiding it as a prerequisite for mastery.

Rivers (52) speaks for many methodologists when she says that "Only through active attempts at expressing meaning does the student become confident in using the rules to express personal messages" (p. 82). This statement runs counter to the Natural Method hypothesis that meaningful speech will emerge spontaneously after an extended period of comprehensible input. Many other methodologists believe that both knowledge of the rules and practice in applying the rules to express personal meaning are necessary. Paulston and Bruder (49) have suggested that acquisition is not dichotomous with drill and practice, but rather can result directly from it as the student moves from mechanical to meaningful to communicative use of language (p. 5).

A major point of vulnerability of the Natural Method is the implied analogy of its label. Historically, critics of the method have jumped upon the obvious fact that the environment in which a child acquires the mother tongue is in no way similar to the environment of the classroom. As Hammerly (28) stated in 1987, "the language classroom is not a natural second language acquisition environment and . . . a natural sociolinguistic language acquisition setting cannot be reproduced in the classroom. There is nothing natural about learning another language within four classroom walls" (p. 398). A strikingly similar statement was made by Thomas (55), more than a hundred years earlier: "You can no more teach a person to speak a foreign language by means of class instruction given at stated intervals, than you can teach him to swim by giving courses of illustrated lectures in a 7 by 9 bathroom. The thing never has been done, never will be done by the Natural Method or by any other method; and anyone who professes to be able to do it may be safely set down as a quack" (p. 22). In Gattegno's (19) opinion both "natural" and "direct" approaches are inefficient because they fail to draw fully upon intellectual skills that the child has unconsciously picked up while acquiring the first language: "My proposal is to replace a 'natural' approach by one that is very 'artificial' and, for some purposes, strictly controlled, and to use all that there is to be tapped in every mind in every school" (pp. 12–13).

The focus upon the problem of interference from the first language onto the foreign language is questioned by advocates of the Natural Approach. The explanation by Krashen and Terrell (39) is that the student is simply "falling back" on the native language grammar for lack of having "properly acquired" the foreign language (p. 41). However, this redefinition of the term "interference" does not get at the central problem of "fossilization" as described by Omaggio (48, pp. 276–84). For example, many first-generation immigrants to the United States have exhibited fossilized forms in phonology, morphology, and word order. In popular parlance, this is called "having a foreign accent." The degree of severity of the accent determines how well U.S. native-speakers can comprehend what the immigrant is saying. In some instances the speaker is virtually unintelligible to anyone other than those who have acquired the same "interlanguage." For some reason, the self-designed "acquisition approach" often failed to work with immigrants, and according to Hammerly (28), there is evidence that "natural" methods that rely on acquisition procedures also show problems in the area of fossilization. In short, in the Natural Approach, it may be true that speaking and writing may emerge only when the student is ready, but there is no apparent way to ensure that the "output" will be acceptable or even intelligible to a native speaker of the target language when it does emerge. As a result, some practitioners still advocate aural discrimination drills based upon an analysis of the native and target languages. Rivers (52) has suggested that problem areas in the foreign language can be practiced based upon how different they are from the native language.

The New Emphasis: Communication and Proficiency _____

By the early 1970s the professional literature showed an increasing concern for developing a more student-centered, communicative approach to classroom teaching. In 1974, for example, Grittner (22) suggested that foreign language programs be modified to "capitalize on student interests" and to "get students actively involved in using the foreign language to express their own perceptions of reality" (p. 28). In 1982 Birckbichler (5) prepared a publication that contained learning activities that encouraged students to use the foreign language creatively (e.g., role playing, open-ended questions, combining activities, personal reactions to visuals, small group work, and many others). These activities were organized around the concept of encouraging fluency, flexibility, elaboration, and originality, which were seen as "abilities that will enhance a person's ability to communicate effectively in a second language" (p. 5). Initially, communicative techniques of this sort were regarded as supplements to the standard, grammar-based curriculum as represented by available textbook content. They were activities that could be used by the teacher to enable students to make meaningful or communicative use of what they had learned from the grammar sequence. In 1983 Savignon (53) challenged this concept when she suggested that "The development of the learner's communicative abilities is seen to depend not so much on the time they spend rehearsing grammatical patterns as on the opportunities they are given to interpret, to express, and to negotiate meaning in real-life situations" (p. vi). She further stated:

> Where the focus is on meaning, on getting one's message across, it is impossible to remain within the structures that have been presented. Learners will initially acquire vocabulary and then use it creatively to convey their meaning. The vocabulary and structures they use will come from experiences in interpreting meaning in both spoken and written discourse (p. 31).

In Savignon's schema, the ideal communicative approach would be built around topics that are appealing to students. Grammar discussion, if needed, would *follow* communicative activities, and would be treated functionally. For "A person demonstrates grammatical competence by using a rule, not by stating a rule" (p. 37). In short, the development of communicative abilities can begin only with meaningful texts or chunks of meaningful discourse. This version of the Communicative Approach clearly rejects the idea of drill and practice in which the student progresses from rote structure drill to meaningful language use and from discrete linguistic objectives to communicative objectives (p. 29). Instead, in Savignon's view one learns to communicate by communicating, and "formal accuracy in the beginning stages should be neither required nor expected" (p. 24). As with the Natural Method and with affective approaches, classroom procedures should be designed to reduce student anxiety to a minimum. According to Savignon, "Communicative language teaching requires a sense of community— an environment of trust and mutual confidence wherein learners may interact without fear or threat of failure" (p. 122). Thus, student errors are to be treated gently, and, as long as communication is taking place, tolerance for student "interlanguage" is recommended.

Proficiency Specifications and Grammar

There are advocates of communicative teaching who disagree with Savignon's position. They feel that grammatical accuracy has been neglected by advocates of "communicative competence." For example, Higgs and Clifford (31) have indicated their concern about

> the tendency to think of communicative competence in terms of the simplest communicative tasks in the context of sharing the communicative

burden with an apparently intelligent, willing, and forgiving interlocutor. [This] has resulted in the widespread impression that communicative competence is a term for communication in spite of language rather than communication through language. As a result, the role of grammatical precision has been downplayed." (p. 61).

Thus, the question arises once more whether grammatical accuracy will develop automatically (as in Natural Method doctrine) or whether it must be systematically taught as a means of preventing the fossilization of incorrect forms.

In advocating the use of the ACTFL Proficiency Guidelines, Heilenman and Kaplan (30) supported the idea of communication as a curricular goal while at the same time de-emphasizing "the role of conscious knowledge of language rules" (p. 60). In the ACTFL Guidelines, proficiency is viewed as having three parts: (1) function; (2) topic or context, and (3) accuracy. In this regard Heilenman and Kaplan express the belief that "these three components of proficiency are equally important, and curricula as well as classroom activities must be based on various combinations of them" (p. 60). Higgs and Clifford (31) are of the opinion that grammar must be taught from the beginning, and they cite evidence that early emphasis upon grammatical accuracy tends to reduce the problem of fossilization while early neglect of grammatical precision tends to promote it. They conclude that "It is when students are regularly rewarded for linguistically inaccurate but otherwise successful communication of meaning or intent that the threat of proactive interference in the form of fossilization looms largest. Given the profession's goal of communicative competence, this problem cannot be ignored, and must not be taken lightly" (p. 78).

Although the term *communication* seems to imply conversation only, most advocates of communicative competence include reading and writing as part of the entire communicative approach to instruction. However, there is a demand for genuine content. For example, instead of learning dialogs about hypothetical families, students would learn to describe their own family including friends, pets, type of housing, and so forth, or they would write a diary about events in their lives. Using an outline map of a city, they might be asked to decide where they would like to go and asked subsequently to prepare a paragraph for written or oral delivery describing how they would get there. In summary, communicative teaching involves some degree of personal choice, an "information gap" of some kind, and a need to convey or receive a message based on real-world situations or credible simulations of them.

In the late 1930s Kaulfers (34) advocated techniques of this sort, and he recommended that students use partner work to master what today we would call topics and functions that relate to survival in the target culture (Grittner, 23). Nevertheless, Kaulfers sided with those who demand that grammatical accuracy be part of communicative competence: "Do not try to say anything whatsoever for which you cannot find a correct model or vocabulary either in this lesson or in previous classwork" (p. 191).

Content of the Communicative Syllabus ─────────────

Historically, all communicative movements have become embroiled in controversy over the question of the need for phonological, morphological, and syntactic accuracy. On the one hand, voices are raised to the effect that it is not meaningful to talk about communication without paying attention to accuracy. On the other hand, there are those who feel that undue attention to accuracy undermines the students' ability to convey meaning and to engage in discourse involving authentic cultural and literary content. A statement by Kramsch cited by Savignon (54) indicated that the ACTFL Proficiency Guidelines were inappropriate for American schools because "the oversimplified view of human interactions taken by the proficiency movement can impair and even prevent the attainment of true interactional competence within a cross-cultural framework and jeopardize our chances of contributing to international understanding" (p. 5). According to Kramsch (cited in Savignon, 54), communication involves interaction, and "The suggested proficiency-oriented ACTFL/ETS goals differ from interactional goals on three accounts: (1) they focus on behavioral functions rather than on conceptual notional development; (2) they have static rather than a dynamic view of content; (3) they emphasize accuracy to the detriment of discourse aptitude" (p. 5). Clearly, during the 1980s two highly vocal groups emerged in the foreign language community; although both groups believed in communicative outcomes, they were strongly at odds over how to define and achieve communicative competence.

It is apparent that something as deceptively simple sounding as communication has become clouded by the inability of groups within the profession to agree upon such basic items as defining goals, specifying methods, and testing proficiency. Specifying curricular content relating either to "communicative competence" or "language proficiency" is also a controversial topic. Traditional grammarians could at least claim that their syllabus covered the grammar of a given language. To contemplate the potential array of notions and functions that any language offers, however, plus the cultural, literary, historical, and anthropological data that are available, is to view the pedagogical equivalent of infinity. In addition, since the possibilities for curricular content are illimitable, the choice of content becomes largely arbitrary. For example, in the past the teacher could choose a reading passage because it contained excellent examples of the present subjunctive. However, to select material that contributes to communicative competence or language proficiency is less definite in terms of available options. The Wisconsin Curriculum Task Force (Grittner, 23) selected the following three categories as a way to delimit the syllabus for beginning, intermediate, and advanced levels of high school instruction:

Level I: Basic Survival in the Classroom.   During Level I, students will learn to interact and survive linguistically in the target language in the classroom, primarily using memorized materials and functions that recur on a daily basis (e.g., greetings, describing weather, telling how they are).

Level II: Basic Survival in the Target Culture.   By the end of this level, students will possess the listening, speaking, reading, and writing skills necessary to be able to handle simple everyday survival tasks in the target culture (e.g., handling routine travel needs or taking care of their physical needs).

Level III and Beyond: Living and Functioning Socially in the Target Culture. By the end of Levels III and IV, students will carry out all the functions of Level II but have greatly increased the content areas they can discuss. Going beyond the linguistic focus of primarily personal welfare and survival of Level II, students at these levels are beginning to discuss other people, places, and external events by describing and narrating in past, present, and future time.

The Wisconsin *Guide to Curriculum Planning in Foreign Language* contains eighty-eight pages of suggested cultural and linguistic content developed in accordance with the categories listed above. These scope-and-sequence items attempt to mingle cultural and linguistic material. The items were chosen by classroom teachers according to their perceptions of what would interest students and what was important to know for communicative purposes. In each language, supplementary instructional units based on the guide are being developed and field-tested in high school and college classrooms. Although this process is still arbitrary, it does have the advantage of drawing upon practical experience and "consumer" feedback. There will probably never be an easy way to avoid subjectivity in content selection where communicative syllabi are concerned. As knowledge proliferates, we will be faced with selecting from an immense array of alternatives.

Conclusion

Most of the bandwagon movements discussed in this chapter have their origin in the belief that there is some best way to teach, learn, or acquire a second language, and, indeed, that the way has been found, described, field-tested, and found to work with real students in normal classroom situations. In some cases, the new "breakthrough" approach is said to have a sound theoretical foundation based upon the latest psycholinguistic research findings. Yet, according to Ferguson and Huebner (16), "the emergence of a single dominant second language acquisition paradigm" has not taken place (p. 4). Simply stated, there is no single agreed-upon theory to explain how one best learns (or acquires) a second language. Thus, since there is no "one true theory" upon which to base instruction, the practitioner must either select from among conflicting theories or else become "eclectic" and choose whatever seems to work in a given situation. In fact, if we consider the variables that confront teachers throughout the profession, it becomes almost ludicrous to contemplate a single set of teaching strategies that will be appropriate for every age group, proficiency level, learning style, class size, socioeconomic background, motivational mindset, ethnic background, teaching style, teacher preparation level, and administrative support system, to name but a few of the most common teacher-learner variables. In view of the lack of a single unified theory for language teaching and of the many variables, the task force of teachers that prepared the Wisconsin *Guide to Curriculum Planning in Foreign Language* endorsed the eclectic approach to methodology: "No teaching method is suggested for any one teacher, for any one class, or for any one individual. The teacher should be cognizant of current trends and innovative techniques in foreign language methodology, and should employ the best methods to achieve the desired goals" (Grittner, 23, p. 26).

The term "eclecticism" should not be equated with the use of "filler" activities, busy-work assignments, or unfocused games that do nothing to advance the students' use of the language or knowledge of the culture. Eclecticism implies the judicious selection of teaching strategies that are aimed at producing specific outcomes in terms of what a given group of students can do with the language. The approach also tends to be pragmatic in that a specific technique is not judged by its conformity to a particular pedagogical theory but rather by how well it works. For example, if a drill that is based on articulatory phonetics helps a student to eliminate a persistent pronunciation error, then the teacher will use it without worrying about whether the technique is consistent with some particular acquisition or learning theory. The ACTFL Proficiency Guidelines reflect a similar philosophy in that student outcomes are specified rather than the methods one should use to achieve them. Heilenman and Kaplan (30) believe that "A proficiency-based curriculum is eclectic. It starts with outcomes; it does not prescribe practices" (p. 62). Part of the rationale for this contention is that students need different methodologies for different levels of proficiency. Thus, structural drill work may be appropriate at the beginning levels, while a notional-functional syllabus implemented with communicative techniques may be suitable for the advanced levels. Any single method imposed at all levels would be considered inappropriate. Heilenman and Kaplan state further that "this suggests a rationally based eclecticism in which instructors pick and choose among the available methods, approaches, and techniques on the basis of their effectiveness at each given level" (p. 62).

The trouble with the eclectic approach is that its success requires constant experimentation and validation by the classroom teacher, who must monitor the progress of students with respect to program goals in order to determine the effectiveness of each classroom strategy. A teacher with five or six large classes daily may well be intimidated by such demands. Thus, it is tempting to jump on the newest bandwagon (which may well be a very old bandwagon embellished with contemporary jargon). Bandwagons are attractive because it is reassuring to believe that someone has discovered a simple, magic way to teach a foreign language. The teacher can feel reassured in the belief that a "new key" to proficiency has been discovered and that one need only follow a prescribed set of teaching procedures developed by experts in order to reach pedagogical salvation. Yet the history of foreign language education suggests that evangelistic bandwagons can end up inhibiting teacher creativity as well as promoting it. A too-suddenly acquired belief in a methodological doctrine can impel teachers toward a willing suspension of common sense, resulting in the abandonment of techniques that were working quite well and the adoption of procedures that fail to function in the local setting.

Why have bandwagons been consistently unreliable as guides to classroom practice? Part of the answer lies in the fact that teaching is an art that involves initiating students to a particular mode of behavior relating to a particular subject area or discipline. Where foreign languages are concerned, virtually all aspects of learning are involved including psychomotor skill development, knowledge of culture, and appreciation of literature. Since there is no general agreement on which of these aspects should be emphasized, however, there can be no method that will be satisfactory for all the potential goals of language teaching. Choice of content is also a problem. Some foreign language leaders emphasize national needs; others international understanding; others literary analysis; others self-actualization; others international trade and commerce; and still others mental discipline. In this chaos of instructional purpose, it seems quixotic to search for a unified, scientifically supported theory of instruction, one that can be converted to pedagogical practice and can be implemented within a few hundred available contact hours. After his review of twenty-five centuries of language teaching, Kelly (36) concluded that "given the prime role of educational objectives in language teaching, we must view with skepticism the notion of a cause-and-effect relationship between human sciences and language teaching" (p. 404).

For this reason, the reliance upon expert opinion to specify teaching methods is futile. Prominent figures from prestigious institutions can be found in support of all contending theories of instruction. Since each expert has a somewhat different image of what kind of student performance should emerge from a foreign language course of instruction, however, the methods for producing such outcomes will vary greatly. Do we want, for example, people who have been rigorously trained in the discipline, or are we looking for people who have subconsciously acquired a language in a low-anxiety, personally relevant classroom environment?

Such questions are so value-laden that they can never be answered through research. We do know, however, from surveys of student expectations that learning to converse has been the main goal of most students. Citing evidence from the 1930s, Kaulfers (34, p. 189) reported that "The ability to converse in a language is the primary objective of a large plurality of students who enroll in modern language classes in junior and senior high schools and adult education centers." The same course expectations were found by Arendt and Hallock (1) in 1979. Therefore, the trends of the late 1980s appeared to be in line with student perceptions of what foreign language instruction is all about. An eclectic summary of elements from current language movements would include the recommendations listed below (although opinion is far from unanimous on several issues):

1. The focus in defining course objectives is shifting from teacher performance in class to what the student can do communicatively with the language in and out of the class.
2. Grammar is not to be discarded completely, but has a greatly reduced role within the syllabus. In fact, the curriculum is now to be defined in terms of communicative functions that students can perform and topics they can

discuss. Grammar is taught in relation to those functions and topics rather than for its own sake.

3. The target language is to be used almost exclusively for classroom communication as well as for drill and practice. The native language might be used initially for homework assignments, test directions, cultural notes, or grammar explanations.
4. All four skills are taught; however, the order of presentation and style of teaching varies with the age of the learner and the goals of the course.
5. There should be regularly scheduled periods where students try to communicate their real ideas and feelings without fear of correction (for example, in pair work and small group situations). There should also, however, be a focus on error correction so that phonological, grammatical, and syntactical errors do not fossilize.

These are a few of the conclusions reached by a considerable number of foreign language practitioners from around the world. Where methods are concerned, the current mood in many countries favors eclecticism. Current jargon calls for implementing a communicative, proficiency-oriented curriculum. Many teachers feel that the best bandwagon is all of them: Decide where you want your students to go and then use whatever helps to get them there.

References, Bandwagons Revisited

1. Arendt, Jermaine D., and Marcia Hallock. "Windmills and Dragons," pp. 124–45 in Jermaine D. Arendt, ed., *Foreign Language Learning, Today and Tomorrow.* New York: Pergamon, 1979.
2. Asher, James J. *Learning Another Language through Actions.* Los Gatos, CA: Sky Oaks, 1983.
3. Bagster-Collins, E. W. *The Teaching of Modern Languages in the United States.* Reprinted from *Publications of the American and Canadian Committees on Modern Languages.* Vol. 17, Studies in Modern Language Teaching. New York: Macmillan, 1930.
4. Berlitz, M. D. *Berlitz Method for Teaching Modern Languages.* New York: Berlitz, 1907.
5. Birckbichler, Diane W. *Creative Activities for the Second Language Classroom.* Washington, DC: Center for Applied Linguistics, 1982.
6. Brooks, Nelson. *Language and Language Learning: Theory and Practice.* 2nd ed. New York: Harcourt, 1964.
7. Buchanan, M. A., and E. D. MacPhee. *Modern Language Instruction in Canada.* Volume 1. Toronto: Univ. of Toronto Press, 1928.
8. Carroll, John B. "Foreign Language Proficiency Levels Attained by Language Majors near Graduation from College." *Foreign Language Annals* 1 (1967): 131–51.
9. Chomsky, Noam. *Language and Mind.* Enl. ed. New York: Harcourt, 1972.
10. Cochran, Emory E. *A Practical German Review Grammar.* New York: Prentice-Hall, 1947.
11. Curme, George O. *A First German Grammar.* New York: Oxford Univ. Press, 1914.
12. Curran, Charles A. *Counseling-Learning in Second Languages.* Apple River, IL: Apple River Press, 1976.
13. Curtain, Helena A., and Carol Ann Pesola. *Languages and Children—Making the Match.* New York: Addison-Wesley, 1988.
14. de Sauzé, E. B. *The Cleveland Plan for the Teaching of Modern Languages.* Philadelphia: Winston, 1959.
15. Diller, Karl C. *The Language Teaching Controversy.* Rowley, MA: Newbury, 1978.

16. Ferguson, Charles A., and Thom Huebner. *Foreign Language Instruction and Second Language Acquisition Research in the United States*. NFLC Occasional Papers. Washington, DC: National Foreign Language Center at the Johns Hopkins University, 1989.

17. Fife, Robert H. "A Survey of Tendencies in Modern Language Teaching, 1927–33: Retro-Spect and Prospect," pp. 1–50 in Algernon Coleman, ed. *Experiments and Studies in Modern Language Teaching*. Chicago: Univ. of Chicago Press, 1934.

18. Galyean, Beverly. "A Confluent Approach to Curriculum Design." *Foreign Language Annals* 12 (1979): 121–27.

19. Gattegno, Caleb. *Teaching Foreign Languages in Schools: The Silent Way*. New York: Educational Solutions, 1972.

20. Gouin, F. *The Art of Teaching Languages*. Trans. H. Swan and V. Bétis. New York: Scribner's, 1892.

21. Grittner, Frank M. "Barbarians, Bandwagons and Foreign Language Scholarship." *Modern Language Journal* 57 (1973): 241–48.

22. _____. "The Teacher as Co-Learner: Interest-Centered Materials," pp. 11–29 in Frank M. Grittner, ed., *Student Motivation and the Foreign Language Teacher*. Proceedings of the Central States Conference on the Teaching of Foreign Languages. Lincolnwood, IL: National Textbook Company, 1974.

23. _____. *A Guide to Curriculum Planning in Foreign Language*. Madison, WI: Department of Public Instruction, 1985.

24. _____. *A Three-Year Evaluation of the NEH German Summer Institute Program Conducted at the University of Wisconsin–Stevens Point*. Unpublished report. Madison, WI: Department of Public Instruction, 1987.

25. Hagboldt, Peter. *The Teaching of German*. Lexington, MA: Heath, 1940.

26. Halsted, Henry. "Foreign Language Instruction in Elementary Schools." *The Wingspread Journal*, July 1988.

27. Ham, Roscoe J., and Arthur N. Leonard. *Brief German Grammar*. New York: Ginn, 1908.

28. Hammerly, Hector. "The Immersion Approach: Litmus Test of Second Language Acquisition through Classroom Communications." *Modern Language Journal* 71 (1987): 395–401.

29. Handschin, Charles H. *Modern Language Teaching*. New York: World Book, 1940.

30. Heilenman, Laura K., and Isabelle M. Kaplan. "Proficiency in Practice: The Foreign Language Curriculum," pp. 55–78 in Charles J. James, ed., *Foreign Language Proficiency in the Classroom and Beyond*. The ACTFL Review of Foreign Language Education Series, vol. 16. Lincolnwood, IL: National Textbook Company, 1984.

31. Higgs, Theodore V., and Ray Clifford, "The Push toward Communication," pp. 57–79 in Theodore V. Higgs, ed., *Curriculum, Competence, and the Foreign Language Teacher*. The ACTFL Review of Foreign Language Education Series, vol. 13. Lincolnwood, IL: National Textbook Company, 1981.

32. Jagemann, H. C. G. "On the Use of the Foreign Language in the Classroom," pp. 171–85 in *Methods of Teaching Modern Languages*. Heath's Pedagogical Library Series. Lexington, MA: Heath, 1896.

33. Joynes, Edward S. "Reading in Modern Language Study," pp. 29–45 in *Methods of Teaching Modern Languages*. Heath's Pedagogical Library Series. Lexington, MA: Heath, 1896.

34. Kaulfers, Walter V. *Modern Languages for Modern Schools*. New York: McGraw-Hill, 1942.

35. Keating, Raymond F. *A Study of the Effectiveness of Language Laboratories*. New York: Institute of Administrative Research, 1963.

36. Kelly, L. G. *25 Centuries of Language Teaching*. Rowley, MA: Newbury, 1969.

37. Kennedy, Dora F., and William DeLorenzo. *Complete Guide to Exploratory Foreign Language Programs*. Lincolnwood, IL: National Textbook Company, 1985.

38. Knop, Constance K. "Notional-Functional Syllabus: From Theory to Classroom Applications," pp. 105–21 in Maurice W. Conner, ed., *A Global Approach to Foreign*

Language Education. Proceedings of the Central States Conference on the Teaching of Foreign Languages. Lincolnwood, IL: National Textbook Company, 1981.

39. Krashen, Stephen D., and Tracy D. Terrell. *The Natural Approach: Language Acquisition in the Classroom.* New York: Pergamon, 1983.

40. Lado, Robert. *Language Teaching: A Scientific Approach.* New York: McGraw-Hill, 1964.

41. Long, Donna R. "What's Really Going On in the Classroom?" pp. 28–37 in Barbara Snyder, ed., *Second Language Acquisition: Preparing for Tomorrow.* Proceedings of the Central States Conference on the Teaching of Foreign Language. Lincolnwood, IL: National Textbook Company, 1986.

42. Lorge, Sarah W. "Language Laboratory Research Studies in New York City High Schools: A Discussion of the Program and the Findings." *Modern Language Journal* 47 (1964): 409–19.

43. Lozanov, Georgi, and Evalina Gateva. A workshop announcement on how to use *The Foreign Language Teacher's Suggestopedic Manual.* New York: Gordon and Breach Marketing Department, 1988.

44. Modern Language Association. *Modern Spanish: A Project of the Modern Language Association.* New York: Harcourt, 1960.

45. Nearhoof, Orrin E. "An Examination of Teacher-Pupil Interaction in Third-Year French Classes." Ph.D. diss., Iowa State University (AMES), 1970.

46. Nerenz, Anne. "Utilizing Class Time in Foreign Language Instruction," pp. 78–89 in David P. Benseler, ed., *Teaching the Basics in the Foreign Language Classroom: Options and Strategies.* Proceedings of the Central States Conference on the Teaching of Foreign Languages. Lincolnwood, IL: National Textbook Company, 1979.

47. O'Connor, Patricia. *Modern Foreign Languages in High School: Pre-Reading Instruction.* Washington, DC: Office of Education, 1965.

48. Omaggio, Alice C. *Teaching Language in Context: Proficiency-Oriented Instruction.* Boston: Heinle and Heinle, 1986.

49. Paulston, Christina B., and Mary N. Bruder. *From Substitution to Substance: A Handbook of Structural Pattern Drills.* Rowley, MA: Newbury, 1975.

50. Prokosch, E. *Deutsche Sprachlehre.* New York: Henry Holt, 1930.

51. Quilter, Daniel. *Do's and Don'ts of Audiolingual Teaching.* Waltham, MA: Blaisdell, 1966.

52. Rivers, Wilga M. *Teaching Foreign-Language Skills.* 2nd ed. Chicago: Univ. of Chicago Press, 1981.

53. Savignon, Sandra J. *Communicative Competence: Theory and Classroom Practice.* Reading, MA: Addison-Wesley, 1983.

54. _____. "Foreign Language Education: Traditions and Trends." *The Lasso: Wyoming Humanities Newsletter,* February 1989, pp. 4–9.

55. Thomas, Calvin. "Observations upon Method in the Teaching of Modern Languages," pp. 11–28 in *Methods of Teaching Modern Languages.* Heath's Pedagogical Library Series, Lexington, MA: Heath, 1896.

56. Twaddell, Freeman. *Foreign Language Instruction at the Second Level.* New York: Holt, Rinehart and Winston, 1963.

57. UNESCO. *Problems in Education—The Teaching of Modern Languages.* Paris: United Nations Educational, Scientific and Cultural Organization, 1955.

58. van Ek, J. *Threshold Level English.* New York: Pergamon, 1975.

59. Wilson, Virginia, and Beverly Wattenmaker. *Real Communication in Foreign Language.* New York: Humanistic Education Center, 1973.

60. Zeydel, Edwin H. *The Teaching of German in the United States—A Historical Survey.* New York: Modern Language Association, 1961.

2

Language Instruction in the United States: Policy and Planning

June K. Phillips
Tennessee Foreign Language Institute

Introduction

Here we are—in the late twentieth century—where the globe has become smaller thanks to improved transportation and telecommunications. At the same time, internationalization has become greater as a result of expanded trade, global economics, international politics, and an increasingly interdependent world. The United States, this melting pot that has historically accepted and absorbed (if not always embraced) peoples from diverse cultural and linguistic backgrounds, has chosen this time to develop language policies and plans that on one front reek of the parochial, the restrictive, and the isolationist, while on another they encourage international communication and understanding. While a major segment of the business and governmental communities rallies to support foreign language instruction in schools at all levels, another segment of the populace strives to close ranks and mandate English (sometimes only English) as the language of all political, social, and economic activity in the United States.

Before one can study the impact of language policy or planning on instruction, one must be knowledgeable about the history and status of language policy in the large arena of everyday life and citizenship. The reality has been, at least until very recently, that most individuals in the United States assumed that English was, is,

June K. Phillips (Ph.D., The Ohio State University) is Executive Director of the Tennessee Foreign Language Institute. She edited several earlier volumes in the ACTFL Foreign Language Education Series, chaired the Northeast Conference on the Teaching of Foreign Languages in 1984, and currently serves on the ACTFL Executive Council. She has written numerous articles, monographs, and textbooks and has conducted workshops and seminars throughout the nation and abroad. Professional affiliations include ACTFL, MLA, AATF, and TFTLA.

our official language. In fact, Di Pietro (11) used to begin his graduate course on bilingualism by querying his relatively informed audience on the "official language" of the United States and found that most responded unhesitatingly with "English."

Many Americans find it difficult to believe, much less accept the fact, that the founding fathers failed to designate a common tongue in the Constitution. While the bicentennial celebration of the Constitution glorifies the foresight of the signers and the viability of the document, the very groups that pride themselves on conservative interpretations of its doctrines are busy trying to fix it with a constitutional amendment declaring English to be the nation's official language. In a fashion similar to that of theologians placing diametrically opposed interpretations on the same scriptures by attributing motivations to those long dead, so do the advocates of the English Only movement suggest that the founding fathers simply forgot, assumed, or lacked the clairvoyance needed to see what the future would require.

Other historians note that the realities of that era and the linguistic diversity in colonial times alerted the framers of the Constitution to the fact that bestowing primacy to any one language would have been a grave political error. Moreover, educated men such as Jefferson and Franklin had no phobia about other languages; indeed they pursued them and vaunted their personal expertise in communicating in several tongues. Of course, Franklin was of divided opinion. He delighted in French with the young ladies in the ballrooms of Paris while fearing the influence of German in southeastern Pennsylvania. Finally, it is difficult to conceive that the men who decreed freedom of speech as a basic right would restrict the languages in which that freedom might be expressed. But then, that, too, is interpretation.

This chapter will begin by reviewing briefly the history of language planning in this country in order to see what the lack of an explicit plan for language policy in the United States has meant implicitly. Language instruction will be interpreted to include native language, foreign language, and English as a second language. Coverage will, however, be concentrated upon the English Only movement and foreign language teaching; ESL and bilingual education will be less comprehensive, for any major discussion of this topic requires separate treatment. We shall look at both federal and state actions as they relate to language policy as well as the increased influence of business and commerce in the late twentieth century. Finally, we shall see how the profession itself has succeeded in providing input into language policy through language centers and coalition building.

History of Language Policy in the United States

Heath (23, 24) in several articles provides a thorough and spritely review of language policy and of language heritage in this country. She traces developments from colonial times through the heavy immigration period of the nineteenth century as English and ethnic languages battled for a role. Almost until the end of the nineteenth century, bilingual instruction in urban schools was a natural companion to the large enrollments of immigrant youngsters. Churches and communities assisted newcomers in learning English and in maintaining native tongues. Social and economic factors encouraged immigration to the United States, because new workers were needed for the factories and industries that were booming. U.S. immigration and naturalization laws placed no barriers upon non-English-speaking persons until the Nationality Act of 1906 required that applicants for citizenship speak English. From the early twentieth century through the period of the world wars, the lack of a common language and maintenance of native ones was not envisioned as a divisive factor. After that period, a swing toward English and the consequent withdrawal of support for bilingual schools became the norm. Later the Internal Security Act of 1950 added citizenship requirements in reading and writing English.

Contemporary History

How does the immigrant fare in the late twentieth century? Today's regulations for literacy and educational requirements state that "unless he is physically unable to do so, an applicant for naturalization must be able to speak and understand simple English as well as read and write it" (United States Department of Justice, 43, p. 14). Exceptions are made for those over the age of fifty who have lived in the United States for at least twenty years. Applicants must also be able to sign their names in the English language (whatever that means). The test of simple English as outlined in the regulations states that "the questions the examiner asks are in simple English and to be able to answer them requires knowledge only of subjects that anyone who has really tried to learn will be familiar with." (One must conclude that ending sentences with prepositions is a sample of simple English.)

The real point here is that even without a constitutional designation of an official language and the consequent establishment of policy, the reality of day-to-day regulations through administrative bodies such as the Immigration and Naturalization Service renders English the de facto language of the nation—at least for its newest citizens. Furthermore, the leniency or strictness with which the tests of "simple English" are conducted has a great deal to do with who is naturalized and who is not. Rubin (33) has culled from research on speech, literacy, and ethnic group relations factors that show the tremendous impact language has on "sense of self" and calls for a rational language policy for immigrants and refugees.

Bilingual education has also experienced its ups and downs in recent years. Less than a decade ago, Ferguson and Heath (15) could quite accurately write that "the use of the ethnic language at school is now often considered natural and even praiseworthy, and bilingual education programs may even use the ethnic language as the medium of instruction for serious content courses" (p. xxxv). The sands had shifted drastically by 1987. Language policy, as reflected in bilingual regulations under the Reagan administration and in initiatives such as English Only, has moved away from language maintenance and gradual transitional programs to language switch, a switch that is to take place with all possible speed.

The history of languages in the United States has been one bereft of steadfastness and deliberateness; instead, it has been one in which the changing tides of economic, social, and political pressures have influenced whether English has been actively or passively promoted, whether foreign language study has been advocated or ignored, and whether ethnic languages have been preserved, protected, or abolished. We have not been a nation that has planned and developed policies consistent with overriding principles. Instead, our language policies have fluctuated to the degree that educational practice has thrived or faltered with the shifting winds. Perhaps that very volatility underscores why language professionals should be concerned with understanding the processes and results of language planning and policy.

Language Planning and Policy as Problem and Practice   _____

What does language planning mean and how does policy affect the teaching and learning of languages among people in a nation? In those countries with official languages, the concept acquires immediate visibility because legislation usually requires bilingual signs or documents as part of everyday life. In these countries the school curriculum is often taught in several languages and the study of official languages is promoted for all citizens. Policy and planning play a major role and exhibit the chief characteristics of language planning as defined by Cooper (9), that is, "the organized pursuit of solutions to language problems usually at the national level" (p. 27). As we shall try to demonstrate later, the situation in the United States fails to operate according to this definition in many instances. The pursuit of solutions here has been reactive for the most part, and the states have jumped in to make explicit policy—whereas the federal government has allowed policy to evolve with the times and current issues. In contrast, many other countries, by setting policies first, plan in accordance with national guidelines and deal with linguistic problems from a proactive stance.

The thrust of planning and the format of solutions differ greatly from nation to nation. Canada continues to struggle with official language policy but does so through legislation, implementation, and revision. Bill C-72, passed in 1988, updated the Official Languages Act of 1969; the legislation does not require that every individual be bilingual, but it does stipulate that access to government, its services, and its opportunities be equally available to speakers of English and of French. Furthermore, the bill provides for the *promotion* of both official languages in Canadian society ("Official Languages," 29).

A country such as Finland, which is officially bilingual in Finnish and Swedish, seeks to ensure that all citizens attain fluency in both languages even though native speakers of Swedish today are a minority geographically concentrated in the Helsinki area. It might be noted that having to learn two languages in school does not impinge upon the learning of other "foreign" languages, and most Finns communicate comfortably in a third tongue such as English, French, German, or Russian. In Soviet republics where Russian is not the native tongue, language policy establishes Russian as the one language all must know (the common element), but native languages may also be the language of instruction in the schools. This principle was not always evident in practice, but under *glasnost* the policy for national languages has become a rallying point for ethnic independence in the non-Russian republics. Throughout the world, language policy takes many different directions; in most cases, however, evidence points toward an "organized pursuit at the national level."

And in the United States?

This nation has thus far existed without having designated an official language in its constitution, in its national code of law, or in statutes at large. Yet the absence of an official language does not mean that no implicit policies have influence on the use of language by citizens. Grant (20) describes language planning and policy more broadly as "what the government—federal, state, and local—says and does with respect to one or more of the languages it represents" (p. 1). Under the umbrella of an "anything goes" approach, language policy has had an effect throughout our history. For the government, at its various levels, has said and done, and continues to say and to do, much that affects language in all its dimensions, be it foreign, second, English, or minority languages. As Grant points out, our laws, legislative statutes, regulations, and practices by dint of their role in society serve to establish policy. Of course, one might also ask whether policy, well thought out in advance, might better precede the creation and establishment of legislation.

Ruiz (34) identifies three perspectives of language planning that frequently set the stage for subsequent legislation and educational directions. The first views "language as problem." The remedy sought under this construct is linguistic unity. The plan for achieving this takes quite distinct forms. Currently in the United States, the search for linguistic unity surfaces in the English Only movement. Linguistic diversity is seen as divisive and "make 'em learn English" as the solution. Such a perspective, in a kinder and gentler nation, would probably promote the teaching of English as a second language, a solution proposed by the English Plus forces. In fact, many of the advocates of new state laws take the opposite path by denying support for ESL in the twisted view that non-English speakers are responsible for their own acquisition of the dominant language.

The second perspective identified by Ruiz envisions "language as right." Under this orientation, individuals have rights to their own languages, and governments are responsible for ensuring the basic human rights of linguistic minorities. This view generates policies that would assure bilingual ballots, social services, and education.

The third perspective is that of "language as resource." When nations embrace this outlook, foreign language study thrives, for diplomatic, military, business, or education endeavors necessitate a multilingual citizenry to work abroad or at home. Recent instances of those "good times" for the foreign language profession included the post-Sputnik decade of the sixties and the Carter years with the spotlight on the President's Commission on the Teaching of Foreign Languages and International Studies (31).

U.S. policy had adopted one or more of these perspectives, some simultaneously, at various periods in our history.

Fishman (17) identifies four language problems as they relate to specific language-planning processes. The first problem involves "code selection," whereby one or more languages (or one variety of a language) is chosen over others and the planning process renders the decision official. Examples of such planning processes include the Canadian Official Languages Act (where two languages are official), India's choice of Hindi as the official language, or even when state laws require bilingual education or ESL for students of limited English proficiency.

A second problem indicated by Fishman concerns regional or social linguistic variability. The resolution is generally found in "standardization or codification." This requires either elevating one variety of language or creating a composite. In the United States "broadcaster's speech," with its midwestern regularity, is an attempt to erase regional pronunciation, and speech clinics now offer programs, especially in the southern states, for aspiring managers who wish to sound more neutral. Governmental attempts at "plain English" in official documents may be another example (although not an entirely successful one). Indeed, that touches upon Fishman's third problem area, that of adding new functions to a linguistic code. English, especially its American variety, has adapted itself easily to new terms to accommodate technology and science. Contrast it with the French effort to keep the language pure (i.e., untainted by English) even as they need to describe new technologies and cultures.

The final problem is that of functional differentiation among registers and "correctness" that language planners confront by cultivation or the production of style manuals. Popular critics such as Edwin Newman and William Safire in his *New York Times Sunday Magazine* column, "On Language," desire to standardize language, but generally the United States has avoided policy in this area and American English has been free to develop in its own fashion.

Another perspective on planning as it relates to language spread and language change is offered by Cooper (9). He defines language spread as "an increase, over time, in the proportion of a communications network that adopts a given language variety for a given communicative function . . . the expansion of a language variety's users or uses" (p. 23). Language spread is a process, language shift an outcome. The former is not always a replacement issue either; individuals can add a language system without losing their native one. In earlier waves of immigration to the United States, English was the language to which people shifted, somehow. But they often lost their native tongues in the process, or at least the next generation did. Under the bilingual programs of the seventies and early eighties, an effort was made to effectuate shift without replacement. The pendulum is moving back toward spreading English with little attention to whether native languages are replaced.

As Fishman (17) concludes, the success of language planning is measured by the extent to which planned change actually occurs. It remains to be seen whether recent policy and planning efforts in the United States, such as English-language amendments and constraints in bilingual programs, unite the nation's people into a single language group, whether economic competitiveness and political realities cause more Americans to learn other languages, or whether requirements for proficiency measures for certification of new foreign language teachers improve instruction.

The Federal Government: Policy and Influence

Given the absence of a constitutional provision to designate the language or languages of the nation's business, one might presume an insignificant federal role or influence on instruction. To the contrary, policy requires no affirmation by legal or statutory status; it quite effectively wields its influence through funding mechanisms, through program priorities, and in reaction to judicial interpretations. Over the years, national policies have played a major role in emphasizing and de-emphasizing bilingual education, in supporting or detracting from a role for ethnic tongues according to the times. National priorities have brought about change and sometimes initiated controversy in the content and orientation of foreign language programs in the schools and in higher education.

English Only, English Plus

The issue of English as an official language has arisen in most recent congressional sessions; while it has never reached a voting stage there, it has received media attention not just in hard news but on the talk-show circuit. Hearings on an English Language Amendment (ELA) were held in May 1988 before the House Subcommittee on Civil and Constitutional Rights. Testimony was given on both sides of this issue, which has given birth to two coalitions. The nonprofit group U.S. English claims S. I. Hayakawa (22), former California senator, as its honorary chairman and states that its goal in declaring English as the official language of the United States is the abolishment of multilingual ballots and the limitation of bilingual education to a transitional role. It takes great pains to assure supporters that "we also want our English-speaking students to become fluent in foreign languages—but that's another matter" (quote from "Dear Friend" undated letter from S. I. Hayakawa received in bulk mailing in fall 1988). It must be evidence of the power of the foreign-language lobby that U.S. English attempts not to alienate it.

In October 1987, the English Plus Information Clearinghouse (EPIC) was launched to promote the concept of English Plus. EPIC is a coalition established under the auspices of the National Immigration, Refugee and Citizenship Forum and the Joint National Committee for Languages (JNCL). Over forty-five organizations, including ACTFL, have endorsed their statement of purpose, which "holds that all members of our society have full access to effective opportunities to acquire strong English language proficiency *plus* mastery of a second or multiple languages" (EPIC, 13). [Appendix A contains the complete text of this statement.]

Bilingual Education

Support for bilingual programs on the federal level has taken its direction from a variety of political, economic, and judicial issues. Rarely has the overriding concern been the best possible education for youngsters with native languages other than English. Instead, programs have responded to decisions in the courts, passions of the public, and even special interests of the entrenched bureaucracy. Planning could never take firm hold because the exigencies of a particular era were reflected in the constantly changing regulations and amendments in the authorizations that cover bilingual programs.

For example, if one traces the evolution of Title VII of the Elementary and Secondary Education Act (1968, reauthorized 1974), one can readily observe the effect of policy on implementation. The 1968 act sought to establish equal opportunity in education by funding bilingual programs through assistance to state and local agencies. Even though entitled the Bilingual Education Act, it did not require that districts offer *bilingual* programs, and the focus of assistance was compensatory. With the emergence of the 1969 *Lau* v. *Nichols* case and the subsequent decision in 1974 of the United States Supreme Court that "sink or swim" was unacceptable as educational practice, a whole series of planned remedies took effect. As the *Lau* case wound its way through the courts, language policy was also affected by social factors. In 1970, the Office for Civil Rights entered the fray and directed school districts to make their programs available to students with deficiencies in English if there were more than 5 percent "national-origin-minority group children" in the district. Existing practices such as assigning these children to classes for the handicapped because of their English-language scores or to vocational tracks were deemed to be discriminatory. Furthermore, the OCR determined that school administrators would henceforth have to communicate with parents in a language they comprehend (Crawford, 10).

In 1975, Terrell Bell, then Commissioner of Education, drew up the Lau remedies that dealt with issues such as the evaluation of Limited English Proficiency, appropriate instructional treatments, approval of mainstreaming, and professional standards for teachers. Bilingual education *plus* ESL was mandated; ESL alone was deemed to be insufficient as a remedy. While no legal status was attached to the Lau remedies, the full force of the government lay behind them, and the Office of Civil Rights had the authority to enforce compliance by negotiating with offending districts.

Reauthorization of the Bilingual Education Act occurred in 1974 when support for programs was strong. Consequently, this version of Title VII expanded programs to encompass students not eligible under poverty guidelines and accepted both *maintenance* and *transitional* approaches. Most significant was the mandate for instruction in the student's native language and culture. But an examination of what happened in reality is interesting. If any doubt remains about the effect of policy as derived from program regulation, compare these two sets of instructions to grant applicants for Title VII funding:

1971: "It must be remembered that the ultimate goal of bilingual education is a student who functions well in two languages on any occasion."

1974: "The cultural pluralism of American society is one of its greatest assets, but such pluralism is a private matter of local choice and not a proper responsibility of the federal government. [The goal of Title VII is] to assist children of limited- or non-English speaking ability to gain competency in English so that they may enjoy equal educational opportunity—and *not* to require cultural pluralism." (Frank Carlucci, H.E.W. Undersecretary, in Crawford, 10, p. 24)

The shift demonstrated in these statements effectively targets English as the language to be learned by all children in the nation's schools and relegates maintenance programs outside the federal agenda. Even President Jimmy Carter, lauded for his efforts in support of foreign language and international studies, is alleged to have told his Cabinet officers "I want English taught, not ethnic culture" (Crawford, 10, p. 24).

The pendulum continues to sway for the various types of bilingual programs. Title VII's 1978 reauthorization ruled out maintenance programs and accepted native language instruction only to the degree necessary for students to develop competency in English. A 1981 review of bilingual programs conducted by the Department of Education determined that the research on various approaches was so weak that schools were now encouraged to experiment and to innovate. The Reagan administration could safely be characterized as "pro-English" or "anti-native language" and William J. Bennett, replacing Bell as Secretary of Education, tried to implement that philosophy by striking the "bi" from bilingual education wherever possible. Title VII managed to be reauthorized in 1984 partly because it was an election year in which Reagan was forced to court the Hispanic vote. Rather than create new definitions for eligible programs, one strategy was to cut actual funding amounts. Another tactic involved giving greater access to programs based on an English-only approach.

Most probably, the bilingual issue will remain in flux and be subject to political pressures and prejudices. As with other areas in language acquisition, it suffers from the lack of a strong and viable research base on the most effective ways to acquire a second language and on the role of the native tongue in that process. As long as research is sparse and no consensus is reached on "best ways" to teach in terms comprehensible to the public, the field remains open to the political whims of the nation. Practitioners have also been guilty of politicizing the issue, because enormous sums of money were available and a significant number of administrative and instructional positions were at stake. Readers interested in a more thorough treatment of bilingual education and the role of the federal government are directed to Baker and de Kanter (3), Crawford (10), Grant (20), and Kloss (25).

Rights to Language

Federal legislation and policy have played a considerable role in protecting the use of languages other than English through antidiscrimination statutes. Without an official language, no justification exists for denying the full benefits of citizenship to those who cannot function in English. The Voting Rights Act of 1965 enjoins states from linking the right to vote to English; this provision, in effect, opened the door to bilingual ballots in many places. The 1975 amendment, which sought to abolish discrimination by outlawing English-only elections and by establishing means for compensation, included the prohibition of literacy tests and any other criteria that have discriminated against minority languages (Grant, 20).

The importance of federal policy in this area is crucial, for states were wont, either by law or by past practice, to require English for voting privileges, for jury duty, for court proceedings, and for education. The supremacy of federal law and the ascendancy of civil-rights legislation preserved privileges of suffrage, court action, and schooling for speakers of other languages.

Today, the right to a language manifests itself most prominently in this country within Hispanic communities. As Tonkin (40) observes,

> The situation of Spanish in the United States highlights for us the problem of reconciling individual rights with the larger public interest as Spanish-speakers insist on access to social services in their own language; and others call on them to assimilate, regardless of the pain involved and the potential cultural deracination (p. 32).

It is no surprise then that the states that have most recently sprung into action to promote an English-language amendment are those experiencing a backlash against a highly visible "foreign" language.

Foreign (or World) Languages and Federal Influence _____

On a day-to-day basis and on the surface, foreign language classrooms appear to be relatively free from the control of the federal government. Similarly, instructional approaches seem to have evolved independently of national bureaucracies. Yet a bit of eavesdropping in a faculty lounge or at a conference where more than two slightly gray-haired (or dyed), experienced foreign language teachers come together eventually produces from one of them "Oh, remember that summer at the NDEA Institute in _____!"

Lessons from the Past

The instructional method—i.e., audiolingualism, promulgated in the United States through the massive in-service teacher training efforts of the National Defense Education Act Institutes—testifies to the power of policy on a profession through funding mechanisms. Government agencies, in response to the political and scientific events surrounding Sputnik, worked with institutions of higher education and the dominant professional organization at that time, the Modern

Language Association, to devise a federally funded program that resulted in a unified approach to the teaching of foreign languages, one that remains a dominant paradigm in many of today's secondary school classrooms.

The first NDEA Summer Institutes went into operation in 1959 and continued into the late sixties. Brod (5) estimates that approximately 30,000 teachers, that is, one-third of all in-service teachers at that time, received instruction in 587 NDEA institutes. While first-level institutes were held on college campuses in the United States, second-level institutes for participants were hosted in target-language countries, providing linguistic and cultural opportunities to many teachers who had never traveled, studied, or lived abroad.

How easy it is to view the past from the perspective of the present and to attack certain aspects of that plan, in particular the methodology espoused for the teaching of other languages. The accuracy of the premises upon which the methodology was based aside, government intervention through funding did manage to turn a profession from curricular goals that relied almost totally on language as translation and the study of grammar to goals that granted recognition to the development of aural/oral skills. Thus, the NDEA institutes performed their mission, as defined, superbly.

The methodology also spawned a generation of teaching materials that, at the outset, relatively few publishers controlled. As the market expanded, others jumped on the same bandwagon, and little deviation from audiolingual practices occurred. School districts that had never before had foreign language programs, particularly at junior high levels, instituted them, largely due to the lure of the federally funded language laboratory, a technological showpiece for the proud school of the sixties. German reentered the curriculum after its banishment during the Second World War, and Russian was introduced for the first time in many schools.

This chapter is not the place to discuss methods per se; suffice it to say that the instructional practices advocated in the NDEA days did reflect the best thinking of their times. They matched the psychological orientation of the era, behaviorism, and they drew their language knowledge from the fields of descriptive and applied linguistics as then practiced. Colleges and universities were also affected, because the opportunities to host and to teach in these intensive programs created a corps of language-education specialists for the first time. The institutionalization of foreign language methods courses and of graduate programs leading to degrees in foreign language education trace their origin to the "NDEA" days. The Modern Language Association, whose membership rolls had formerly attracted English language and literature and foreign literature faculty, found a new audience in the foreign language teaching and foreign language education professoriat. Because this group soon became large enough and developed specialized interests, the MLA supported the establishment in 1967 of a new organization to address that constituency, the American Council on the Teaching of Foreign Languages (ACTFL).

The orientation of the NDEA institutes was not without critics; yet the bottom line was that a funding mechanism influenced the training of several generations of teachers. The existence of the NDEA institutes and the act itself promoted the study of foreign languages in the nation's schools and of foreign language pedagogy in the institutions of higher education. In a nation where a federal curriculum does not exist, the NDEA institutes constituted a clear example of language policy as advocated by governmental and academic leaders.

Lessons for the Present

Are there currently areas where federal policy influences the direction and teaching of world languages in the United States? Today, the influence of government on language teaching is weaker partly because monetary allocations are so much less. Instances that most closely parallel the NDEA era coalesce around three issues: (1) proficiency-based curriculum, (2) the broadening of foreign language instruction as a practical and ancillary skill, and (3) language training and area studies. These orientations gained strength following the Report of the President's Commission on the Teaching of Foreign Languages and International Studies, *Strength through Wisdom: A Critique of U.S. Capability* (31).

Policy and Proficiency

The secondary and the college curriculums had been undergoing change before the commission was established by President Jimmy Carter. Brod (4) reports that the reduction in foreign language requirements that took place between 1966 and 1974 forced institutions to react to student demands for specific languages (gains in Spanish and Italian, losses in French, German, and Russian) and to make the courses themselves more relevant, i.e., practical, to perceived learner needs.

Additional incentives for change emanated from the more than thirty national commissions that existed in the early 1980s; most of the reports on American education issued by these groups of high-powered business, government, and educational leaders contained statements or exhortations for more and better foreign language instruction in the nation's schools. Recommendations in the reports became the policies, which in turn determined program support and priorities for funding.

In essence, the strong endorsement of foreign language study did not affirm the status quo in curriculum. The arguments were not couched in terms of protecting language requirements nor increasing significantly the number of belle lettrists in departments. The policymakers' interests centered upon producing Americans who could speak languages, who could use languages for practical purposes; they sought people who were proficient to conduct their occupations and their lives in other languages and in other cultures. They wanted *proficiency,* by which they meant the ability to perform real-world tasks:

> Study of foreign language introduces students to non-English speaking cultures, heightens awareness and comprehension of one's native tongue,

and serves the nation's needs in commerce, diplomacy, defense, and education (National Commission on Excellence in Education, 28, p. 26).

From a national perspective, young men and women with proficiency in foreign languages are sorely needed now that we are increasingly involved in competitive trade and investment with the rest of the world (Twentieth Century Fund, 41, p. 12).

Geno (18) and subsequently Edwards and Hanisch (12) provide detailed chronicles of policy initiatives and public activities that preceded and followed the President's Commission on the Teaching of Foreign Languages and International Studies.

It is difficult to ascertain whether the push toward proficiency as an outcome for foreign language study resulted from the policymakers or from the profession itself. It may also be one of those serendipitous occasions when several forces happened to move simultaneously toward a goal. In any case, the President's Commission brought together at regional meetings members of the language-teaching profession from academe, government schools, and business. The ensuing dialog soon generated cooperative projects and laid the basis for proposals to funding sources, private and government. Most of this early work focused on proficiency as a central theme; the government schools shared their descriptions of proficiency in the four skills as well as their testing procedures. Shortly thereafter, ACTFL received grants to develop proficiency guidelines for academic purposes, to train faculty to administer an academic version of the Oral Proficiency Interview, and to rate speaking skills in a manner that was compatible and transferable to government scales.

Just as with audiolingualism in the 1960s, there is disagreement within the profession concerning, in particular, the influence of government agencies in the testing of proficiency in academic environments. Some of the questions arise from university faculty who claim there is no acceptable research base for the performance descriptions. Others object in principle and see any governmental role as interference, whether it be in course or programmatic goals, teaching approaches, or testing. Without further elaborating on all the issues surrounding the so-called proficiency movement, the point of this chapter is to underscore the fact that policy at the highest national levels has, once again, initiated a series of events that have resulted in the profession's having taken significant steps to change curricular goals, materials, and testing procedures in many institutions of higher education and in secondary schools.

A Broader Base and Longer Sequence

The commissions and reports also influenced policy by increasing support for and momentum in developing longer sequences for foreign language study. This parallels the rush to FLES programs that occurred in the 1960s, but the content and goals of today's programs differ notably. Organizations such as the National Association of State Boards of Education (see Sullivan, 38) have issued strong calls for sustained sequences of foreign language study beginning in the early grades. A recent Wingspread Conference, sponsored by the Johnson Foundation, has produced a set of recommendations for programs in the elementary schools for which endorsement from foreign language and other professional associations and institutions is being sought (Halsted, 21). The intent of these recommendations is to prevent erosion of high standards and appropriate curriculum as a result of the mandate for earlier second language experiences.

If the United States is ever to emulate the rest of the world's schools by offering instruction in other languages in elementary schools, the time is now. Consensus exists at the policy level. Planning and implementation depend upon funding, upon creating a corps of teachers and materials appropriate to programs, and most importantly, articulation so that students build upon previously learned skills. Policymakers do not see these early experiences as isolated activities but as prerequisites for developing skills needed by adults to live and work in the global economy.

Language Proficiency and Area Studies

Area studies are where the full force of policy in determining the direction of language instruction is felt. The government's funding for international studies is concentrated significantly in the programs established under Title VI, the National Resource Centers and Foreign Language and Area Studies Fellowships. Since the 1985 federal fiscal year, the government has awarded approximately $12,200,000 for centers and $7,550,000 for fellowships. Federal policy was translated into program regulations that carried the force of law. Colleges and universities nationwide competing for Title VI funds are among our most prestigious research institutions. Applicant institutions are required either (1) to build upon a strong language department that could demonstrate successful performance in language proficiencies, not in terms of seat time, or (2) to provide training and staff development in the proficiency approach. With each funding cycle, the regulations on foreign language study have become tighter and more prescriptive by requiring institutions to develop proficiency-based programs, to teach languages through intensive or immersion models, and to assess students' skills according to accepted measures of communication. Proposals for centers had to include information on how the foreign language department was involved in staff development on proficiency teaching and testing.

Excerpts from the Request for Proposal (RFP) for the 1988 competition illustrate how federal regulations modify teaching and program in foreign languages. Priorities set forth in the 1988 competition included:

1. Develop and implement a comprehensive plan for evaluating and improving their foreign language programs in ways compatible with developing national standards.

2. Strengthen their language programs by adding advanced third- and fourth-year language-skill courses (not including literature and tutorial courses).
3. Initiate or strengthen intensive summer language programs that offer instruction in languages not taught on a regular basis during the summer in the United States, provide instruction in introductory and intermediate courses of not less that 20 hours per week, and provide the equivalent of a full academic year's work of language training.
4. Strengthen their language programs by increasing to ten hours of instruction per week their introductory and intermediate language-skill courses (U.S. Department of Education, 42, pp. 3–4).

Not only do program regulations influence approach, they also provide stimulus for including less commonly taught languages in the centers. A report from the Department of Education on the distribution of funds for priority projects in fiscal year 1988 reveals the impact of policy and planning. Table 2-1 shows the distribution of funds allocated for priority projects (set-asides), within the foreign language portion of center activities.

Table 2-1

Allocations for Priority Projects

Title VI Centers FY88

Department of Education, Center for International Education

PROJECT	FUNDS	PERCENT OF TOTAL
Primarily foreign language		
Intensive language instruction	$ 51,285	3.7
3rd / 4th-year language courses	185,549	13.4
Cooperative summer language programs	225,939	16.4
Language program evaluation and proficiency testing	235,376	17.0
Foreign language and international studies		
Teacher education (Outreach)	288,881	20.9
Professional school linkages	175,270	12.7
Filling disciplinary gaps	220,258	15.9

One can trace similar influences on the teaching of world languages in any federally funded program. The National Endowment for the Humanities has, over the last two administrations, allocated its funds for foreign languages to programs grounded in literature and has refused to consider the teaching of the skills. In 1988, the secretary's Discretionary Fund for Critical Languages only entertained proposals on K–6 projects. Should programs approved most recently by the Congress ever be funded, increased emphasis will be placed on linkages of foreign languages and international business at the postsecondary level and in magnet schools at the precollegiate level.

In the United States, however, federal language policy enforces no direct mandate on instructional programs. Should an institution choose a direction in opposition to national guidelines, it can easily circumvent them by developing programs internally without federal funding.

The State Role: Where the Action Is

Whereas the federal government sets policy at the national level, state action determines the reality of language planning, use, and instruction for the majority of citizens. State policies often reflect national priorities, but they are just as likely to clash with them, given that the agendas of the states and of the nation often follow divergent paths.

In terms of bilingual issues, the states are bound to adhere to federal guidelines; some exceed them by implementing substantial programs in ESL and bilingual instruction, drawing upon both transitional and maintenance models. Others obey only the letter of the law by providing minimal state support for students with limited English proficiency and by relegating much of adult English language learning to community agencies such as the YMCA, continuing-education units in local school systems, particularly large urban ones, or literacy programs in the workplace. The enormity of the bilingual issue militates against treating it in detail here and requires limiting this discussion to the three most active areas of state language planning: (1) English as an official language; (2) requirements for foreign language programs in the schools; and (3) foreign language study as part of international education, which is in turn tied to economic development.

English as an Official Language in the States

While passage of a constitutional amendment declaring English to be the official language has thus far failed nationally, sixteen states have so declared either by statute, resolution, or amendment to the state constitution. Table 2-2 contains a listing by state, date, and the legislative action taken.

A perusal of the dates reveals that with the exception of early initiatives in Nebraska (1923), and Illinois (1969), the decade of the 1980s has spawned the most activity. The roots of the Nebraska amendment can be traced to the anti-German sentiment that fermented in the period between the world wars. The Nebraska law prohibited schools from teaching in any language other than English. That law was challenged in *Meyer v. Nebraska* in 1932 when a case was brought against a teacher for having conducted his classes in German in a private church school. The Nebraska Supreme Court upheld the state's prohibition against instruction in a language other than English, but the U.S. Supreme Court overturned it. It did so, however, under protections of freedom of religion and the fundamental rights of families, since the case involved worship and religious instruction in German. Thus, the Nebraska language law remains intact in its requirement for instruction in English in the public schools (Heath, 24; Lyons, 26).

Table 2-2

States with English as an Official Language

STATE	YEAR	LEGISLATION
Arizona	1988	Constitutional amendment
Arkansas	1987	Statute
California	1986	Constitutional amendment
Colorado	1988	Constitutional amendment
Florida	1988	Constitutional amendment
Georgia	1986	Resolution
Illinois	1969	Statute
Indiana	1984	Statute
Kentucky	1984	Statute
Mississippi	1987	Statute
Nebraska	1923	Constitutional amendment
North Carolina	1987	Statute
North Dakota	1987	Statute
South Carolina	1987	Statute
Tennessee	1984	Statute
Virginia	1981	Statute

In the present decade, the motivations and reasons that explain the passage of some of these acts remain ambiguous. Legislators questioned, in hindsight, offer no explanation for these actions, and until recently media coverage was negligible and the public was apathetic toward the issue. In the absence of written policy or documentation, the table and distribution of states suggests certain hypotheses. Of those states enacting laws in the 1980s, eight are in the South with Indiana bordering them. On the map these states form a contiguous block. Most of the laws resemble one another, with Tennessee's statute being typical:

> English is hereby established as the official and legal language of Tennessee. All communications and publications, including ballots, produced by governmental entities in Tennessee shall be in English, and instruction in the public schools and colleges shall be conducted in English unless the nature of the course would require otherwise. (*Tennessee Code of Laws*, 39)

State legislators in office at the time could provide little information on why the statute was introduced or what discussion evolved. They surmise that the impetus arose from a sense of "protectionism" in a time when such international expansion was going on.

Although on the surface this attitude may seem to be inconsistent, conflicting loyalties in these states (parochial Americanism versus the need for international investment) caused legislators to express constituents' concerns for things American, such as language (also an import!) even as governors and mayors provided incentives to foreign industry and trade. No great debates occurred in these states over the issue; indeed, passage was probably achieved in collegial acknowledgment of "someone's bill," as are other nonissues. The results of this legislation in most of these central/southern states today is nil, primarily because few discriminatory behaviors can be attributed to them (few multilingual services or signs existed, so there was little to abolish!), and most citizens are unaware of their existence.

The most recent cases of new English-language laws entail distinct and potentially divisive histories. Arizona, Colorado, and Florida followed California's 1986 precedent and passed their own laws in November 1988. These states share a common and visible concern, that is, integrating a large non-English-speaking immigrant population. Whereas the South may have succumbed to protectionism, these states have capitulated to a backlash with grave economic, social, and political implications. The presumption is that most of these laws will be challenged in the courts, because their intent is to deny many of the benefits of American society to speakers of other languages, including access to the courts, health care, voting, education, and even life style (as evidenced in an office where a supervisor used the new law to forbid employees from conversing behind his back to one another in Spanish).

A few states have established policies that contrast dramatically with English-language amendments by encouraging the use of other languages. In 1989 the New Mexico state legislature unanimously adopted the purposes of English Plus (13—see Appendix) as a resolution. Hawaii in 1978 passed a constitutional amendment rendering English and Hawaiian as coequal official languages. Louisiana's 1974 statute upholds the preservation of and promotes minority languages and cultures. Ancelet (2) traces the state's policy concerning Cajun and discusses the role of the schools in maintaining the language and culture.

Foreign Language Study in the Schools: Revitalization and Requirements

The states, acting primarily through their boards of education, create policies with immense influence on the amount and sometimes the content of foreign language instruction in their schools. Most efforts are targeted at the secondary curriculum, but in some instances elementary and postsecondary mandates also exist.

Numerous surveys track the growth and decline of foreign language programs at various levels of instruction; unfortunately, data are outdated almost as soon as they are reported. Yet a trend toward increased enrollments and/or requirements is clearly visible at present.

Rhodes and Oxford (32) surveyed elementary and secondary program offerings during the 1986/87 academic year. Rather than gather limited numerical data from district offices, they collected information on an extensive questionnaire from a stratified random sample of 5 percent of all 106,000 public and private schools in the United States. Results of this survey, conducted as part of a project by the Center for Language Education and Research (CLEAR), show that 87 percent of responding secondary schools offer foreign language classes (72 percent of junior high schools and 95 percent of senior high schools). At the elementary level, 22 percent offer them, but 55 percent of private and 48 percent of public schools would like to start a program. The survey also reports on types of programs, languages taught, instructional problems identified, and teacher certification. In addition, they offer recommendations that could be used by policymakers and those interested in elementary programs.

The other question that arises relates to whether the availability of language courses is accidental, a local option, or a result of implementation of state policy. Policy may mandate course offerings, it may require students to spend time in a discipline or it may pursue a "carrot" rather than a "stick" path and encourage study without insisting upon it.

In a survey conducted by the author in 1989 for this article, 42 states, through their foreign language supervisors, responded to the following questions:

1. Are schools in the state *required to offer* foreign language instruction? If so, how many years? How many languages? At what grades?
2. Are *students required* to take foreign languages? If so, for how long? Which students (all, honors diploma, college admission)?

Of the states that responded, 31 require public schools to offer at least two years of foreign language study at the high school level; only 11 are exempt from so doing. The mandate for required language courses may come from the state or local school system (e.g., for an honors or regents diploma) or increasingly from higher education. Table 2-3 summarizes in column one whether the schools are required to offer foreign language instruction and if so, what the minimum offerings are. Column two presents requirements for students and whether these are for special diplomas, admission to higher education in the state, or for all students. Readers should be aware of the constantly changing nature of the data contained in table 2-3.

Recent efforts at raising standards in state university systems have resulted in admission criteria that now include two or more years of foreign language study at the secondary level. Thus, policies set in higher education create an impact on precollegiate offerings. Contrary to Ferguson and Huebner's (16) conclusion that private universities have taken the lead in reinstating language requirements, today's huge increases in many states arise from enhanced requirements by state systems of higher education. Granted, many private institutions maintained foreign language entrance requirements when state schools had none, and as liberal arts colleges, their exit requirements still tend to include more language.

Requirements and enrollments do not operate in tandem, however. In many of the states where policy, by requiring language study for college admission, has made courses available in most school systems, the actual number of students taking those courses remains relatively small. Thus, a state such as Tennessee has seen enrollments in second-year high school courses increase 45 percent in the two years prior to the beginning of new admission requirements. At the same time, the number of schools without foreign language courses decreased, so that as of 1988 only four secondary schools lack foreign language offerings. Yet only 29.9 percent of 1987 high school students studied a foreign language. On the other hand, Connecticut requires its schools to offer only a single language for an unspecified number of years and does not require students to take them; nonetheless Connecticut has led the nation in the percentage of secondary students studying languages. Moreover, 90 percent of middle schools voluntarily

Table 2-3

Summary of State Requirements for Course Offerings
in Foreign Language and for Student Enrollment

State	Requirement for Schools; Number of years, languages	Requirement for Students
AL	2 yrs. of 1 lang.	*For adv. dipl.*
AK	None	No
AZ	None	No; 2 yrs. FL may substitute for Eng. IV
AR	2 yrs. of 1 lang.	*For honors dipl. (locally)*
CA	By grade 7	1 yr. FL or arts
CO	None	No; *For U. of CO adm.:* 2 yrs.
CT	None; 90 percent do	No
DE	None; all offer 2 yrs.	*For U. of DE adm.:* 2 yrs.
FL	None; all h.s. do	*For honor dipl./adm. to state higher ed. inst.:* 2 yrs.
GA	2 yrs.	*For adm. to state higher ed. inst.:* 2 yrs.
ID	2 yrs.	No; may satisfy humanities req.
IL	Yes (unspecified)	Part of core with music, computer ed.
IN	2 yrs. of 1 lang.	*For honors dipl.:* 2 yrs. of 2 lang. or 3 of 1
IA	4 of 1 lang. (1989)	*For U. of IA, ISU adm.:* 2 yrs.
KS	2 of 1 lang. (1990)	No; local requirements exist
KY	3 yrs.	*For Commonwealth Dipl.:* 3–4 yrs.
LA	In grades 4–8; no h.s. requirement	5 yrs. in 4–8; *For h.s. honor dipl.:* 3 yrs.; *For LSU adm.:* 2 yrs.
ME	2 yrs. of 1 lang.	No
MD	None	*For Certificate of Merit:* 1 yr. at level 2
MA	None	No; suggested policy
MN	2 yrs. (3 pending) of 1	No; *U. of MN proficiency standard:* 2 yrs. seat time (1991)
MO	2 yrs. of 2 lang. for AAA rating	*For honors:* 2 yrs.
MT	None	No; *U. of MT:* 2 yrs. of FL or 1+ Eng./math/sci./soc. sci.
NB	2 yrs. of 1 lang.	No; position paper being drafted
NV	None	No
NH	3 yrs. of 1 lang; 2 of 2nd	No; requirements for coll.-bound in most districts
NY	4 yrs.; begin by grade 8	2 yrs. in K–9; *For Regents Dipl.:* 3 yrs. plus exam
NC	13 yrs. (1993)	K–5; *For honors:* 2 yrs. h.s.
ND	None	No
OH	3 yrs. of 1 lang. or 2 of 2	*For adm. to state higher ed. inst.:* 2–3 yrs.
OK	None; 2 yrs. for Central Accred. Assoc.	No; most honors require
PA	4 yrs. of 1 lang.; offer 2	No
RI	3 yrs.; 2 lang.	*For coll. adm.:* 2 yrs.
SC	2 yrs. of 1 lang.	*For honors dipl.:* 2 yrs.; *For coll. adm.* (in some districts): 2 yrs.
SD	2 yrs. of 1 lang.	*For coll. adm.*
TN	None	*For adm. to higher ed. inst. (1989):* 2 yrs.
TX	2 yrs. of 1 lang.	2 yrs. in adv. h.s. program
VT	3 yrs. of 1 lang.	No
VA	3 yrs. of 1 lang. by grade 8	*For adv. studies dipl.:* 3 yrs. of 1 or 2 of 2
WV	2 yrs. of 1 lang.	No
WI	4 yrs. of 1 or more	No
WY	2 yrs. of 1 lang.	No

offer foreign languages and every 9–12 school offers at least two, according to Kenneth A. Lester, state foreign language consultant.

The existence of courses provides testimony to state policy, but the most important impact may relate to those rarer instances in which states actually mandate the content of instruction. In the past, little interference occurred as discipline-specific consultants, texts, and past practice combined forces to produce state curriculum guidelines that ruffled few feathers. This tendency may be changing, partly because the public and politicians, in becoming supporters of language study, have agendas of their own.

Teacher Certification: A State Issue

State policy wields strong control over foreign language in the area of standards for teacher education programs and certification. Recent efforts at testing in the certified discipline in addition to that in basic skills and pedagogy have created controversy in foreign language programs. In essence, states have thus far translated policies calling for improved control over subject matter in divergent ways. One complaint in the foreign language field has been the perennial lack of testing of the speaking skill even at a time when the ability to speak becomes increasingly important to classroom performance. Several states have therefore opted to include speaking. Some, such as Texas, will use the Oral Proficiency Interview; others, Georgia for example, use an adaptation or some as yet unidentified equivalency. In other cases, states have issued curriculum guides for the schools that require the teaching of spoken skills and contemporary language, yet test their teachers with outdated instruments that concentrate on language forms, civilization, and a literary orientation in a fill-in-the-blank format. A fuller review of teacher-education issues as affected by state policy can be found in Phillips (30), and Jarvis and Taylor (chapter 5 in this volume) addresses teacher education in a broader sense.

The principal issue here relates to the fact that initiatives at improving teachers' language skills evolve from state policies on teacher education in general and from the schools' need for foreign language teachers who are themselves proficient in order to reach today's objectives.

International Education and Economic Development

Today's state initiatives originate at higher levels than boards of education, for they emanate directly from governors' offices. Of particular interest and importance are economic competitiveness and an international citizenry. The recent report of the Task Force on International Education of the National Governors' Association (28), *America in Transition: The International Frontier,* encourages governors to exert their leadership to promote the study of foreign languages and geography in the schools. The motivations of governors are linked directly to the marketplace and national security.

> How are we to sell our products in a global economy when we neglect to learn the language of the customer? How are we to open overseas markets when other cultures are only dimly understood? Virginia Governor Gerald L. Baliles (28, p. iii).

> More than ever before, our economic well-being is intertwined with that of other countries through expanding international trade, financial markets, and investments. More than ever before, our national security—indeed, world stability as a whole—depends upon our understanding of and communication with other countries. New Jersey Governor Thomas H. Kean (28, p. vii).

As governors translate their concerns for foreign language study into policies for educational institutions, the agenda for language courses includes outcomes measurable in terms of proficiency and the less commonly taught languages. The NGA report (28) laments the fact that

> children in other nations begin to learn a second language in elementary school. American children who have learned languages have learned through outdated methods, with little emphasis on speaking and listening skills. . . . In the United States, instruction is seldom offered in some major languages such as Japanese, Russian, Arabic, and Chinese. Yet these languages are spoken by three-fourths of the world's population, including some major U.S. trading partners (p. 4).

Meeting the Needs of the States

Our discipline enjoys renewed support from the highest levels of state government. The profession, however, must assume responsibility to meet the new goals being set in curricula that focus on practical, measurable, relevant performance in other tongues. Furthermore, ways will need to be found to introduce less commonly taught / most commonly spoken languages into the curriculum rather than adding to the reasons that it cannot be done. Either the profession is part of the solution or it is part of the problem, as the adage goes.

Naturally, state governments should be expected to have to pay for the expansion of programs into elementary grades and into other languages. The profession will have to use that support to learn more about how younger students learn, to create a cadre of teachers for that level, to prepare new teachers at all levels to achieve the stated proficiency goals, to train native speakers of languages to become teachers of those languages. This is a much broader mission than that of teaching two years' worth of language forms to students several times in their educational cycle.

Many states are already active in carrying out the new mandates. All eyes are upon North Carolina as it seeks to implement a K–12 foreign language curriculum by 1993. In an era with dire pronouncements of teacher shortages, one wonders where instructors will be found, especially at the elementary level. Wisconsin, California, Illinois, and several others have undertaken major efforts to create curriculum, to develop materials, and to prepare teachers of Japanese. Wisconsin created a State Superintendent's Advisory Council for Japanese Language and Culture, which formulated policy and implemented an action plan. (Wisconsin Department of Public Instruction, 45.)

The international and global view that motivates the states also causes concern in many language departments at school and university levels. Political leadership wants proficiency as an outcome, whether they know the jargon or not. Professionally, national organizations such as ACTFL, the AATs, regional conferences, even the College Board's Educational Equality Project (7) have dealt extensively with issues of proficiency. State departments of education and local schools have developed curriculum guides using the ACTFL Guidelines (1) as a resource. Yet many states will find that at the classroom level, little has changed to ameliorate the NGA (28) report's complaint about outdated methods and minimal emphasis on communication.

In reality, some of the stagnation occurs because teaching behaviors change ever so slowly. Some of the resistance comes from professionals who have legitimate concerns about the research base and about the lack of theoretical models to support the instructional practices being advocated. Thus, a professional priority must be that of conducting research and improving both teacher preparation and direct classroom instruction in ways that either implement the goals of policy and planners or that amend those goals if they are not appropriate.

Business and Corporate Influences on Policy

There is no denying that both federal and state policies move in directions compatible with perceived needs of business, commerce, and industry in the United States. On the other hand, academic priorities for foreign language study in the liberal arts preparation of students tend to remain stable and loyal to a more narrow definition of humanities; granted the periodic cries for abandonment or for reinstatement of requirements are heard, but generally the cycles settle in and *"plus ça change . . ."*

The impact of business and the corporate world on language instruction in educational institutions is minimally felt in the traditional academic sequence, but it gains prominence in areas where expanded programs are occurring. Specifically, it affects enrollments in uncommonly taught languages, in double majors / minors, and in the continuing education units of universities.

Enrollment Increases in Marketable Languages

The survey conducted by the Modern Language Association and discussed by Collison (8) links the four languages with the greatest three-year growth directly to international business needs. The report shows that between 1983 and 1986 enrollments in Japanese grew by 45.4 percent, Chinese by 28.2 percent, Portuguese by 14 percent, and Russian by 11.8 percent. While raw numbers are still small in comparison to Spanish, French, or German, the students in these courses tend to be there out of choice and in pursuit of specific career goals. These students are primarily business, economics, management, marketing, or finance majors with a smattering of journalists and political scientists.

Many literature departments experience great difficulty in absorbing, evaluating, and promoting teachers of less commonly taught languages (LCTs). Walker (44) explores the dilemma faced when the LCTs meet the "bulk" languages. The solution is either one of creating two distinct programs or one of integrating languages being studied for business purposes and by business students with the more conventional mission of departments. At many universities today, traditional courses are taught in colleges of arts and sciences, while Japanese, Chinese, Arabic, and other LCTs are housed in continuing education, area centers, international studies centers, or weekend colleges. In other words, language instruction at the university level chooses to meet policy initiatives or to operate independently of them.

Nontraditional Majors and Programs

Certainly, today's professional literature is replete with reports of campus initiatives at designing special degree programs that attract dual majors and that promote foreign languages as an ancillary skill. Almost every issue of the *ADFL Bulletin* (Association of Departments of Foreign Languages) contains an article describing such a program; Spinelli (36) reviews some of these in her report and Eastern Michigan's annual conference on foreign languages and international business attracts ever greater numbers. New federal legislation in support of International Business Centers should provide additional support for cooperative ventures with foreign language study. Numerous graduate-level programs are being developed on the models of the former Thunderbird School, the Lauder Institute at the University of Pennsylvania, and the MIBs (Master of International Business) program at the University of South Carolina. Ventures into schools other than business, such as the five-year international engineering program (B.S. in Engineering; B.A. in German) at the University of Rhode Island, provide models for new linkages (Grandin, 19).

Business Learns Language Commercially

Once having exited the groves of academe, businesspeople learn their languages in commercial schools. The world of business finds that language instruction in academic institutions is often too slowly paced, not sufficiently communicative in its objectives, not offered at convenient times, too bound to credit and tuition, and not innovative enough in approach and method. Consequently, commercial schools thrive and many businesses actually contract for on-site teaching that meets their direct needs.

Berlitz no longer dominates the market, although its U.S. enrollments jumped 27 percent last year. Newspaper and magazine articles report constantly on new companies entering the market. Inlingua estimates that revenues for specialized schools topped $100 million last year. Former language teachers, freed from institutional constraints, have even been successful entrepreneurs. Sharon and Karen Whitely operate International Language Services of Dallas, where instruction is based upon the Lozanov approach. While still a small operation ($150,000 in 1988 revenues), it exemplifies the small-business model of language teaching (Buchholz, 6).

The business community recognizes the importance of greater foreign language skills for individuals in their organizations. Consequently, leaders in those companies continue to pressure the government and the educational establishment to provide instruction. When policy does not result in desirable programs, businesses will continue to seek that training elsewhere. They will not, however, stop pressing for better and wider opportunities in the schools.

Professional Input on Policy

Certainly, this article has dealt primarily with the impact of policy on foreign language instruction, but the time has finally arrived in which the profession has the power to act, to help shape policy at national, at state, and at local levels. This has not always been the case. Indeed, prior to the President's Commission on the Teaching of Foreign Languages and International Studies, little dialog occurred between policymakers and foreign language professionals.

A great deal of credit for having changed this state of affairs must be given to the Joint National Committee for Languages, its leadership, and the many professional organizations that gave birth to it and that continue to nurture it. The JNCL and its political-action branch, the National Council for Languages and International Studies (NCLIS), have built the necessary connections to government so that they act as the eyes, ears, and voice of the foreign language profession as they present issues to policymakers.

Recent years have also witnessed foundations acting in support of foreign language projects and in the creation of various centers to consolidate research opportunities, to provide for discussion on language issues, and, last but not least, to influence policy. The role of these centers is not without controversy, because their funding often results from successful proposal writing, which may or may not reflect a consensus of the group supposedly being served.

The National Foreign Language Center, under the leadership of Richard D. Lambert, has received major funding from four foundations: The Exxon Education Foundation, the Ford Foundation, the Andrew W. Mellon Foundation, and the Pew Memorial Trusts. While its mission is multifaceted, it claims that proactive and reactive foreign language education policy is a priority. At the same time, it concentrates its efforts on adult learning and the acquisition of advanced language skills for specialists.

More recently, the Coalition for the Advancement of Foreign Languages and International Studies (CAFLIS), under the directorship of Lillian Pubillones, has been working on a consensus document to identify institutional and policy changes that should take place if international competence is to be achieved in the United States. CAFLIS has focused much of its energy on the concept of endowment in the model of the National Endowment for the Humanities. CAFLIS is a two-year project supported by monies from the Ford, Hewlett, McDonnell, and Rockefeller Foundations.

At a state level, the Tennessee Foreign Language Institute serves as an arm of state government, with a broad mission to improve teaching, to conduct research in language learning, and to increase opportunities for foreign language study by all citizens in the state. On a policy level, it provides information to state government and business and responds to their requests.

Numerous campus-based centers have also arisen in the last few years. Some are coalitions of institutions sharing a common interest, such as the eleven institutions in the Consortium for Language Teaching and Learning headquartered at Yale University under the direction of Peter C. Patrikis. Others are dedicated to topics such as CALICO at Brigham Young for computers (Frank Otto, Director) or PICS at the University of Iowa for international video (James Pusak and Sue Otto, Directors). Finally, single-institution centers act as a conduit for language-related activities on a campus and outreach into the region. Their interest in policy is probably minimal, except that funding opportunities are tied to current national, state, or regional priorities.

Conclusion

In comparison with many nations, the United States has no strong or explicit history of language policy. It designates no official language in its constitution; it enforces no code of standardization on the implicit language, English; it does not require that any school at any level offer instruction in world languages. In fact, it is almost alone among nations in not staffing embassies and missions abroad with speakers of the native languages (Simon, 35).

With implicit policy the reality, planning likewise becomes sporadic, reactive, and changeable. Advantages and disadvantages combine under this framework. On one hand, the United States has not had to deal with some of the divisive issues facing countries such as Canada, where recent official language acts to develop bilingualism have caused much upheaval. Even now, the European Economic Community is grappling with language issues as it readies for a unified Europe in 1992. Should English Only succeed as policy, then planning for implementation could cause problems that remain dormant in its absence.

As for language instruction, states exert more direct control over programs at the classroom level than does the federal government, but even that influence is minimal in terms of day-to-day teaching. Interactions between federal and state government flow in two directions. In the Sputnik era, the federal government provided the impetus and support for new programs. Currently, while Washington plays a funding role, the governors are asserting leadership in pressing for internationalism as a means of developing jobs, trade, and investment in their states.

Putting aside discussions about the humanistic and intellectual value of language study, it is clear that from a policy perspective our discipline is inextricably linked to economic, social, and political factors. While other countries have exhibited more exact planning, their policies are based on similar rationales and goals—communicating in other tongues to enrich one's life intellectually, but also to enhance it socially, politically, and materially.

References, Language Instruction in the United States

1. American Council on the Teaching of Foreign Languages. *Proficiency Guidelines.* Hastings-on-Hudson, NY: ACTFL, 1986.
2. Ancelet, Barry Jean. "A Perspective on Teaching the 'Problem Language' in Louisiana." *French Review* 61 (1988): 345–56. [EDRS: EJ 366 215.]
3. Baker, Keith, and Adriana de Kanter, eds. *Bilingual Education: A Reappraisal of Federal Policy.* Lexington, MA: Lexington Books, 1983.
4. Brod, Richard I. "Options and Opportunities: New Directions in Foreign Language Curricula." *ADFL Bulletin* 10, 4 (1979): 13–18.
5. _____, personal communication.
6. Buchholz, Brad. "Sisters of Other Tongues." *American Way* (1988): 30, 32, 34, 36–38.
7. College Entrance Examination Board. *Academic Preparation in Foreign Language: Teaching for Transition from High School to College.* New York: College Board, 1986.
8. Collison, Michele N-K. "Fascination with Business and the Orient Fuels Enrollment in Asian Languages." *The Chronicle of Higher Education,* February 17, 1988.
9. Cooper, Robert L. "Language Planning, Language Spread, and Language Change," pp. 23–50 in James E. Alaitis and G. Richard Tucker, eds., *Language in Public Life.* Georgetown University Roundtable. Washington, DC: Georgetown Univ. Press, 1979. [EDRS: ED 219 968.]
10. Crawford, James, ed. "Bilingual Education: Language, Learning, and Politics." *Education Week,* April 1, 1987, pp. 19–50. [EDRS: ED 284421.]
11. Di Pietro, Robert J. *U.S. English: Filling a Need?* Paper presented at the 15th Annual LACUS Forum, Michigan State University, East Lansing, MI, August 1988.
12. Edwards, J. David, and Melinda E. Hanisch. "A Continuing Chronicle of Professional, Policy, and Public Activities in Foreign Languages and International Studies," pp. 167–96 in Alice C. Omaggio, ed., *Proficiency, Curriculum, Articulation: The Ties That Bind.* Report of the Northeast Conference on the Teaching of Foreign Languages. Middlebury, VT: The Northeast Conference, 1985.
13. English Plus Information Clearinghouse. "Statement of Purpose." *EPIC EVENTS* 1, 1 (1988): 2.
14. Ferguson, Charles A. "National Attitudes toward Language Planning," pp. 51–60 in James E. Alaitis and G. Richard Tucker, eds., *Language in Public Life.* Georgetown University Roundtable. Washington, DC: Georgetown Univ. Press, 1979. [EDRS: ED 219 968.]
15. _____, and Shirley Brice Heath, eds. *Language in the USA.* Cambridge, Eng.: Cambridge Univ. Press, 1981.
16. _____, and Thom Huebner. *Foreign Language Instruction and Second Language Acquisition Research in the United States.* NFLC Occasional Papers. Washington, DC: National Foreign Language Center at the Johns Hopkins University, 1989.
17. Fishman, Joshua. "Language Modernization and Planning in Comparison with Other Types of National Modernization and Planning." *Language in Society* 2 (1973): 23–43.
18. Geno, Thomas H. "A Chronicle: Political, Professional, and Public Activities Surrounding the President's Commission on Foreign Languages and International Stud-

ies," pp. 13–45 in Thomas A. Geno, ed., *Foreign Languages and International Studies: Toward Cooperation and Integration.* Report of the Northeast Conference on the Teaching of Foreign Languages. Middlebury, VT: The Northeast Conference, 1981.

19. Grandin, John M. "German and Engineering: An Overdue Alliance." [unpublished paper]

20. Grant, Steven A. "Language Policy in the United States." *ADFL Bulletin* 9, 4 (1978): 1–12.

21. Halsted, Henry. "Foreign Language Instruction in Elementary Schools." *The Wingspread Journal,* July 1988.

22. Hayakawa, S. I. "Make English Official: One Common Language Makes Our Nation Work." *Executive Educator* 9, 1 (1987): 36. [EDRS: EJ 345 333.]

23. Heath, Shirley Brice. "Our Language Heritage: A Historical Perspective," pp. 23–51 in June K. Phillips, ed., *The Language Connection: From the Classroom to the World.* The ACTFL Foreign Language Education Series, vol. 9. Lincolnwood, IL: National Textbook Company, 1977. [EDRS: ED 161 257.]

24. _____. "English in Our Language Heritage," pp. 6–20 in Charles A. Ferguson and Shirley Brice Heath, eds., *Language in the USA.* Cambridge, Eng.: Cambridge Univ. Press, 1981.

25. Kloss, Heinz. *The American Bilingual Tradition.* Rowley, MA: Newbury, 1977. [EDRS: ED 145 680.]

26. Lyons, James. "Language and Loyalty: A Comment on the ELA Hearing." *EPIC EVENTS* 1, 2 (1988): 5, 7.

27. National Commission on Excellence in Education. *A Nation at Risk: The Imperative for Educational Reform.* Washington, DC: Government Printing Office, 1983.

28. National Governors' Association. *America in Transition: The International Frontier.* Report of the Task Force on International Education. Washington, DC: National Governors' Association, 1989.

29. "Official Languages: Reconciliation and Tolerance: An Interview with the Prime Minister of Canada." *Language and Society / Langue et Société* 23 (Summer 1988): 7–8.

30. Phillips, June K. "Teacher Education: Target of Reform," pp. 11–40 in Helen S. Lepke, ed. *Shaping the Future: Challenges and Opportunities.* Report of the Northeast Conference on the Teaching of Foreign Languages. Middlebury, VT: The Northeast Conference, 1989.

31. President's Commission on the Teaching of Foreign Languages and International Studies. *Strength through Wisdom: A Critique of U.S. Capability.* Washington, DC: Government Printing Office, 1979.

32. Rhodes, Nancy C., and Rebecca L. Oxford. "Foreign Languages in Elementary and Secondary Schools: Results of a National Survey." *Foreign Language Annals* 21 (1988): 51–69.

33. Rubin, Gary. "Language Policy and the Refugees." *Journal of Refugee Resettlement* 1, 3 (1981): 59–63. [EDRS: EJ 248062.]

34. Ruiz, R. "Orientations in Language Planning." *NABE Journal* 8 (1984): 15–34.

35. Simon, Paul. *The Tongue-Tied American: Confronting the Foreign Language Crisis.* New York: Continuum Publishing, 1980.

36. Spinelli, Emily L. "Beyond the Traditional Classroom," pp. 139–58 in Helen S. Lepke, ed., *Shaping the Future: Challenges and Opportunities.* Report of the Northeast Conference on the Teaching of Foreign Languages. Middlebury, VT: The Northeast Conference, 1989.

37. Stewart, Whitney. "State Initiatives in Foreign Language Study: ERIC/CLL Interviews Jamie Draper." *ERIC/CLL News Bulletin* 12, 2 (1989): 1, 3–4.

38. Sullivan, Candace J. "Foreign Language Study: A Call for State Board Action." *The State Board Connection: Issues in Brief* 7, 7 (1988): 1–2.

39. Tennessee Code of Laws, Acts 1984, Chapter 821, 1.

40. Tonkin, Humphrey. "Grassroots and Treetops: Collaboration in Post-Secondary Programs," pp. 27–60 in John M. Darcey, ed., *The Language Teacher: Commitment and*

Collaboration. Report of the Northeast Conference on the Teaching of Foreign Languages. Middlebury, VT: The Northeast Conference, 1987.

41. Twentieth Century Fund. *Making the Grade.* Report of the Task Force on Federal Elementary and Secondary Education Policy. New York: Twentieth Century Fund, 1983.

42. U.S. Department of Education. Application for Grants under Title VI of the Higher Education Act of 1965: National Resource Centers and Foreign Language and Area Studies Fellowships (1988 competition). CFDA Number 84.015.

43. U.S. Department of Justice, Immigration and Naturalization Service. *Naturalization Requirements and General Information.* Form N-17 (Rev. 5-5-83)Y.

44. Walker, Galal. "The Less Commonly Taught Languages in the Context of American Pedagogy," pp. 111–37 in Helen S. Lepke, ed., *Shaping the Future: Challenges and Opportunities.* Report of the Northeast Conference on the Teaching of Foreign Languages. Middlebury, VT: The Northeast Conference, 1989.

45. Wisconsin Department of Public Instruction. *Preliminary Report of the State Superintendent's Advisory Council for Japanese Language and Culture.* Madison, WI: Department of Public Instruction, 1987.

Appendix A:
English Plus Information Clearinghouse
Statement of Purpose

The core of the strength and vitality of the United States is the diversity of our people, and our constitutional commitment to equal protection under the law. Now, more than ever, our commitment to cultural and democratic pluralism is essential to enhance our competitiveness and position of international leadership. In an interdependent world, the diversity of our people provides a unique reservoir of understanding and talent.

In order to sustain and strengthen these values and the national interest, the undersigned organizations have come together to address more effectively the role of language in the national and international community. We have agreed to a statement of principles and objectives, and to establish EPIC, the English Plus Information Clearinghouse.

The "English Plus" concept holds that the national interest can best be served when all members of our society have full access to effective opportunities to acquire strong English language proficiency *plus* mastery of a second or multiple languages. "English Plus" holds that there is a need for a vastly expanded network of facilities and programs for comprehensive instruction in English and other languages.

"English Plus" rejects the ideology and divisive character of the so-called "English Only" movement. "English Plus" holds that national unity and our constitutional values require that language assistance be made available in order to ensure equal access to essential services, education, the electoral process and other rights and opportunities guaranteed to all members of society.

The undersigned organizations have agreed to establish a national clearinghouse to facilitate the exchange of information in order to strengthen programs and advocacy consistent with our shared values, common objectives and the national interest.

In establishing EPIC, the founding member organizations have agreed to the following resolution:

WHEREAS English is and will remain the primary language of the United States, and all members of our society recognize the importance of English to national life, individual accomplishment, and personal enrichment; and

WHEREAS many U.S. citizens have native languages other than English, including many languages indigenous to this continent, and many members of our society have not had an equal opportunity to learn English; and

WHEREAS the ability to communicate in English and other languages has promoted and can further enhance American economic, political and cultural vitality; and contributes to our nation's productivity, worldwide competitiveness, successful international diplomacy and national security; and

WHEREAS our fundamental values and national documents ensure tolerance and respect for diversity and guarantee all persons equal protection under the law; and

WHEREAS "English Only" and other restrictionist language legislation has the potential for abridging the citizen's right to vote, eroding other civil rights, fostering governmental interference in private activity and free commerce, and causing social disunity; and

WHEREAS the organizations establishing the English Plus Information Clearinghouse are committed to the principles of democratic and cultural pluralism and encourage respect for the cultural and linguistic heritages of all members of our society;

BE IT RESOLVED THAT:

1. There is a need for a vastly expanded network of facilities for comprehensive English language instruction and services to ensure all persons the ability to exercise the rights and responsibilities of full participation in society.
2. There is a need to foster multiple language skills among all of our people in order to promote our position in the world marketplace and to strengthen the conduct of foreign relations.
3. There is a need to encourage the retention and development of a person's first language, to build upon the multiple language skills of all members of our society, and to strengthen our commitment to cultural and democratic pluralism.

4. There is a need to retain and strengthen the full range of language assistance policies and programs including bilingual assistance, in order to ensure all members of society an equal opportunity to exercise their rights and responsibilities in regard to the electoral process, education, the legal system, social services and health care.
5. There is a need to reject the objectives and premises of "English Only" and promote the concept of "English Plus" in order to promote public civility and the fundamental values and objectives of our society.
6. There is a need to defeat any legislative initiative on the federal, state or local level which would mandate English as the official language and thereby restrict the civil rights, civil liberties or equal opportunities of all persons, including persons with limited English proficiency.
7. There is a need for an English Plus Information Clearinghouse to facilitate and enhance: the exchange of information, public education, advocacy, effective policies and programs, and cooperation among a wide range of communities, private organizations and public sector entities.
8. The National Forum and the Joint National Committee for Languages will provide the auspices for the staff and information activities of the English Plus Information Clearinghouse.

3

Sketching the Crisis and Exploring Different Perspectives in Foreign Language Curriculum

Dale L. Lange
University of Minnesota, Twin Cities Campus

Introduction

In the simplest way of stating it, most people consider curriculum to be the determination of what is to be taught, how to organize the "what," and how to teach it. In other words, *curriculum* is a learning plan; *instruction,* on the other hand, is generally considered to be a coupling of such a plan to students as they learn. The teacher serves as mediator and "coach" between the plan and student learning. Curriculum and instruction are both necessary elements in developing and delivering any program for students, including foreign languages. Although the emphasis in this chapter is on foreign language curriculum, its relationship to instruction cannot be ignored.

In the foreign language context, there seems to be no lack of programs designed to illustrate how curriculum and instruction are associated. Two recent examinations of this relationship have categorized the several ways in which language curriculum and instruction are allied. Crawford-Lange (16) suggests that process, content, and instruction together affect curricular options.

Dale L. Lange (Ph.D., University of Minnesota) is Professor of Second Languages and Cultures Education and Associate Dean in the College of Education at the University of Minnesota–Twin Cities Campus. He edited volumes 2 and 3 and coedited volume 4 of the ACTFL Foreign Language Education Series; he also served as editor of the ACTFL Annual Bibliography from 1968 to 1972. He served as President of ACTFL in 1980. His articles have appeared in many professional journals, including *Foreign Language Annals, French Review, Modern Language Journal, Review of Educational Research,* and *Die Unterrichtspraxis.*

In reviewing curricular designs (*process:* systems-behavioral and problem-posing), content alternatives (*content:* functional-notional syllabus, interdisciplinary, and cross-disciplinary approaches), and instructional alternatives (*instruction:* Suggestopedia, Counseling Learning, and cooperative learning), Crawford-Lange assumes the validity of all alternatives, with no one of them being monolithic in its ability to resolve all curricular or instructional problems. Instead, the conscious choice of one or more approaches over others results from considerations of student, school, community, context, instructor, and desired outcomes. In a second analysis, using Stern's (92) now-classic conceptualization of the four contents of language curricula (the linguistic, communicative, cultural, and general language syllabi), Lange (56) demonstrates the ability of systems-behavioral, proficiency, and content-oriented curricular designs to accommodate the integration of these contents. The result of this exploration reveals that content-oriented curricula (a process-governed culture content and a framework directed toward world knowledge) have the potential for integrating the four contents, whereas others (systems behavioral, communicative, and proficiency-oriented) fail that test in various ways.

These analyses are provocative mainly because they display extensive curricular designs and approaches, including those that are instructional in nature. This abundance of choice is mostly theoretical, however, because the options remain unrealized. The real curriculum is not necessarily determined from speculative deliberations by academics or by practical requirements of classroom teachers. It is determined more by publishers and textbook authors than curricular theorists, curriculum supervisors, and teachers. In simple terms, we have handed the design of elementary, secondary, and college curricula to commercial interests that have determined both the content and direction of language programs. What sells is what gets printed; what gets printed is used; what is used is considered authentic because it has been published! The circle is closed.

In the past decade, at least three statements about the articulation of language programs have appeared in print. Lafayette (49) listed three types of articulation: internal articulation (uniting progress toward desired outcomes with classroom instruction within a course), sequential articulation (unity in direction from one course to program, school, and university), and external articulation (relating to the content of other areas of the curriculum, e.g., social studies or global education).

In a subsequent article, Lange (55) standardized Lafayette's concepts, using terms understood more broadly in the curriculum field itself: relationship of performance objectives to outcomes and horizontal, vertical, and interdisciplinary articulation. He also suggested means by which articulation can be resolved through dialog and action, use of the curricular process itself, coordination of programs, individualized instruction, course content, and text selection. Even though these definitions, explanations, and resolutions are easily understood, their actual application in schools and colleges and universities remains ignored.

In a 1988 article, Lange (58) approached the issue once again. In this analysis, he defines articulation in the following way: "*Articulation* is both the interrelationship and continuity of contents, curriculum, instruction, and evaluation within programs which focus on the progress of the student in learning to both comprehend and communicate in a second language" (pp. 16–17). This global statement is different from the earlier statements of both Lafayette and Lange. It suggests considerable complexity in the relationships indicated. Furthermore, its focus is clearly on the student's competence *to comprehend and use* language. Where earlier emphasis on language teaching attended to the *language* content of the curriculum (phonology, morphology, syntax, lexicon), this statement connects comprehension with content, supplies the obligation to express meaning, provides meaning for the learning environment, furnishes the occasion for the student and teacher to find the discourse needed to negotiate both the expression and comprehension of meaning, and evaluates the individual's ability to express and comprehend meaning within a context of a program designed for these purposes.

The definition of content, used in this context, is not that of grammar, vocabulary, pronunciation, and fluency of language production only. It includes the personal and social contexts of the learner and anticipates the learner's application of language within those contexts. In other words, the foreign language permits the learner to think in another language, to comprehend, know, and interpret the environment in which it is used. It allows the student to "know" himself or herself and the environments in which she or he uses different languages. The content of the language curriculum contains the parts and pieces of language as well as the use of language by the individual for knowing the self and the interrelationship of the self with that which is to be known. Widdowson's (105) lengthy discussion of language as communication approaches this definition. Yet his definition is incomplete, because its focus remains on the structure of language and what is to be known with the language tool. He does not recognize the contribution of language learning to the development of the relationship of thought to "word" in a second language in the Vygotskyan sense (102) where thought is not clearly separable from language. Language or the word expresses the innermost thoughts of the individual, not just abstractions represented by the word.

In this different vision, there are new relationships to be built. Classroom language learning will not only be structured for the learning of aspects of language, but will also be open to the knowledge, background, and experiences of learners and teachers together. The resulting context will be replete with a variety of interactions among the suggested relationships. Kramsch (45) conveys the importance of these interactions in her description of different discourse options in using the foreign language in the classroom and their implications for teaching and learning, as well as for the development of a social context, including the negotiations for power, all of which impinge on "the plan" for foreign language learning and teaching. The simple solutions of choosing the same text, the same method, and the same testing procedures for everyone are superficial responses to this exceedingly complicated set of conditions.

The foreign language curriculum can be viewed as (1) complex in terms of existing curricular and instructional choices, at least in theory, (2) controlled by outside factors such as publishers and textbook authors (maybe even some linguists), and (3) elaborate in terms of the many relationships among the elements of its makeup in responding to a different view of language learning that is more personal and more desirous of both the expression and comprehension of meaning. Because of this complexity, it is clear that designing and organizing curriculum for foreign language programs is formidable. In the view of this writer, these three conditions present also important evidence to suggest that the necessary concentration, energy, and attention are *not* being directed to curricular considerations in school and college and university foreign language programs. In simple truth, the foreign language curriculum is in crisis.

Having raised the concern for a crisis in foreign language curriculum in the introduction to this paper, it is the author's intention to document its existence, discuss current mainstream conceptualizations of curriculum, examine foreign language curriculum in their shadows, and from this examination imply directions for the future of curriculum development in this field.

A Crisis in Second Language Curriculum: Seven Indicators

In order not to alarm anyone, the concept of curriculum, in the broader sense of our school and college and university cultures, *is* in crisis (Boyer, 8; National Commission on Excellence in Education, 71; President's Commission on the Teaching of Foreign Languages and International Studies, 80; Sizer, 88) in the general sense. The crisis announced by such documents is largely a public perspective of education and is supported by viewpoints from private philanthropic organizations. Though important, these arguments are not specific to language education and will not be repeated here.

The crisis in language education has a more internal nature and is similar to the crisis in curriculum in general in 1969, a situation that has not been substantially ameliorated. Schwab (86), a general curriculum theorist who announced this 1969 crisis, characterized it as having six "flights," to which I add a seventh. In the following discussion, each of Schwab's signs is briefly described and then related to foreign language education. There is no attempt to review the substantial body of literature related to foreign language curriculum; instead the examples used have been chosen to support Schwab's metaphor and to create the image of flight.

Flight 1: From the Field

This flight suggests relocation of the field's problems to another place and resolution of the problems by those who have little to do with them or the field itself. In many ways, foreign language education solicits solutions to issues and problems within by seeking resolution in outside disciplines such as linguistics, psycholinguistics, educational psychology, and psychology. In order not to be misunderstood, I suggest that these areas may certainly contribute to our broad knowledge of language and learning. Yet they are incapable of resolving questions of a curricular and instructional nature because their conceptualization is directed almost exclusively toward the learning of linguistic aspects of language, with little intent to consider either the intellectual, social, and emotional development of individuals in classrooms (Egan, 23) or the purpose of language study in their theories.

Foreign language education has always allowed itself to be influenced, for example, by the field of linguistics, "the scientific study of language." Largely as a result of Bloomfield's (7) conceptualization of how language should be examined, namely by the "scientific method," an aura of truth was allocated to linguists who classify and codify a set of synchronic rules to explain observed language behavior. In turn, the explanation of that behavior is used to predict and determine how languages are learned and taught. In a chapter of his book, however, "Application and Outlook," Bloomfield alludes to the practical problems of the application of scientific linguistics to foreign language learning and other endeavors and carefully avoids direct utilization of linguistics in the resolution of specific issues. Some years later, Chomsky (13) states openly that he is skeptical about the significance of linguistics for the teaching of languages. But, in the same publication, Ferguson (25), while attempting to show two examples of the application of linguistics to language teaching and a set of general principles for the same basic purpose, is not very convincing in making the argument for the connection. Certainly, any interpretation of the most recent article that examines broadly the research in the field of second language acquisition (Ferguson and Huebner, 26) finds that attempts to both use and create theory to answer questions about language acquisition and learning in the classroom from either linguistics or psychology are problematic, to say the least.

These general perceptions, which I have presented here as evidence of this "flight," suggest that linguistic theory is of some importance to language learning but that it is not sufficient to explain how language is either learned or acquired in the classroom.

Flight 2: Upward

This flight is a theoretical discussion about theory moving from use of principles and methods to discussion about them, or in theoretical jargon, metatheory. There is an increasing demand for clarification of the language learning/acquisition process from those who think and write about the nature of that process. A relatively recent extrapolation of many of the theories in this regard has been accomplished by Gardner (32). He reviews seven theories of language acquisition, adding an eighth of his own: (1) the monitor model (Krashen, 46 and 47; Krashen and Terrell, 48); (2) a conscious reinforcement model (Carroll, 11); (3) a strategy model (Bialystok, 6); (4) a social psychological model (Lambert, 53 and 54); (5) an acculturation model (Schumann, 85); (6) a social context model (Clément, 15); (7) an intergroup model (Giles and Byrne, 35); and (8) his own socioeducational model. In his discussion of these theories, Gardner moves from a description of the principles of each model to a metatheoretical discussion of all of them. He extrapolates five major themes common to all models: There is a presumption of motivation; motivation is social in nature; language learning requires learners to make adjustments of a social nature; individual differences relate to differential learning or acquiring of language; and all of the models are descriptive, they are not predictive. Clearly, these models do not account for all aspects of language learning. Gardner's specific focus, for example, is on motivation. Such a singular focus tends to ignore the myriad of other factors, some of which can be examined and some not. Similar kinds of emphases are apparent for the other models as well.

A curious fact arrives from this examination. None of the models focus on the development of the individual in school settings in relationship to language learning or acquisition with the purpose of developing learners' knowledge and use of another language, culture, and experience that causes them to grow socially, emotionally, spiritually, and intellectually. What has the flight upward contributed to our understanding? Can we have confidence that the theoretical discussion and its meta-conclusions are useful?

Flight 3: Downward

In this flight, according to Schwab, the movement is by practitioners who move without consideration from the theoretical, to a completely innocent and virginal examination of the subject to be studied. The single best example of the "flight downward" is a book by Oller and Richard-Amato (73), which contains a subtitle, "a smorgasbord of ideas for language teachers," announcing an uncritical examination. It is a book that serves as a dramatic example of movement from the theoretical to the practical. In so doing, the editors send the message to teachers that they have many alternatives from which to choose. While the presentation of these concepts is not virginal in the Schwabian sense, it is somewhat naive, suggesting that those for whom the book is intended are unsophisticated and should remain in that state.

By using the term *uncritical* in the above paragraph, I am not suggesting that the authors should conduct a logical or empirical critique of these ideas. I do mean, however, that these "ideas" require careful examination in the light of the implications of their use in connection with curricular and instructional realities that cannot be ignored. The contextualizations that "these ideas" are given in the book raise more questions than they answer. The need for a critical pedagogy, that is, the examination of the "relationship between power and knowledge" (McLaren, 68), arises from the superficial treatment given the ideas in the book. In the "flight" being discussed here, the "ideas" about language teaching are treated as being technical or instrumental in the achievement of language competence. At the same time, there is virtually no assessment of the use of these instrumental procedures in accomplishing the larger task of developing the learners' broader understanding of the world and their development in it. Some of the questions that *must* be asked in this regard are the following:

1. What is the contribution of language learning to the social, economic, and political contexts in which these "ideas" may or may not be employed?

2. What is the effect of social, political, and economic contexts on the use, modification, or nonuse of these "ideas" in language learning?
3. What are the contributions of these "ideas" to the development of the ability of children, adolescents, and adults to know themselves and their world(s)?
4. What are the contributions of these "ideas" to the learning of language in various school, college, or university contexts that are always influenced by the social, political, and economic context?

The lack of a critical examination of these "ideas" has several effects. It suggests that language learning in schools, colleges, and universities is disconnected from a meaningful world. It eimplies also that a mindless choice of strategy, "method" (whatever that means), or activity is all that matters. Further, it demonstrates a lack of understanding, coherence, and connectedness of the field to students' need for meaning in their lives. I would argue that the import of this condition is a demonstration of lack of intellectual will and vigor in both knowing and understanding the importance of language learning. From my perception, there is no more potent tool for the discovery of meaning for ourselves and our world than the development of cultural sensitivity and competence in languages other than the one(s) given to us by our mother culture.

Flight 4: To the Sidelines

Instead of participating in the problems of the field, there is movement to the sidelines to observe, comment, review the past, or critique the contributions of others. While there are several examples of this tendency, among them the President's Commission on the Teaching of Foreign Languages and International Studies (80), the most visible one is that contributed by Richard Lambert. Lambert, a sociologist whose comments on the field from the sidelines are intended to save second language education from itself, believes that his perceptions exhibit truth that others do not recognize. In two of his recent books (50 and 51), Lambert focuses largely on three observations of the field. In his opinion, second or foreign language education (1) lacks concentration on the development of language competency for adults; (2) is disaggregated or organized of separate, noncommunicating parts; and (3) demonstrates a weak association with and tradition of empiricism. In disputing these observations, Lange (57) suggests that adult language learning problems cannot be resolved in isolation, that centralization of power eliminates discovery and choice, and that empiricism is but one means of discovering knowledge of how languages are learned and acquired.

Based on his work, it appears that Lambert believes that the concentration of power in the now established National Foreign Language Center and in a proposed Foundation for Foreign Language and International Studies will eradicate the failures of foreign or second language education. These proposals come not from participating in the field, but from its observation, from the sidelines, if you will.

In his "Monday morning quarterback" role, Lambert displays a veritable misunderstanding of the field. At the same time, he conveys solutions that largely discount and disregard the field for which they were intended. His action solutions to treat the problem focus largely on the learning of the "truly foreign languages" (e.g., Chinese and Japanese) by adult learners. While it is important to recognize these language as crucial and this population as critical, the attention given to them is out of proportion with the many issues and problems that face second language education in general (e.g., curricular directions; content; articulation from elementary school through university level; research needs; development of meaningful, reliable, and valid tests and evaluation procedures) in a variety of contexts and circumstances (elementary and secondary schools, college/university, government language schools, to name a few). In arriving at his action solutions, Lambert drew people in the field together to outline the problems and to create a national agenda (Lambert, 52). He used the arguments developed to solicit money for this agenda. He created certain expectations and excitement. Once he received the money, however, he abandoned the consensus agenda in favor of his own. This behavior suggests a strange personal ethic that does not match the original purpose of creating a national agenda. One unfortunate result of his rhetoric is the deception of well-intentioned colleagues, associations, and funding sources into giving support for his hidden agenda.

In this particular instance, it appears as though the flight to the sidelines may have "boomeranged," since the National Foreign Language Center is largely unproductive, an ironic twist of fate for the center and an unhealthy result for a field in crisis.

Flight 5: Preservation of the Familiar

This flight is characterized by repetition of the known in new language, by repetition of known principles as a means of critique, or simply by minor alterations. The intent is preservation of what exists.

Perhaps the best-known examples of this flight with which many readers are familiar are the hypotheses of Krashen (46 and 47). It is my contention that these assertions represent partial restatements or repetitions with some "new twists" or minor alterations. In a general sense, Krashen's five hypotheses (distinction between learning and acquisition, natural order of acquisition, monitor, input, and affective filter) affirm in provocative terms a renewed importance for the learning and acquisition of linguistic content mostly for adults. The learning of linguistic content is, however, really nothing new (see Kelly, 44; especially pp. 34–59). Furthermore, these hypotheses do not speak directly to the development of the ability to communicate either with text or people and should not be transferred automatically to that context. Within this understanding, then, it appears that Krashen supports the tendency to preserve the familiar," but also provides some new "insights." The "familiar" in this case is the focus on linguistic structures and features. Thus we are given seventeenth century wine in twentieth century bottles with better glass and different shapes, representing either regions whence the wine comes or better design for storage.

Learning-Acquisition Distinction. The elements of Krashen's first hypotheses have been known for some time and have been treated in a similar fashion.

Krashen defines learning and acquisition as "picking up a language" and "conscious knowledge of a language" (46, p. 10) and believes these concepts are distinct and independent. Palmer's (77) earlier discussion of spontaneous and studial capacities (pp. 1–22) parallel in many ways Krashen's concepts of acquisition and learning. Palmer too sees the distinction and the separation of the spontaneous from the studial capacities. In fact, he seems to argue that learning inhibits acquisition. Palmer's focus seems to be more on the acquisition of language for communication, whereas Krashen's focus is on the acquisition of linguistic structure. Palmer, like Krashen, outlines a series of scenarios where learning may be useful. While the debate over the distinction between these terms and their usefulness is certainly not over, it appears that previous discussions of the distinction have perhaps been ignored.

Natural Order. This hypothesis, which has its roots in the research of Dulay and Burt (22), states that grammar is acquired in a predictable order. While Krashen's unique contribution to this hypothesis as well as the uniqueness of the hypothesis itself are not disputed here, there is significant controversy over the concept (Spolsky, 89). This hypothesis represents a new "twist."

Monitor. According to this hypothesis, the monitor is the editor of our utterances, either during or after speaking or writing. In order for the monitor to function, the language performer must have sufficient time, must focus on form, and must know the rule. Here again, Palmer's (77) earlier discussion of "our studial capacities" should be noted. Palmer explains that these capacities are used to learn how to read and write (considered unnatural aspects of language by Palmer), for purposes of correction ("to replace faulty material by sound material," p. 19), and "to learn its structure and peculiarities just as a mechanic" (p. 21). The parallelism of Palmer's notions with those of Krashen is certainly provocative. Is the idea of the monitor new?

Input. This hypothesis is certainly not new. Every teacher knows intuitively that contextualization of new linguistic material is important for meaning of that material to be established, that the linguistic material to be learned must always be just slightly beyond the place where the learner currently functions, and that student learning needs to be both gradual and challenging. Kelly's (44) comments on staging the sequence of skills and gradation, particularly on productivity, suggest that elements of input have been in the discussion of language teaching for several centuries. Palmer's definition of gradation, which he describes as "passing from the known to the unknown by easy stages, each of which serves as a preparation for the next" (p. 76) also sounds vaguely reminiscent of Krashen's concept of $i + 1$.

Affective Filter. The affective filter hypothesis suggests that motivation, self-confidence, and levels of anxiety affect the outcome of language acquisition either positively or negatively. There is not sufficient opportunity to discuss this issue at length, except to say that the evidence from the research of the past two decades is not clear in this regard. While this hypothesis is a unique contribution of Krashen to a theory of second language acquisition, I tend to side with Spolsky (90) who argues that the evidence to support the hypothesis is weak.

This discussion, while not intended as a critique of Krashen's five hypotheses, has demonstrated that there is some repetition of old and familiar knowledge in new language in hypotheses 1, 3, and 4. Perhaps the most surprising development is that there is no reference to Harold Palmer in either Krashen's *Principles and Practices in Second Language Acquisition* (47) or *Second Language Acquisition and Second Language Learning* (46).

Flight 6: Contentious Debate

Simply stated, this flight refers to the abundance of quarrelsome interchange and *ad hominem* debate in the literature and at conferences about issues related to the curriculum. The literature on language as communication contains competing tenets and structures that seem to have both personal and political import. Is it communicative competence or language proficiency? Whose description, principles, and procedures should endure? How do we "test" oral language competence? Which came first? Examples of responses to these questions are found in several professional publications.

The American Council on the Teaching of Foreign Languages (ACTFL) has attracted the rancor of several foreign/second language scholars by publishing a set of proficiency guidelines (ACTFL, 1 and 2) and by pursuing a "testing" procedure, the oral proficiency interview (OPI). The reader should examine Byrnes and Canale (10), Higgs (38 and 39), and James (40) to understand the guidelines, their perceived implications for teaching, curriculum, and evaluation of learning, and the history and structure of the OPI. The examples of opposition to the ACTFL effort comes from discussions, research, and conference proceedings. It is not my intention here to take sides in the debate or to argue with the point of view of the writers, but rather to indicate that discord exists and to provide a few important examples of it.

Several discussions of the ACTFL effort demonstrate the squabble. One of the first articles to "tackle" the ACTFL project was that of Lantolf and Frawley (59). Although the critique presented in the article is reasonable, it offered a direct challenge to both the guidelines and the OPI by arguing that (1) the definitions of the guidelines are analytic, reductive, and norm-referenced; (2) the OPI as a testing procedure is not criterion-referenced and does not reflect the world; and (3) the building of language learning curricula on the guidelines is very undesirable. Lantolf and Frawley question the statements and judgment of the proponents of the ACTFL project by juxtaposing their arguments against those of Gasparro, Higgs and Clifford, Lowe, and Omaggio. In their 1988 article, Lantolf and Frawley (60) use the same procedure to direct their critique, but they also provide the beginnings of a different model of proficiency, in spite of protesting that they are not required to produce one. Needless to say, this critique "rattled" the "proficiency movement," though documentation in this regard is difficult to find. Lowe's article (64) is probably the most useful comment on the criticism of both the guidelines and the OPI, but not necessarily on the Lantolf and Frawley articles.

Savignon's critique (83) is more personal. It appears that at least one of her arguments revolves around the fact that the concept of communicative competence, which she proffered extensively and almost exclusively in the 1970s, was not considered part of "the proficiency movement." She also emphasizes the narrow definition of proficiency that appears in the guidelines, such as lack of focus on sociolinguistic, discourse, and strategic competencies. This emphasis is linked directly to the model of proficiency that Bachman and Savignon (3) have stipulated as the concept of "communicative language proficiency." Savignon (83) attacks directly what appears to be an overly heavy emphasis on grammar, which comes not from the guidelines themselves but rather from the literature that explains the guidelines and their use in the OPI. She is also critical of the attempts to base specific curricula on the guidelines and the OPI.

Up to this point, the situation is understandable. However, those persons associated with the ACTFL "proficiency movement" need to understand that they had created certain relationships between the ACTFL Guidelines (1 and 2) for reading, hierarchies of reading skills (Phillips, 79; Omaggio, 74), and text types (Child, 12). Since there is little data to support those associations, Lee and Musumeci (61) chose to research them. The results of their research indicate that neither hierarchies of reading skills or text types nor a cross section among hierarchies of reading skills and text types across four semesters show any statistical relationship with those hypothesized in the assumption of Phillips (79), Omaggio-Hadley (75), Child (12), or in the Guidelines. While it is clear that this research is disturbing to at least three proponents of the Guidelines (Dandinoli, 20; Galloway, 31; and Omaggio-Hadley, 75), it is at the same time important for them to listen to and read carefully what the research expresses. They cannot simply argue that associations about which they have clearly been writing are not related to the Guidelines. Lee and Musumeci's response (62) continues the debate by suggesting that ACTFL "serve up the model of reading underlying the *Proficiency Guidelines*" (p. 457), which appears to me to be a reasonable request.

Finally, conferences are used to bring "opposing sides" together to debate issues that have become emotional and political rather than intellectual. This intent served as the impetus for a symposium on proficiency evaluation sponsored by Indiana University (Valdman, 100). Having been an attendant and presenter, I have no doubt that the atmosphere was charged. This was the time to confront ACTFL on its project. Several of the presentations, discussions, and critiques were so harsh, acerbic, and caustically given that debate and discussion was for all purposes cut off. The result was a publication, but hardly a useful discussion. The most reasonable voice was that of Tucker (97), who articulated three needs that arose from the symposium: (1) the need to develop operational definitions of crucial, important terms; (2) the need to develop "a vigorous proactive research agenda"; and (3) the need to "undertake a broadly-based information dissemination campaign." To date, none of these efforts has been undertaken.

Certainly, little of the rhetoric of these discussions has been useful. Anger, distrust, frustration, inflammatory oratory, and division seem to rule where dialog and discussion, cooperation, trust, and anticipation could help resolve problems and differences.

Flight 7: Exhaustion

This flight (added by the author) refers essentially to the lack of willingness to consider further developments in a field because of the inability to sort out those that already exist. Secondary school language teachers, college and university language coordinators, instructors, and professors, those who deliver the language learning curriculum, are overwhelmed by the task and the demands of the context. There is little time to reflect on the tasks involved in language learning to know even that those tasks are appropriate. The important changes that could be made are not even contemplated. The opportunities to examine the newest textbook, to read the latest research report or interesting journal article, and to teach an experimental course all go begging. There is hardly any energy or time for renewal!

In a 1978 article, DeLorenzo et al. (21) describe the attitudes of teachers who find the expectations of their jobs almost impossible to realize. The teacher is expected to know how to develop and write materials, to organize each and every learning task effectively, to remember enormous detail, and to furnish answers and develop instruction for all levels. Teachers are expected to fulfill all these responsibilities simultaneously *and* with few resources or little support. Jarvis (chapter 5 in this volume) makes similar observations. The demands on elementary and secondary teachers are immense. They are no less gargantuan for professionals at the college level where, in addition to all the previously mentioned duties, professors must "publish or perish." While difficult to document, it is this atmosphere that makes the professional life of foreign language teachers exhausting.

When the day is done and the weariness of the many problems are resulting decisions begin to take hold, how is it possible to grasp new ideas, teaching strategies, or texts? One approach to ease this burden has been the establishment of collaboratives (Gaudiani, 34) of the Academic Alliance movement. Although these helpful and resuscitative groups work well, they provide only a minor portion of the solution to an immense problem.

This situation must be placed into a broader perspective because it holds not only for foreign language teachers but for almost all who really care about their students and their profession. Tensions exist between the requirements of school and university systems, the manner in which teachers are treated, and the teachers' own views of education, all of which contribute to a kind of intellectual, ethical, and emotional exhaustion. This condition is exemplified in a study by Freedman, Jackson, and Boles (27) of Boston-area elementary school teachers who found themselves viewed by the public as incapable of making appropriate decisions, who are constantly monitored, who were treated to work conditions that were sexist, and who were restricted to the most rote and mechanical orientations toward teaching. As explained by the authors, this climate existed while simultaneously the public expected schools to prepare students for adult life, to encourage students to act independently, to prepare students to understand the implications of their decisions in a democratic society, and to teach and encourage students to understand the implications of their decisions in a democratic society, and to teach and encourage students to be risk-takers. In addition to the conditions and expectations of schooling detailed in this study, it is important to add that teachers, for the most part, serve large numbers of students, have little time for planning, may teach too much, possess few opportunities to work together collectively to make decisions about teaching and curriculum, and may be working with teacher-proof materials, which deskill teachers and devalue their decisions.

The above paragraphs describe the kinds of responsibilities, tasks, expectations, and responses of teachers to the demands of their positions. There is no question that teaching is complicated and exhausting! It may even seem impossible! It may also seem that precious few improvements can be made in the teaching environment. In two important books, Giroux (36 and 37) presents the concepts of teachers as intellectuals and critical pedagogy as means by which these conditions can be alleviated.

Summary

Simply put, the foreign language curriculum is in crisis. The broad evidence presented here does not suggest that the foreign language curriculum is moribund, but it does nudge us into the realization that curriculum in foreign language education evokes quite differing thoughts, reactions, and actions, all of which lack focus on student learning. In other words, the various "flights" examined here essentially point away from the central concern of foreign language curriculum which is the development of students' ability to function in another language and to understand its culture(s). I do not propose that a single, unified direction for foreign language curriculum be attempted, but rather that the curriculum should be consolidated around the learner, an idea supported and discussed by Galloway in chapter 4 of this volume. To conclude from the preceding examination of the crisis, that focus has not occurred.

Further, narrow curricular emphases must be examined in the light of broader discussions. While many examples were revealed above, another such focus is mentioned here, namely the emphasis associated with the assumed, ubiquitous, and highly developed technology of behavioral objectives and learning outcomes designation, task analysis of language learning and language use, the evaluation of learning that is currently en vogue. State departments of education seem to be flocking to the notion of learner outcomes, associated learning tasks, and evaluation procedures. The crisis suggests that the narrow confines of curricular organization and design cannot be the sole arbiter of curriculum. The foreign/second language profession must connect itself to other, more general, theoretical, and critical discussions of curriculum about which it knows extremely little. It is this connection that is discussed in the next section.

Sorting Out the Conceptualizations of Curriculum ───────

The purpose of this section is not to define the concept of curriculum, for there are hundreds of definitions in education textbooks. Instead, the purpose of these next paragraphs is to categorize tendencies from theoretical discussions about the nature and purpose of the curriculum, or "the plan for student learning." While there is not necessarily complete agreement on the metacategorization of curriculum theory, there seems to be some agreement on a threefold categorization described in the work of Schubert (84): (1) scientific-technical, known also as the empirical-analytic or systems-behavioral inquiry; (2) practical or hermeneutic inquiry; and (3) critical or emancipatory inquiry. A description and critique of each mode of inquiry is provided below.

Scientific-Technical, Empirical-Analytic, or Systems-Behavioral Inquiry

This category combines a group of tendencies that are both analytical and prescriptive. Tyler (98; or see Tyler, 99, for a succinct summary of the "Tyler rationale") is generally "blamed" for having oriented curriculum in this direction. While his orientation to the study of curriculum was specifically analytic, the use of his work has been largely prescriptive. His original intent was the description of curricular practice in schools. What he found appears to be a systematic process consisting of four elements (1) statement of purpose; (2) learning experiences to fit the purpose of learning; (3) ordering of learning experiences for the purpose of efficient learning; and (4) evaluation of learning to demonstrate that the goals had been achieved. His work has, however, been misused. Instead of looking at the four elements through which Tyler described curriculum activity in schools as explanation of curriculum development, teachers, administrators, and curriculum consultants have widely used his analysis to restrict the elaboration of curriculum in a highly technical manner. This direction has largely been interpreted as being canon. As a result, much of curricular theory, inquiry, orientation, and decision making in schools, and even in colleges and universities, is characterized as being "scientific."

Within this prescriptive mode of thinking, the logical breakdown of what is to be learned into its constituent parts is a central concern. The beginning of the process is a statement of purpose or goal. Those purposes having been determined, "scientific knowledge" of the field and of the teaching-learning process is used to analyze the "experiences" needed to achieve those purposes. In order to observe that learning has taken place, the "required" behavioral activities for teaching/learning are then arranged, for example, in an order from easy to difficult, or from simple to complex. The learning of these activities is then evaluated to ascertain if the learning of these parts equals the originally analyzed whole. If the student has "mastered" the elements taught, it is assumed that the purposes of the learning have been reached.

The use of this approach to curriculum is common practice in educational circles today, from kindergarten through graduate school. This model is one that is particularly used in elementary and secondary schools. It is fostered, suggested, and supported by state departments of education throughout this country. One such example is that of the Minnesota Department of Education (Jebe, 41). Because it has the appearance of being efficient and effective, this "model" has become associated with the movement for accountability in the schools. Furthermore, it has become more sophisticated than originally described by Tyler. Learner outcomes, microanalyzed subobjectives or tasks, finetuned and highly refined testing strategies have been added to make curriculum development a technology. In his critique of this "means-end" process, Eisner (24) specifies several consequences of this direction that are important for this discussion. First, the technical orientation of this direction is *never* value-neutral. Thus, even the technical direction itself is a value and produces consequences for the "form, content, and aims of schooling" (p. 68). It suggests that knowledge is neutral and that learning is the same for all students. In addition, a scientific curriculum leads to complete specification of objectives in its most extreme position, learning units based on limited time intervals, and standardization of evaluation practices. While perhaps efficient and effective from a management point of view, such direction limits learning. Instead, form and technique drive what is to be learned, while process and values are essentially ignored. The objective is to be able to measure and account for what has been learned. Efficiency, effectiveness, and system are what function in the curricular machine of this category. The focus of this approach is not on the student, the student's learning, or the quality of that learning, but rather on the amount of knowledge, the methods used to teach that knowledge, and the standardized approaches to evaluation to ascertain that everyone has attained the prestated outcomes.

Practical Inquiry

This direction for inquiry, in spite of its name, does not refer to the practical concerns of day-to-day teaching. In this category, *practical* indicates rather the quest for meaning and comprehension of the world as individuals strive to grasp an awareness of their own worth and identification, as well as the capacity to develop those attributes. This is not a superficial perception of the "everyday" world, but rather a deep probing of existence to fathom the connections of persons to a similar context, whether social, political, economic, or historical. The resulting dialog, both within the self and with others, turns on an ethic that connects people to actions that allow all people to develop in more human manner.

Macdonald's (66) description of such curriculum inquiry, which he labels hermeneutic, discloses it as antithetical to a scientific or technical exploration. He terms it instead contemplative, where individuals bring their background into dialog with theory to understand it in the light of their person, experience, and value. Contrary to the scientific experience, where explanation is for the establishment of a general authority, this difference constitutes individual experience as a firmer basis for the reinterpretation of reality.

According to Schubert (84), there are four assumptions that explain the practical. (1) Curriculum deliberation takes place locally. (2) It involves those who live in the local community, namely teachers, students, parents, and principals. (3) The learning content is situational, where students, along with teachers, create curriculum for their lives. (4) The result of this curriculum is the growth of individuals in their ability to live and act morally and ethically in association with others in that situation.

A brief explanation of these principles is in order. The site for curriculum deliberation in this category is the local site. In fact, Schwab (87) specifically declares the classroom as the place for this kind of reflection to occur. It is in this context that the determination of the curriculum takes place, not in publishing houses or by national commissions, state education agencies, and school boards. Those who negotiate the curriculum are those most closely related to it. Teachers, principals, other administrators, and parents discuss with students the content and processes of the curriculum. In these deliberations, the classroom serves as the basic "society" in which students help determine the learning that is to take place. That learning is interactive in nature between teacher and students and among students. The content and processes of these interactions are related to the importance of the local context and the needs of learners to comprehend and function in it. The resulting curriculum prepares the individuals to act morally and ethically within a framework to which a process of knowledge and under-standing has been applied. Such a process allows learners to grow personally by understanding and constructing their own meanings within the local situation. It also allows that comprehension and growth be applied to situations that are outside of those in which the original knowledge, comprehension, and growth initially occurred.

Eisner (24) would categorize this approach as being associated with personal relevance. Among his most important criticisms, he would be concerned about the considerable responsibility that this curriculum inquiry category places upon the teacher's intellectual load in that he or she must be aware of the various needs, aptitudes, and interests of a variety of students with whom she or he interacts. He would reserve judgment about the efficiency in which the private and individual needs of students could be accommodated. Class size in these instances would have to be rather small. In addition, evaluation procedures would have to be notably different in order to relate to individual needs and different contexts.

Critical or Emancipatory Inquiry

This category takes the "practical" one step further. It is oriented toward an emancipation of the individual to enable growth and development from accepted social conventions, beliefs, and modes of functioning that operate with the established ideology. Critical inquiry, the process of knowing, understanding, reflecting, and acting, is the vehicle through which the established ideology is discussed, critiqued, and changed. As a consequence of this process, people are empowered to question the political, economic, social, and psychological aspects of life and to recreate them. The implication for education rests on understanding that knowledge is not neutral, that it is constantly changing, and that it exists in a political, social, and economic context or culture in which people have to learn to live. In order to survive within this culture, and to make it work better for all of its members, the citizen must not only have knowledge, but also understand its biases, reflect on that knowledge as part of the cultural context, and act morally and ethically on those issues of importance to the benefit of both the individual and the other participants. While there are several important writers to consider who have written in this vein, perhaps the most important are Freire (28 and 29) and Giroux (36 and 37).

Schubert (84) refers to critical inquiry as a unity of reflection and action that is political in nature. Meaning for life is developed within a social, economic, and political context. Critical analysis of the conflicts between and among elements of this context are related to human development. The inequalities of educational access, opportunity, and quality within and without subordinate cultures and subcultures, including class, race, gender, and age, dominate the consideration of this inquiry. But it is not just the contemplation of these injustices that is important here, but rather how they may be surmounted. In other words, a key ingredient in this inquiry is *praxis*. Praxis is defined as the integration of political and cultural action with critical reflection. In other words, contemplation of named inequalities is not sufficient. Such analysis and consideration must be associated with acts intended to create a broader awareness of societal inequities and to bring fairness and social justice. In terms of schooling, critical inquiry identifies how the inequities in schools and classrooms and among individuals occur as a reflection of the broader society and how those inequities can be alleviated within that environment as a means of giving learners preparation for acting similarly in their adult lives. The following questions serve as a means of perceiving the direction of such inquiry in schools and how it relates to curriculum (Schubert, 84, p. 315):

1. How is knowledge recreated by schools?
2. What are the sources of such knowledge?
3. How do both teachers and learners dispute and contest their in-school classroom knowledge and experience with outside established sources of knowledge?
4. What is the impact of schooling on the outlook of both learners and teachers? In other words, how do learners and teachers interact and communicate in ways which are sensitive enough to allow each to *truly* benefit from each other's experience and knowledge?
5. Does schooling perpetuate support for the socioeconomic, class, and racial structure of the prevailing culture, or does schooling instill a vision of equity, a sense of justice, and emancipation for all learners which would apply to all, regardless of race, creed, age, and social class?
6. Are the interests of equity, justice, and emancipation for all learners actually communicated to students and clearly a broad goal of the educational effort?

7. What aspects of schooling actually transcend the exhibition of knowledge and use knowledge to resolve inequities, injustices, and restrictions of freedom for individuals and groups? Or how do we prepare humans to "create a society that perpetually renews itself through education"? (Schubert, 84; p. 330)

Eisner (24), who can continue to serve as foil or general critic of any of these categories of curricular inquiry, would probably declare that critical or emancipatory inquiry falls within the framework of social reconstruction. In this model, the learner becomes aware of the "ills" of society and is prompted to learn how to reduce them. In programs where this reduction occurs, learners tend to concentrate on controversial issues and "closed" areas such as corruption, politics, prejudice, race relations, religions, sexual orientation, values, and the like. The purpose of education is not simply to help students adapt to such issues, but to generate basic modifications of the culture. The curriculum for such learning would come from the issues and problems of humans living together in a seemingly common culture, but in which there is much diversity. The result of such a curriculum would be the betterment of the human condition. Or would it?

Examination of Second Language Curricula According to Three Categories of Curricular Inquiry

Under this heading, the definitions of the three categories of curriculum inquiry will be used to both discuss and categorize the curricular writings of a number of authors who have made proposals about foreign or second language curriculum: the scientific-technical, the connective, the practical, and the critical or emancipative; because strict adherence to the three categories is not possible, I have added a fourth, *the connective*.

This category seemed necessary because I perceive a distinct overlap between the scientific-technical and the practical orientations. From my perspective, there is a blurring of the definitions and functions of a scientific-technical model of the foreign/second language curriculum, represented by a focus on the linguistic aspects of language, and of a practical orientation, which could best be explained as dedicated to communication. While communication is certainly oriented to some aspects of the individual developing meaning in a broader context of the culture in which she or he exists, it appears that such direction is confused by an unfulfilled desire on the part of teachers to satisfy an allegiance to the scientific-technical. This confusion controls teachers through an intimidation of guilt, asserted by feelings connected to the abandonment of the known (the scientific-technical) for a somewhat unknown (communication). Uncoupling the constraints of the scientific-technical for the unknown of the communicative appears to be extremely difficult. Teachers understand the scientific-technical to be the model that they are supposed to know and use because it is ubiquitous, pervasive, and required by the system of accountability by which teachers' professional lives are determined. Everything else is foreign and therefore suspect.

While not a historical overview, the following analysis includes curricular conceptualizations covering approximately two decades, but not in chronological order, and demonstrates that the categories of inquiry already presented have relevance to the creation of a vision for the foreign/second language curriculum. The implications from this inquiry for the foreign language curriculum and the already determined crisis will be explained in the final section of this chapter.

The Scientific-Technical

Although not established by this inquiry, it is the consensus of many writers in the curriculum field that scientific-technical inquiry is the dominant and most diffused curricular orientation in American education. (See especially Schubert, 84.) It is my assertion that this same domination rules in second language education. One way of supporting this assertion would be to examine most textbooks for an orientation to a scientific-analytic direction based on criteria for such direction. Another would be to examine the literature on curriculum development. There are at least three examples of this direction that I should like to present here from that literature: Banathy and Lange (5), Brooks (9), and Phillips (78). They are described in chronological order.

Brooks (9) helped to shape a different direction in describing the audiolingual approach for *teaching* foreign languages. In distinct ways, Brooks used the "sciences" of both linguistics and psychology as underpinnings for the definition of the so-called audiolingual approach. In his work, structural linguistics and behavioral psychology were major suppliers of principles for language teaching. In this context, Brooks saw language as rule-governed behavior and language learning as habit formation where the practice of language forms (phonology, morphology, syntax, lexicon) would lead to ability to use language. In other words, the aforementioned "sciences" contributed an analysis of the elements of language and of language learning to a vision of language teaching. The additive practice of these parts and processes, resembling a manufacturing model where the sum of the parts equals the whole, was supposed to culminate in the ability to mainly speak, but also to understand oral language. Yet Brooks contributed a broader awareness of language (and culture) than that of grammar-translation, the prevalent practice in language teaching and learning prior to the 1960s, even though both audiolingual and grammar-translation teaching can be viewed as belonging to a linear, analytic, and scientific orientation.

The contribution of Banathy and Lange (5) rests on the systematization of the scientific orientation to curriculum development for foreign language teaching and learning. In an earlier publication, Banathy (4) shaped the work of Gagné (30), Mager (67), and Tyler (98)—as well as numerous others whose work is associated with a linear, objective, and technical approach to curriculum—into a specific process that is applicable to any content and any context where a curriculum could be devised. Banathy and Lange then applied this process to the foreign language curriculum. Although certainly not new in current times, the resulting process for curriculum elaboration emerges as a procedure that guides decisions from the level of broad abstraction of a philosophic nature to goals, objectives, specification of content and tasks, ordering of the content and tasks, determination of how and with what the learning is to take place (materials, equipment, persons), presentation of learning content and tasks, and finally how the learning is to be evaluated. This theoretical process of curriculum development is commonplace, both in education in general and no less so in foreign language education.

Although not as carefully associated with a systems-analysis approach, the Phillips volume (78) represents, however, a next step in the application of an analytic, linear process to curriculum development. That step elaborates the "curriculum cycle," as it is labeled, for the practitioner. The so-called curriculum cycle constitutes a vision of the analytic, linear process that constitutes four components or steps: (1) the statement of goals, objectives, and outcomes; (2) refinement of content; (3) designation of human resources; and (4) processes of evaluation (formal and informal). The chapter by Medley (69) is a clear example of linear analysis: he discusses needs analysis, the determination of goals, and the setting of objectives. The determined steps (eleven steps and seven poststeps), as well as the flowcharts, give practitioners what appears to be a formula for this first part of the process. Content is discussed in two chapters (Johnson, 42; Mollica, 70). In the former, the acceptance of the text as curriculum is presented as inevitable; in the latter, materials are offered for adaptation and use with textbooks and as standalone items. The nature of the content to be chosen and its actual choice, however, are basically left to forces outside the classroom, namely publishers. Human resources are discussed in two chapters (Christensen, 14; Westphal, 104). The first one emphasizes the classroom and the teacher; the second describes a variety of "methods" of language teaching, focusing on the "eclectic" as being the most prevalent. In either case, little time is spent on the most important ingredient in the learning process, the student. Three chapters, devoted to testing, evaluation, and feedback to the system (Valette and Linder, 101; Omaggio et al., 76; Loew, 63), complete the technical, analytic loop. Here, it is assumed that tests based on prespecified objectives assure that what is being taught and tested is what is being learned, and that what is tested is important to learning and the student. In addition, testing is used as one of several means of determining the success of a program of foreign language study. And finally, tests and evaluation serve as a means of feeding information back into the program for consideration of change. Changes made are then fed back into the loop and the process begins again.

The image of the scientific, analytical, and technical curriculum represented in these works supports my contention that, in an overall manner, the message presented by that model is prescriptive in nature through the process that is used to determine it. As a result, it seems that the definition of this orientation, established above, fits the works cited.

The Connective

Although the definition for this category is essentially my own, I think that I can justify and demonstrate that the works to be discussed here, namely Johnson (43), Nunan (72), Omaggio (74), Richterich (81), Savignon (82), and Yalden (106) connect the analytic, scientific, and technical with the practical. In my opinion, recent trends in language curriculum indicate that the scientific has been extended in the quest for the development of language competence/proficiency as a means of expressing individual meaning and discovering meaning in the world of the individual, but that the tie to the scientific is still very strong.

In the work of the Council of Europe (Richterich, 81), even though the emphasis is on communication, the analysis of language use is scientific. Instead of focusing analysis on the standard grammatical features, the analysis has shifted to functional and notional categories. Functional categories of analysis are those that indicate how the language can be used, such as the category of suasion or persuading, suggesting, urging. Notional or "semantico-grammatical" categories are exemplified by duration in use of verbs expressing time as well as prepositions suggesting length. The result is that a new analytic grammar is created. Further in this process, communicative needs have been analyzed in extreme detail. Having this analysis allows the teacher or curriculum developer to match needs with specific communicative goals, objectives, and tasks. In a very interesting visual representation, Richterich specifically points up the match between communicative needs and communicative curriculum where needs can be specifically matched by communicative curriculum and instruction.

In further amplifying the European system, Johnson (43) demonstrates how a curriculum could be organized for different groups with different needs. His curriculum is organized according to function, setting, and notions. In dealing with a variety of proficiency levels where students are learning language for the same purpose, he indicates the importance of a common core of functions, settings, and notions for student learning. Student competence with this core is tested at the appropriate time. After the testing phase, students move to further practice or an advanced module, beyond which they may engage in simulations of language use. This is but one view of the organization of such a curriculum using this model.

The North American context seems to have been differently influenced. Although the European unit-credit system is known here, it has not been as widely discussed and hardly used. Instead, the focus has been on extending the whole of language learning based on information from a variety of subfields of linguistics, namely sociolinguistics and psycholinguistics, accumulated from research on second language acquisition. Here the science of linguistics, using the results of both empirical and analytic research, have contributed to the view expressed by Savignon (82) that communicative language proficiency is constructed of different competencies: grammatical, discourse, strategic, and sociolinguistic. The reader can see that the whole of language learning is directed toward language as communication. The whole has been expanded, however, beyond grammar to include the three other mentioned aspects.

As an example of curriculum design in the North American context, Yalden (106) provides a bridge between the European and North American conceptualizations of communication. She incorporates the notional-functional syllabuses into the linguistic, discourse, strategic, and sociolinguistic elements of Savignon's definition. Yalden recommends a proportional organization that is constructed of three phases: linguistic, communicative, and specialized. For complete beginners, the linguistic phase is included, suggesting that some focus on the concrete features of language is necessary before proceeding to other phases. In the communicative phase, proportional emphasis or de-emphasis is given to the formalistic features of language as competence in the functional, discursive, and rhetorical aspects of communication is developed. The specialized phase allows systematic treatment of highly developed features of language as they merge with special content as in language for special purposes. Within this general organization, themes and situations are used to organize individual units or modules according to the tasks required. Nunan's (72) very clearly analytical examination of tasks in communicative language teaching could fit very nicely into Yalden's structure. Although different from that of Johnson, Yalden's structure suggests that the whole of language is constituted of its parts and that learning the parts will give the learner ability to communicate with the language.

A kind of competing notion of communication is found in Omaggio (74). This work is closely associated with the so-called "proficiency movement," which has been generated from the American Council on the Teaching of Foreign Languages Proficiency Guidelines (1 and 2) for speaking, listening, reading, and writing. These guidelines do not represent any theoretical position or research on language acquisition. Instead, they were derived from analysis of field observations of oral language functioning, originally completed by the federal government, and the application of that analysis to listening, reading, and writing. The analysis offers levels of proficiency (Novice to Superior) as well as elements within the levels (content, function, and accuracy). Omaggio uses this framework to specifically organize curriculum for listening, speaking, reading, and writing by focusing on content ("what" is to be expressed), function ("how" expression will be accomplished), and accuracy ("how well" expression occurs) within the different levels within the scale. Although somewhat different from the European direction and from Savignon, this path to proficiency also exhibits an analytical, technical system, which suggests that communication consists of steps and elements in those steps. When competence is demonstrated in the elements at one level, the curriculum moves to the next one. Progress is made by adding up competencies until the competence of the theoretical "well-educated" native speakers is reached.

From a perspective even broader than a curricular one, Stern (91) reviews the study of language education and its fundamental concepts, detailing how they function in relation to the development of language teaching and its product, language proficiency. In his very systematic analysis, he includes an extensive repertoire of variables: the nature of language, the learner, the nature of language learning, the language teacher, the nature of language teaching, and the context.

The result of his analysis is both additive and integrative because he adds these variables one to another, but at the same time he also integrates them.

Stern (92) also uses this basic formula to present his multidimensional curriculum. The four contents of language learning treated in this discussion are a linguistic syllabus, a cultural syllabus, a communicative syllabus, and a general language education syllabus. After having outlined the content of each syllabus, Stern turns to the important issue of their integration. He demonstrates how these syllabi are added one to another by joining a communicative aspect of language to a linguistic feature, and then adding its cultural meaning and use. Further, he demonstrates that the integration of syllabi through materials dealing with content organized largely around cultural topics and by employing a set of four categories of objectives (proficiency, knowledge, affect, and transfer) could contribute to an integration of the four contents. Yet while this vision of language teaching moves us to broader considerations of language curriculum, it still leaves us in the middle of an analytical model that is mostly imposed on the learner.

This category, the connective, suggests that while curriculum is oriented toward the use of language for communication, the understanding of "the self" and of "the other," as well as any use of language to act upon the human condition, are but very minor byproducts. In other words, the connection from the analytic, scientific, technical to the communicative continues the tradition of "the sum of the parts equals the whole." The intent is new, but the means of achieving the intent is extremely familiar.

The Practical

In this category, we move quite directly outside of the mainstream of language education in the United States and perhaps elsewhere. This orientation to curriculum is characterized as practical or hermeneutic, which, in very general terms, brings dialog between the learner and his or her context so that the meaning of the context can be uncovered. This more personal orientation recognizes the knowledge and experience of the individual as important in the quest for the meaning and understanding of the individual, the group, and social institutions that are necessary for the development of values and direction in a human society. Knowledge and experience are not thought of only as scientific and rational, but include information from the senses and from intuition. Stevick's writings (93, 94, 95, and 96) in which he explains Curran's (19) Community Language Learning, Gattegno's (33) Silent Way, and Lozanov's (65) Suggestopedia, are the major examples of work in this category in second language education.

From my perception, Stevick's work very strongly accommodates learners as they work to understand themselves in relationship to language, learning, and communication as part of their world. While it is not possible to provide a complete review of Stevick's writings here, it is possible to exemplify his work. In *Memory, Meaning, and Method,* Stevick (93) discusses the meaning of memory and of method as he understands them. His personal meaning is displayed in a "psychodynamic" interpretation of language learning, teaching, and materials development, which includes five principles. Each of these principles turns toward the development of the learner's human experience in some way. (For example, Principle 1a: "Language is one kind of purposeful behavior between people.") Through this dialog with himself and the reader, the author works through his own personal credo of language learning and teaching. He uses the work of Curran, Gattegno, and Lozanov to establish and partially represent his principles.

While *Memory, Meaning, and Method* represents a dialog of Stevick with himself and with the reader, *A Way and Ways* (Stevick, 94) portrays him in a lyrical monolog. One of his main themes is illuminated by the phrase "what goes on inside and between" people. One example of this theme is language. Through language, our self-image and our private universe are expressed; through language, we recognize our mortality and struggle against it; through language, we recognize our connection to other private universes; through language, we can act collectively and supportively to shape the world in an affirmation of life. Language represents the values, struggles, and aspirations of the person as well as of the people. Because of the humanistic picture of language as discussed by Stevick, language learning and teaching should desire a similar existence. It is in this context that Community Language Learning, the Silent Way, and Suggestopedia are explored.

It is probably not productive to try to define each of these ways in which language teaching could take place because a definition of one would obscure the intent of the other. Further, although it is somewhat dangerous to represent someone's private meaning, only those methods offered by Stevick in his text will be presented here.

Each involves an important and special relationship between the teacher and learner and the involvement of both in the discovery and uncovering of meaningful expression in a new language. In this regard, the term *curriculum* is applied in a very loose sense. Its connection is shown in a different relationship among learner, content, and teacher.

In Community Language Learning, for example, the teacher serves as the counselor who guides the dialog and learning of a group of learners through stages of dependency upon, codependency with, and independence from the counselor as they express their intended meanings with the group or community. In this context, language is the vehicle by which relationships are established and maintained. Here, a sense of community is developed in which the learner finds support for the self.

In the Silent Way, learners discover the ability to judge the use of their own inner resources and knowledge as they make choices in learning, including a second language. In this sense, learning is not restricted to any particular content. It is for the purpose of being able to reconcile the self with the outside world. Here, the teacher provides the challenges according to the current resources of students. Yet he or she stays silent so that learners can choose among the resources that they have developed within themselves. Under this mode, learning results in independence, responsibility, and autonomy of the self, as well as aloneness. A connection to community is obscure.

In Suggestopedia, the relationship of the teacher and learner takes a slightly different direction. The purpose of the teacher is to arrange for the removal of norms, limitations, and tensions that society has placed on learning and avoid the placement of others in their place. In the environment that is created, learners can use conscious as well as unconscious functions to establish meaningful connections to what is being learned in ways that can be much faster than normal. In this way, learners can understand, retain, and acquire qualitatively more insight in any content. Here also, the tie to community is uncertain.

The other works of Stevick will not be detailed here in any sense. However, they continue the humanistic path in language learning and teaching that was begun in the texts discussed above. *Teaching and Learning Languages* (Stevick, 95) is a text that shows how a variety of classroom procedures fit into the development of personal language competence and proficiency of students. *Images and Options* (Stevick, 96) demands engagement of the teacher-readers to examine both teaching and materials from a perspective that explores their imagination, knowledge, and understanding of the results of teaching and widens the alternatives available to them. While both texts are more practically oriented than either *Memory, Meaning, and Method* or *A Way and Ways,* they are definitely allied to them.

The examples of curricular efforts beyond the analytic, scientific, and technical are difficult to find. Stevick's work, as well as the three language teaching means that he described, give us some awareness of "ways" that extend beyond the usual and the known. They give us examples of curricular orientations that develop fierce individuals, individuals who function within a community, and individuals who have been exposed to new forms of learning. All these modes surround learners with the opportunity to create meaning for themselves.

The Critical or Emancipatory

As stated earlier, a critical or emancipatory direction in curriculum goes beyond the practical. It is the unity of reflection and action within a social, economic, and political context that makes the difference stand out. This unity allows individuals and groups to contemplate *and* to act upon the society in which we live and breathe for the purposes of responding to societal inequities and of finding fairness, justice, and emancipation for all persons regardless of race, creed, age, sex, and social class. The intent is the development of a truly democratic society and the betterment of the human condition.

Crawford-Lange and Lange (17 and 18) and Wallerstein (103), the former associated with foreign language education, and the latter with English as a Second Language (ESL) are among the few to explore the critical or emancipatory dimensions of curriculum. They should be considered as evolutionary in nature and can probably never be as complete as curricula in the scientific-technical or connective categories can be, because they evolve with the problems posed to which reflection and action are attached. Problems resolved create new problems; thus the process of understanding, knowing, reflecting, and acting is an ongoing one.

These examples below reflect that process. In the foreign language education context, Crawford-Lange and Lange (17 and 18) have applied the work of Freire (28 and 29) to specifically reorient the direction of foreign language curricula away from a concentration on language to the use of language as a tool for uncovering the interrelationships, differences, and gaps between the target and the native languages. The result is an eight-step overlapping process that begins with the specification of a cultural theme of a problematic nature, continuing with the examination of representative phenomena that serve to stimulate dialog about the student's original perceptions of the phenomena. Language-learning needs and the actual practice of language aim at the further exploration of the original cultural perceptions (native and target cultures) by whatever means available (text, image, people). Language is then used to describe, analyze, and compare new information with original perceptions. Students then relate the new information to their experience with the cultural phenomena, the language learned, and the verification of perceptions, noting how perceptions have changed as well as both the effect and affect of the process. In the final stage, students demonstrate their ability to respond in the language to some of the issues, contexts, and complications in functioning in another culture as well as in their own. They are acting on the awareness, knowledge, perceptions, and understanding they have gained of both their own and another's culture and language as they deal with problems posed to them around a problematic issue or theme in the classroom.

In Wallerstein's (103) work, the problems posed are of an actual nature and relate largely to the difficulties of refugees and immigrants as they learn to cope with American culture and American English. These difficulties revolve around economic, cultural, and linguistic discrimination. The role of language learning in this context is to provide them with a tool to understand, cope with, and explore their life situations in the classroom with the hope that they can redefine their culture and gain control over their lives in the community. Wallerstein's process is not unlike that of Crawford-Lange and Lange. As teacher and students interact in getting to know each other, the teacher listens to the themes of the adult learners as they talk about their lives and their struggles with the new language and culture. Through dialog, the teacher also becomes a learner, verifying themes, learning new language, and sharing some of his or her life. In this dialog, the learners reflect on such experiences as inflation, discrimination, social conditions, and language learning as examples, sharing their stories and problems. Through problem-posing questions, the teacher orients the learner's reflection toward a common understanding of a particular concern. Stories, pictures, and drawings serve to objectify and direct the dialog toward the specific naming of the problem, understanding how that problem applies to individual cases as well as the collective, and then to find alternative resolutions to the problem upon which one or all can act. Most of the book contains examples of units on themes that have been found to be important to adult learners of ESL, such as neighborhood, immigration, health, and work. Learning to act on one's own culture in relation to a new one through a language that is being learned is a tall order. But it is exactly this plan that can improve the lives of the refugee and immigrant.

Emancipatory curriculum may be very significant to the future of foreign/ second language education as well as of literacy in general. In this category, language has a purpose. It is a tool of understanding, knowing, and communication. But it is also more. It is also an instrument of action for the improvement of the human condition. In developing this resource, the learner authors his or her own voice, responds to the voices of others, and works to form a world that is honest and equitable.

Implications and Directions

In the context of this article, the presence of a crisis in the second language curriculum has been demonstrated, and its various facets have been discussed. As a means of broadening the concept of curriculum, we inspected four formulations of that concept, each of which was illustrated through a discussion of some selected second language curricular literature. What have we learned? The following general statements reflect my own reading of the importance of the discussion:

1. The most significant efforts in second language curriculum are placed in the category of the scientific-technical. Despite movement to connect language curriculum to the world of communication, this change only translates the scientific-technical into the communicative. In this context, communication is viewed as analyzable, parsable; it is also assumed that we can learn and master it because we can create models of its elements. The learning and mastery of the elements, however, is only the learning and mastery of the elements.

2. If most curricular effort is placed on the scientific-technical and if connections to communication are of a heavy scientific-technical nature, learners may be able to listen, read, write, and speak, but will they be able to use another language to know, understand, and act upon their world? In my view, the answer to the question is probably no. Why? The answer is that learners have not been asked to do more.

3. Lest I be misinterpreted, let me clarify that I am not attacking the scientific-technical as evil, negative, or irrelevant. I am only providing a picture of the results we have achieved in applying it exclusively. I believe the scientific-technical contributes an objective investigation of the structures of language and communication that is indispensable to knowing, communicating with, and using another language. But I also believe that the scientific-technical is not sufficient in learning anything. Although language has been removed from the person for study, it must be reconnected to the person as it is learned. Only people can give language sufficiency and purpose.

4. In keeping with the concept of sufficiency and purpose, the two other curricular orientations discussed here, namely the practical and the emancipatory, require our serious consideration. Language learning, and even the link to

proficiency, is insufficient if it is relegated to the assembly of the "parts and pieces" of language and communication. It is in the connection of language to the discovery of one's own culture as well as that of the other, the stranger, that we understand ourselves as well as the other. It is in this relationship that we understand our existence. It is in this relationship that we find direction and purpose to our actions.

5. Specifically, the scientific-technical curricular orientation is insufficient in preparing learners to use language to intersect with their existence. In my view, it is the connection of the scientific-technical with both the practical and the emancipatory that will provide both sufficiency and purpose for language learning. It is in the combination of these three approaches that there can be more fulfillment of the serious goals to which both language teachers and learners aspire.

6. The vision displayed in the extension of foreign language curriculum beyond the known (the scientific-technical and connective) is not an easy one. There is much exploration to do in terrain that is largely unknown. As indicated in the above analysis, few teachers and scholars have ventured into either the practical or the emancipatory. Those who have taken such paths have taken risks: they may have been misunderstood, or they may have been misjudged. However, it is time to recognize the limits of the scientific-technical in learning and teaching a human language. We need to move toward the recognition of the contributions that the practical and emancipatory curriculum orientations may provide to the scientific-technical. In other words, all orientations and those who work with them must communicate and contribute to the language teaching and learning mission. It is in this way that the crisis in foreign / second language education can be overcome and renewal can occur.

References, Sketching the Crisis in Foreign Language Curriculum

1. American Council on the Teaching of Foreign Languages. *Provisional Proficiency Guidelines.* Hastings-on-Hudson, NY: ACTFL, 1982.
2. American Council on the Teaching of Foreign Languages. *Proficiency Guidelines.* Hastings-on-Hudson, NY: ACTFL, 1986.
3. Bachman, Lyle, and Sandra J. Savignon. "The Evaluation of Communicative Language Proficiency: A Critique of the ACTFL Oral Interview." *Modern Language Journal* 70 (1986): 380–90.
4. Banathy, Bela H. *Instructional Systems.* Palo Alto, CA: Fearon, 1968.
5. _____, and Dale L. Lange. *A Design for Foreign Language Curriculum.* Lexington, MA: Heath, 1972.
6. Bialystok, Ellen. "A Theoretical Model of Second Language Learning." *Language Learning* 28 (1978): 69–83.
7. Bloomfield, Leonard. *Language.* New York: Holt, Rinehart and Winston, 1933. [A revised edition of *Introduction to the Study of Language.* New York: Henry Holt, 1914.]
8. Boyer, Ernest L. *High School: A Report on Secondary Education in America.* The Carnegie Foundation for the Advancement of Teaching. New York: Harper & Row, 1983.
9. Brooks, Nelson. *Language and Language Learning: Theory and Practice.* 2nd ed. New York: Harcourt, 1964.

10. Byrnes, Heidi, and Michael Canale, eds. *Defining and Developing Proficiency: Guidelines, Implementations, and Concepts.* The ACTFL Foreign Language Education Series, vol. 17. Lincolnwood, IL: National Textbook Company, 1986.

11. Carroll, John B. "Conscious and Automatic Processes in Language Learning." *Canadian Modern Language Review* 37 (1981): 462–64.

12. Child, James R. "Language Proficiency Levels and the Typology of Texts," pp. 97–106 in Heidi Byrnes and Michael Canale, eds., *Defining and Developing Proficiency: Guidelines, Implementations, and Concepts.* The ACTFL Foreign Language Education Series, vol. 17. Lincolnwood, IL: National Textbook Company, 1986.

13. Chomsky, Noam. "Linguistic Theory," pp. 43–49 in Robert G. Mead, Jr., ed., *Language Teaching: Broader Contexts.* Report of the Northeast Conference on the Teaching of Foreign Languages. Middlebury, VT: The Northeast Conference, 1966.

14. Christensen, Clay B. "Beyond the Desk," pp. 93–117 in June K. Phillips, ed., *Building on Experience—Building for Success.* The ACTFL Foreign Language Education Series, vol. 10. Lincolnwood, IL: National Textbook Company, 1978.

15. Clément, R. "Ethnicity, Contact and Communicative Competence in a Second Language," in H. Giles, W. P. Robinson, and P. M. Smith, eds., *Language: Social Psychological Perspectives.* Oxford: Pergamon, 1980.

16. Crawford-Lange, Linda M. "Curricular Alternatives for Second-Language Learning," pp. 81–112 in Theodore V. Higgs, ed., *Curriculum, Competence, and the Foreign Language Teacher.* The ACTFL Foreign Language Education Series, vol. 13. Lincolnwood, IL: National Textbook Company, 1981.

17. ————, and Dale L. Lange. "Doing the Unthinkable in the Second-Language Classroom: A Process for the Integration of Language and Culture," pp. 139–77 in Theodore V. Higgs, ed., *Teaching for Proficiency, the Organizing Principle.* The ACTFL Foreign Language Education Series, vol. 15. Lincolnwood, IL: National Textbook Company, 1983.

18. ————, and Dale L. Lange. "Integrating Language and Culture: How to Do It." *Theory into Practice* 26 (1987): 258–66.

19. Curran, Charles A. *Counseling-Learning in Second Languages.* Apple River, IL: Apple River Press, 1976.

20. Dandinoli, Patricia. "*MLJ* Readers' Forum: To the Editor." *Modern Language Journal* 72 (1988): 450.

21. DeLorenzo, William E., et al. "New Teachers: Developing Flexible Foreign Language Teachers," pp. 64–113 in Warren C. Born, ed., *New Contents, New Teachers, and New Publics.* Report of the Northeast Conference on the Teaching of Foreign Languages. Middlebury, VT: The Northeast Conference, 1978.

22. Dulay, Heidi, and Marina K. Burt. "Natural Sequences in Child Second Language Acquisition." *Language Learning* 24 (1974): 37–53.

23. Egan, Kieran. *Educational Development.* London: Oxford Univ. Press, 1979.

24. Eisner, Elliot W. *The Educational Imagination: On the Design and Evaluation of School Programs.* New York: Macmillan, 1979. [See especially chapter 4, "Five Basic Orientations to the Curriculum" pp. 50–92.]

25. Ferguson, Charles A. "Applied Linguistics," pp. 50–58 in Robert G. Mead, Jr., ed., *Language Teaching: Broader Contexts.* Report of the Northeast Conference on the Teaching of Foreign Languages. Middlebury, VT: The Northeast Conference, 1966.

26. ————, and Thom Huebner. *Foreign Language Instruction and Second Language Acquisition Research in the United States.* NFLC Occasional Papers. Washington, DC: National Foreign Language Center at the Johns Hopkins University, 1989.

27. Freedman, Sara, Jane Jackson, and Katherine Boles. "The Other End of the Corridor: The Effect of Teaching on Teachers." *Radical Teacher* 23 (1983): 2–23.

28. Freire, Paulo. *Pedagogy of the Oppressed,* trans. Myra Bergman Ramos. New York: Seabury, 1970.

29. ————. *Education for Critical Consciousness.* New York: Seabury, 1973.

30. Gagné, Robert M. *The Conditions of Learning.* New York: Holt, Rinehart and Winston, 1965.
31. Galloway, Vicki. *"MLJ* Readers' Forum: To the Editor." *Modern Language Journal* 72 (1988): 450–52.
32. Gardner, Robert C. *Social Psychology and Second Language Learning: The Role of Attitudes and Motivation.* London: Edward Arnold, 1985.
33. Gattegno, Caleb. *Teaching Foreign Languages in Schools: The Silent Way.* New York: Educational Solutions, 1972.
34. Gaudiani, Claire L. "The Importance of Collaboration," pp. 13–26 in John M. Darcey, ed., *The Language Teacher: Commitment and Collaboration.* Report of the Northeast Conference on the Teaching of Foreign Languages. Middlebury, VT: The Northeast Conference, 1987.
35. Giles, H., and J. L. Byrne. "An Intergroup Approach to Second Language Acquisition." *Journal of Multilingual and Multicultural Development* 1 (1982): 17–40.
36. Giroux, Henry A. *Schooling and the Struggle for Public Life: Critical Pedagogy in the Modern Age.* Minneapolis: Univ. of Minnesota Press, 1988.
37. _____. *Teachers as Intellectuals: Toward a Critical Pedagogy of Learning.* Granby, MA: Bergin & Garvey, 1988.
38. Higgs, Theodore V., ed. *Curriculum, Competence, and the Foreign Language Teacher.* The ACTFL Foreign Language Education Series, vol. 13. Lincolnwood, IL: National Textbook Company, 1981.
39. _____, ed. *Teaching for Proficiency, the Organizing Principle.* The ACTFL Foreign Language Education Series, vol. 15. Lincolnwood, IL: National Textbook Company, 1983.
40. James, Charles J., ed. *Foreign Language Proficiency in the Classroom and Beyond.* The ACTFL Foreign Language Education Series, vol. 16. Lincolnwood, IL: National Textbook Company, 1984.
41. Jebe, Suzanne P., ed. *Model Learner Outcomes for World Languages Education.* St. Paul, MN: Minnesota Department of Education, World Languages Education, 1988.
42. Johnson, Carl H. "Choosing Materials That Do the Job," pp. 67–92 in June K. Phillips, ed., *Building on Experience—Building for Success.* The ACTFL Foreign Language Education Series, vol. 10. Lincolnwood, IL: National Textbook Company, 1978.
43. Johnson, Keith. *Communicative Syllabus Design and Methodology.* Oxford: Pergamon, 1982.
44. Kelly, Louis G. *25 Centuries of Language Teaching.* Rowley, MA: Newbury, 1969.
45. Kramsch, Claire J. "Classroom Interaction and Discourse Options." *Studies in Second Language Acquisition* 7 (1985): 169–83.
46. Krashen, Stephen D. *Second Language Acquisition and Second Language Learning.* New York: Pergamon, 1981.
47. _____. *Principles and Practices in Second Language Acquisition.* New York: Pergamon, 1982.
48. _____, and Tracy D. Terrell. *The Natural Approach: Language Acquisition in the Classroom.* Oxford: Pergamon, 1983.
49. Lafayette, Robert C. "Toward an Articulated Curriculum," pp. 61–76 in Thomas H. Geno, ed., *Our Profession: Present Status and Future Directions.* Report of the Northeast Conference on the Teaching of Foreign Languages. Middlebury, VT: The Northeast Conference, 1980.
50. Lambert, Richard D. *Beyond Growth: The Next Stage in Language and Area Studies.* A Report by the Association of American Universities. Washington, DC: Association of American Universities, 1984.
51. _____. *Points of Leverage: An Agenda for a National Foundation for International Studies.* New York: Social Science Research Council, 1986.
52. _____, ed. "Foreign Language Instruction: A National Agenda." *The Annals of the American Academy of Political and Social Science* 490 (March 1987): 1–247.

53. Lambert, Wallace E. "Psychological Approaches to the Study of Language, Part I: On Learning, Thinking and Human Abilities." *Modern Language Journal* 47 (1963): 51–62.

54. _____. "Psychological Approaches to the Study of Language, Part II: On Second Language Learning and Bilingualism." *Modern Language Journal* 47 (1963): 114–21.

55. Lange, Dale L. "The Problem of Articulation," pp. 113–73 in Theodore V. Higgs, ed., *Curriculum, Competence, and the Foreign Language Teacher*. The ACTFL Foreign Language Education Series, vol. 13. Lincolnwood, IL: National Textbook Company, 1981.

56. _____. "The Language Teaching Curriculum and a National Agenda." *The Annals of the American Academy of Political and Social Science* 490 (1987): 70–96.

57. _____. "The Nature and Direction of Recent Proposals and Recommendations for Foreign Language Education: A Response." *Modern Language Journal* 71 (1987): 258–66.

58. _____. "Articulation: A Resolvable Problem?" pp. 11–31 in John P. Lalande II, ed., *Shaping the Future of Foreign Language Education: FLES, Articulation, and Proficiency*. Proceedings of the Central States Conference on the Teaching of Foreign Languages. Lincolnwood, IL: National Textbook Company, 1988.

59. Lantolf, James P., and William Frawley. "Oral-Proficiency Testing: A Critical Analysis." *Modern Language Journal* 69 (1985): 337–45.

60. _____. "Proficiency: Understanding the Construct." *Studies in Second Language Acquisition* 10 (1988): 181–95.

61. Lee, James F., and Diane Musumeci. "On Hierarchies of Reading Skills and Text Types." *Modern Language Journal* 72 (1988): 171–87.

62. _____. "*MLJ* Readers' Forum: Lee & Musumeci Respond." *Modern Language Journal* 72 (1988): 454–57.

63. Loew, Helene Z. "Modifying the Program and Providing for Change," pp. 271–303 in June K. Phillips, ed., *Building on Experience—Building for Success*. The ACTFL Foreign Language Education Series, vol. 10. Lincolnwood, IL: National Textbook Company, 1978.

64. Lowe, Pardee, Jr. "Proficiency: Panacea, Framework, Process? A Reply to Kramsch, Schulz, and Particularly to Bachman and Savignon." *Modern Language Journal* 70 (1986): 391–97.

65. Lozanov, Georgi. *Suggestology and Outlines of Suggestopedy*. New York: Gordon and Beach, 1978.

66. Macdonald, James B. "Theory-Practice and the Hermeneutic Circle," pp. 101–13 in William F. Pinar, ed., *Contemporary Curriculum Discourses*. Scottsdale, AZ: Gorsuch Scarisbrick, 1988.

67. Mager, Robert F. *Preparing Behavioral Objectives*. San Francisco: Fearon, 1962.

68. McLaren, Peter. *Life in Schools: An Introduction to Critical Pedagogy in the Foundations of Education*. White Plains, NY: Longman, 1988. [See especially chapter 6, "Critical Pedagogy: A Look at the Major Concepts," pp. 166–91.]

69. Medley, Frank W., Jr. "Identifying Needs and Setting Goals," pp. 41–65 in June K. Phillips, ed., *Building on Experience—Building for Success*. The ACTFL Foreign Language Education Series, vol. 10. Lincolnwood, IL: National Textbook Company, 1978.

70. Mollica, Anthony S. "Print and Non-Print Materials: Adapting for Classroom Use," pp. 157–98 in June K. Phillips, ed., *Building on Experience—Building for Success*. The ACTFL Foreign Language Education Series, vol. 10. Lincolnwood, IL: National Textbook Company, 1978.

71. National Commission on Excellence in Education. *A Nation at Risk: The Imperative for Educational Reform*. Washington, DC: Government Printing Office, 1983.

72. Nunan, David. *Designing Tasks for the Communicative Classroom*. Cambridge, Eng.: Cambridge Univ. Press, 1989.

73. Oller, John W., Jr., and Patricia A. Richard-Amato, eds. *Methods That Work: A Smorgasbord of Ideas for Language Teachers.* Rowley, MA: Newbury, 1983.
74. Omaggio, Alice C. *Teaching Language in Context: Proficiency-Oriented Instruction.* Boston: Heinle and Heinle, 1986.
75. Omaggio-Hadley, Alice C. "*MLJ* Readers' Forum: To the Editor." *Modern Language Journal* 72 (1988): 452–54.
76. Omaggio, Alice C., Peter A. Eddy, Lester W. McKim, and Anthony V. Pfannkuche. "Looking at the Results," pp. 233–70 in June K. Phillips, ed., *Building on Experience—Building for Success.* The ACTFL Foreign Language Education Series, vol. 10. Lincolnwood, IL: National Textbook Company, 1978.
77. Palmer, Harold E. *The Principles of Language-Study.* London: Oxford Univ. Press, 1964.
78. Phillips, June K. *Building on Experience—Building for Success.* The ACTFL Foreign Language Education Series, vol. 10. Lincolnwood, IL: National Textbook Company, 1978.
79. _____. "Practical Implications of Recent Research in Reading," *Foreign Language Annals* 17 (1984): 285–96.
80. President's Commission on the Teaching of Foreign Languages and International Studies. *Strength through Wisdom: A Critique of U.S. Capability.* Washington, DC: Government Printing Office, 1979.
81. Richterich, René. "Définition des besoins langagiers et types d'adultes," pp. 33–94 in John L. M. Trim, René Richterich, Jan A. van Ek, and David A. Wilkins, eds., *Systèmes d'apprentissage des langages vivantes par les adultes: Un système européen d'unités capitalisables.* Strasbourg: Le Conseil d'Europe, 1973.
82. Savignon, Sandra J. *Communicative Competence: Theory and Classroom Practice.* Reading, MA: Addison-Wesley, 1983.
83. _____. "Evaluation of Communicative Competence: The ACTFL Provisional Proficiency Guidelines." *Modern Language Journal* 69 (1985): 129–34.
84. Schubert, William H. *Curriculum: Perspective, Paradigm, and Possibility.* New York: Macmillan, 1986.
85. Schumann, John H. "Social and Psychological Factors in Second Language Acquisition," pp. 163–78 in Jack C. Richards, ed., *Understanding Second and Foreign Language Learning.* Rowley, MA: Newbury, 1976.
86. Schwab, Joseph J. "The Practical: A Language for Curriculum." *School Review* 78 (1969): 1–23. [Also found on pp. 26–44 in Arno A. Bellack and Herbert M. Kliebard, eds., *Curriculum and Evaluation.* Berkeley, CA: McCutchan, 1977. See also "The Practical: A Language for Curriculum," pp. 287–321 in Ian Westbury and Neil J. Wilkof, eds., *Joseph J. Schwab: Science, Curriculum, and Liberal Education: Selected Essays.* Chicago: Univ. of Chicago Press, 1978.]
87. _____. "The Practical 4: Something for Curriculum Professors to Do." *Curriculum Inquiry* 13 (1983): 239–65.
88. Sizer, Theodore R. *Horace's Compromise: The Dilemma of the American High School.* Report from A Study of High Schools. Boston: Houghton-Mifflin, 1984.
89. Spolsky, Bernard. "Formulating a Theory of Second Language Learning." *Studies in Second Language Acquisition* 7 (1985): 269–88.
90. _____. "Bridging the Gap: A General Theory of Second Language Learning." *TESOL Quarterly* 22 (1988): 377–96.
91. Stern, H. H. *Fundamental Concepts of Language Teaching.* Oxford, Eng.: Oxford Univ. Press, 1983.
92. _____. "Toward a Multidimensional Foreign Language Curriculum," pp. 120–46 in Robert G. Mead, Jr., ed., *Foreign Languages: Key Links in the Chain of Learning.* Report of the Northeast Conference on the Teaching of Foreign Languages. Middlebury, VT: The Northeast Conference, 1983.
93. Stevick, Earl W. *Memory, Meaning, and Method: Some Psychological Perspectives on Language Learning.* Rowley, MA: Newbury, 1976.

94. _____. *Teaching Languages: A Way and Ways.* Rowley, MA: Newbury, 1980.
95. _____. *Teaching and Learning Languages.* Cambridge, Eng.: Cambridge Univ. Press, 1982.
96. _____. *Images and Options in the Language Classroom.* Cambridge, Eng.: Cambridge Univ. Press, 1986.
97. Tucker, G. Richard. "Evaluation of Foreign Language Proficiency: Synthesis," pp. 307–12 in Albert Valdman, ed., *Proceedings of the Symposium on the Evaluation of Foreign Language Proficiency.* Bloomington, IN: Committee for Research and Development in Language Instruction, Indiana University, 1987.
98. Tyler, Ralph W. *Basic Principles of Curriculum and Instruction.* Chicago: Univ. of Chicago Press, 1949.
99. _____. "The Organization of Learning Experiences," pp. 45–55 in Arno A. Bellack and Herbert M. Kliebard, eds., *Curriculum and Evaluation.* Berkeley, CA: McCutchan, 1977.
100. Valdman, Albert, ed. *Proceedings of the Symposium on the Evaluation of Foreign Language Proficiency.* Bloomington, IN: Committee for Research and Development in Language Instruction, Indiana University, 1987.
101. Valette, Rebecca M., and Cathy Linder. "Measuring the Variables and Testing the Outcomes," pp. 199–232 in June K. Phillips, ed., *Building on Experience—Building for Success.* The ACTFL Foreign Language Education Series, vol. 10. Lincolnwood, IL: National Textbook Company, 1978.
102. Vygotsky, Lev S. *Thought and Language,* trans. Eugenia Hanfmann and Gertrude Vakar. Cambridge, MA: MIT Press, 1962.
103. Wallerstein, Nina. *Language and Culture in Conflict: Problem-Posing in the ESL Classroom.* Reading, MA: Addison-Wesley, 1983.
104. Westphal, Patricia B. "Teaching and Learning: A Key to Success," pp. 119–56 in June K. Phillips, ed., *Building on Experience—Building for Success.* The ACTFL Foreign Language Education Series, vol. 10. Lincolnwood, IL: National Textbook Company, 1978.
105. Widdowson, H. G. *Teaching Language as Communication.* London: Oxford Univ. Press, 1978.
106. Yalden, Janice. *Principles of Course Design for Language Teaching.* Cambridge, Eng.: Cambridge Univ. Press, 1987.

4

From Student to Learner: Style, Process, and Strategy

Vicki Galloway
Georgia Institute of Technology
Angela Labarca
University of Delaware

Introduction

Ask educators about the source of their most vexing problems, and most will refer to change, differences, irregularities, and how best to deal with them (Goodlad, 44). The numerous studies of schooling that have appeared in the past two decades emphasize, above all, the sameness of our nation's educational institutions and depict a "one size fits all factory model" (Walsh, 99), where difference is a defect clogging the machinery and where change, often a goal, is equally often an excuse. Change has been feared and awaited, revered and hated. Institutional change has not come cheaply; for that reason it has not come often or evenly. Individual change, however, has always been expected, for change is something that one must do if one is "different."

Vicki Galloway (Ph.D., University of South Carolina) is currently Associate Professor of Spanish at the Georgia Institute of Technology. She served for six years as State Consultant for Foreign Languages and International Studies in South Carolina. She was formerly Project Director at ACTFL and is presently serving as editor of *Foreign Language Annals*. She has taught at the secondary and university levels and has presented numerous teacher-development workshops at the state, regional, and national level. Her publications have appeared in the ACTFL Foreign Language Education Series, *The Modern Language Journal, The Northeast Conference Reports,* and *The American Educational Research Association.*

Angela Labarca (Ph.D., The Ohio State University) is Associate Professor of Linguistics at the University of Delaware. She has had extensive teaching and administrative experience both here and in Chile. She is a regular presenter at international and domestic conventions and is a member of many professional organizations, among them MLA, AAAL, TESOL, ACTFL, and AILA. She has written books on second language acquisition, has coauthored Spanish and ESL textbooks, and has written articles on a variety of topics that have appeared in journals such as *Studies in Second Language Acquisition, Hispania,* and *The Modern Language Journal.*

In what is commonly labeled the "teaching-learning process," it is the acts and conditions of teaching that have traditionally received the most notable focus, while the learning portion of the process has been variously represented according to the era: In eras of demographic explosion, students have been the problem; in eras of accountability, students have been the proof; in eras of prescriptive innovation, students have been the product. But throughout the eras, the concept of student as *person* has been the most enigmatic and perplexing, for it is the perspective we are perhaps least prepared to handle as educators. The convenient solution to student differences has been to construct typologies, such as the following of Nelson Brooks's (16) day:

> A school typically contains four types of students: those who are able and willing to follow the prescribed regimen; those who are able but unwilling to do so, those who are unable though willing enough, and those who are unable and unwilling, and do not pretend otherwise. (p. 67)

Thus, as students are measured through grades and conduct, their performance has been typically explained away by the existence or absence of only two factors: *desire* and *ability*. The image is one of passive students classified according to perceived motivation and received knowledge as they react to a packaged and fairly rigid chunk of instruction. In the foreign language classroom, the able and willing would learn on their own with mild support; the unable and unwilling would be screened out of this elective; the able but unwilling would have moments of motivation from gimmicks pulled out of the teacher's bag of tricks and tantalizers; and the unable but willing would be "remediated" (given more of the same coursework) or tracked (given less of the same coursework and less of the teacher's expectations). The fact that "bluebirds" have always seemed to remain bluebirds and "cardinals" always cardinals is evidence, perhaps, that our solutions were not as effective as we would have liked.

In education in general, and in foreign language education in particular, new perspectives are emerging. The hint of change is reflected in our professional talk—in the words we use and in the meanings we assign them. Words such as *strategy* and *style,* used in the past to describe teachers and teaching acts, now refer more frequently to learners and learning; individualization refers more often now to the *how* and *why* of learning, than to the *what* and *when* of teaching. The term *accountability*, used most often in the past to refer to teachers rather than students, now assumes more powerful and interesting connotations when applied equally to both. Most importantly, we are beginning to look at what it means to be a *learner,* rather than simply a student.

Thirty years ago, 60 percent of households matched the traditional family pattern of one mother, one father, and two children; today the figure is 4 percent. The proportion of children under six with employed mothers is expected to reach two-thirds by 1995; many of today's children live in poverty (Stern, 93; Strong, 95); and many of today's classrooms are composed of children of immigrant families. Homogeneous classrooms, even in foreign languages, are an artifact of the past—states such as New York, North Carolina, and Louisiana have decreed that *all* students will study a foreign language.

According to Edmonds (35): "We can, whenever and wherever we choose, successfully teach all children whose schooling is of interest to us. We already know more than we need to do that" (p. 15). This chapter will examine what it is that we know or think we know, and what this might mean for a teaching-learning process. The first section will describe *whom we are teaching* and what factors make up their various and individual learning styles. The second section will discuss *how we are teaching* and how well our teaching acts synchronize with the learning process. The third section will examine *how our students are learning* and will focus on current research and implications in the area of learner strategies.

Learning Styles

According to Dunn and her colleagues (Dunn et al., 33), most children can master the same content—*how* they master it is determined by individual learning styles. Every person has a learning style—a set of biological or developmental characteristics, preferences, and tendencies that affect *how*—not how well—one learns. One's learning style says nothing about one's overall intelligence, or ability, or desire to learn. Just as there is no one best teaching style, there is no one best learning style. More often than not, however, teaching and learning styles do not match. Because normal, healthy students absorb, process, and retain information and skills in different ways, the same teaching method that is so pleasant for some may be painful for many others.

Learning style is a composite of environmental and perceptual preferences, which influence our physical and sensing needs; cognitive variables, which determine how we approach, conceptualize, and structure our world; and social preferences, which arise from cognitive, personality, and affective factors and which shape our behavioral tendencies in learning situations. Each person's cluster of traits, preferences, and needs is as distinct and unique as a signature— and as neutral. One can neither be glorified nor stigmatized by learning style.

While we can observe teaching directly, we can only speculate on the less visible acts of learning. A rapidly growing body of research has afforded merely a glimpse of the multitude of factors that form one's learning style. What this research has repeatedly shown is that many different learning styles exist in the same group. Cafferty (19), for example, compared the profiles of teachers in one high school with each of their sophomore and junior students and confirmed 1689 mismatched teacher–student pairs. Results of research also indicate that students achieve higher grades and have significantly more positive attitudes toward a subject when their learning styles are similar to their teachers' teaching styles (Cafferty, 19; Dunn and Griggs, 34).

What the research has not investigated adequately is: (1) the variability of a learner's style from one event to another; (2) the variation among individuals in the manifestations of a shared learning trait; or (3) the extent to which a learning style will resist change. At present, readers reviewing the literature on learning styles will benefit from a high tolerance of ambiguity. Not only do traits studied vary in their specificity of definition, mode of measurement, and nomenclature across disciplines and across learning style inventories, but it is questionable whether investigative focus on a single trait is not unlike isolating the distinct threads of a well-knotted rope. The bulk of research to date has been exploratory in nature, establishing the strength of relationships between traits themselves and between specific traits and student achievement, as indicated by performance on discrete tasks.

This section will examine selected aspects of learning style in terms of some of the most recent research and will raise some questions regarding classroom implications and future research avenues.

People as Learners Sense Differently

Individuals differ in physical needs and comfort requirements as learners. Studies of chronobiological preferences, for example, lead researchers to conclude that no matter when a class is in session, it is the wrong time of day for almost one-third of that population (Dunn and Dunn, 32). While precollegiate schooling adheres to the 8:00–2:00 or 9:00–3:00 time frame divided into 40–55-minute shifts, indications are that not all learners do follow this rhythm. Dunn et al. (33) conclude that while most teachers appear to be early-morning people, in tests of over one million students, only about one-third were morning alert—the majority preferred late morning, afternoon, or evening as the best time for concentration. Experiments with time-of-day matching consistently showed significantly improved performance, especially with dropouts, underachievers, and at-risk students.

While time of day may be an unalterable variable, out-of-class assignments, projects, and research opportunities can allow students flexibility in the selection of optimum performance hours. Homework might therefore be viewed not as workbook chores, but as activity that is comparable or superior in learner engagement to classroom work and valued beyond its mere completion.

Learners have comfort needs as well. Some require mobility and physical activity in order to concentrate; many perform significantly better in low than in bright light; and some concentrate better in a reclined position or seated on the floor. And while the notorious pencil tapper may be admonished for his or her apparent distractibility, this student may indeed be fulfilling a need for sound. Researchers contend that the need for sound (or noise!) increases as adolescence begins and later returns to its previous level (Price, 84). Surprisingly, according to a study by the NASSP Task Force, of all the characteristics that influence achievement, intake preferences (needs for eating or drinking while concentrating) achieved the highest reliability (Dunn and Dunn, 32). Dunn and Griggs (34) describe ten U.S. secondary schools that increased student achievement by, among other things, affording more environmental flexibility to learners. In these classrooms, some students use headsets to block out extraneous sounds; others are permitted to listen to music on Walkman players. Subdivisions of classroom space allow for mobility and preferred seating arrangements.

Dunn and Dunn (32) contend that these physical responses are biological in origin and therefore enduring and pervasive. They conclude that "Those who suggest that children should learn to adapt to their teachers' styles disregard the biological nature of style" (p. 62).

Researchers also categorize preferred perceptual modality as biological. Learners will differ in the senses they use to take in and remember difficult information most easily—through hearing, seeing, speaking, touching and manipulating, moving, or any combination of these. Dunn and Dunn (32) summarize studies revealing that students achieved significantly higher test scores in modality-matched rather than modality-mismatched instruction. They add, further, that these scores increased even more when students were taught with multisensory resources, but *initially through their most preferred modality,* and then reinforced through secondary or tertiary preferences.

Studies of learner sensory needs and reactions to peripheral stimuli hold implications for the foreign language classroom. Many of the "methods" available to teachers capitalize on certain sensory channels—some combine visual and auditory, others include tactile learning through object manipulation, still others incorporate background music. While each method has its *teacher* advocates, no one method will match the modality preferences and priorities of all learners. Rather, what research seems to suggest is multisensory instruction that is not limited to or constrained by a packaged prescriptive approach. Further, if achievement is enhanced by initial teaching through the learner's preferred modality, then ways must be explored to activate a range of senses in the *presentation* of new elements of language. What is called for is not a teaching method, but a teaching repertoire. We may also expect differences in skill development and in the ways learners approach tasks. Visual and tactile processors may require mental imaging or notetaking as they listen, "manipulatives" or visual organizers as they speak or write; auditory and kinesthetic processors may need to subvocalize as they read, and so on.

Certainly, the most profound implication of the diversity of perceptual preferences is that in presentation and practice, instruction should move beyond chalkboard, textbook, and teacher's voice to utilize imagination and the rich resources available in activities that engage students in seeing, saying, touching, hearing, and moving in the language. The foreign language classroom should provide the kinds of whole sensory experiences that real life affords the communicator.

People as Learners Act and Interact Differently

Within the microsociety of the classroom, learners will vary in the ways they react to and interact with teachers and other students, as well as with learning tasks. These social preferences reflect various manifestations of inward (self) or outward (other) direction and derive from the interaction of cognitive, personality, and affective learner variables. Students will thus display distinctly different constellations and degrees of such traits as independence, responsibility, competitiveness, risk-taking tendency, and initiative as demonstrated by varying needs for attention, direction, structure, freedom, and praise. Some of these behaviors and needs may vary from one situation to another.

Individuals as learners differ in their preferences to work alone, with the teacher, or with other students. Price (84) indicates that the higher the grade level, the less teacher-motivated learners become. Thus, the majority of adolescent and adult learners will prefer to learn with and from peers or to work alone in the appropriate setting with the appropriate resources. Dunn and Dunn (32) indicate that most "gifted" students prefer to work alone, to establish their own direction, task timing, and approach, although we suspect that this may be true only of certain tasks. Other learners are more dependent, both on structure (outcomes, time frame, organizational clues) and peer support. Birckbichler (13) notes that there are, however, adolescent learners who will cue their learning directly to the teacher and seek the support and approval of the authority figure. According to Dunn et al. (33), a small percentage of students cannot concentrate with anyone present, yet may not have the skills to work independently. Some of these students may work better with computers or other media than with people.

Students differ, as well, in their response to competitive environments. Scott (88) notes that one of the characteristics of gifted learners is their enhanced "internal locus of control," that is, their capacity to self-assess and feel responsible for their learning. Students tending more to external loci of control, on the other hand, assess their performance through comparison with or approval of others. While Scott observes that the latter will often blame others (teachers, peers, parents) when this comparison falls short of the desirable, it is equally plausible that these learners, lacking a strong internal regulator, may internalize this comparison and become overly self-critical. Classrooms that incorporate competition or external criteria in grading will enhance learners' external locus of control; more collaborative environments can encourage learner problem solving and accountability. Kagan's (62) surveys revealed, however, that approximately 85 percent of college undergraduates had never worked cooperatively to learn.

In some experimental studies designed to reduce competitiveness and foster cooperation in learning, cognitive outcomes included increases in the following (Johnson and Johnson, 59): retention, application, and transfer of information, concepts, and principles; problem-solving ability; and divergent and risk-taking thinking. Affective gains included acceptance and appreciation of individual differences and reduction of bias and more positive attitudes toward learning. Studies indicate further that students in cooperative learning environments have greater self-esteem, greater concern for others, higher levels of reasoning, increased perspective taking, more on-task behavior, and higher overall achievement (Conrad, 27). Cross-cultural studies may reveal to what extent these are cultural phenomena.

The concept of cooperative learning, however, should not be so oversimplified as to be equated with peer grouping. While grouping may be a technique used to foster cooperative learning, it may not always result in a cooperative learning context and may not always lead to cooperative learning strategies. Whether students learn more effectively individually or in groups depends on the nature of the task and expectations, whether students are working with or merely in the presence of others, the size and nature of the group, and whether the outcome is a group product or individual products of component group members.

Learners also differ in their needs for performance reward. While the term *positive reinforcement* has long been key in the teacher's pedagogical lexicon, studies of the effects of praise and the structure of rewards indicate that learners have varying needs and requirements for both the quantity and quality of this type of teacher feedback (Hawley et al., 51). Praise has been found to be effective when tied to specific achievements that make the relationship between behavior and reinforcement explicit. Much of teacher praise, however, does not actually serve to reinforce because it is mere reactive behavior, is not tied to a standard of performance, and lacks either specificity or credibility. There is a tendency for peers to infer and attribute low ability to students who are overpraised and high ability to students of whom teachers are demanding. In fact, studies by Brophy and Good (17) indicate that low-achieving students are sometimes praised more often for marginal and inadequate answers than high achievers.

A comprehensive review of research on the specific cognitive outcomes facilitated by different reward structures (Johnson and Johnson, 59), ties the efficacy of different goal and reward structures to differences in desired cognitive outcomes. Cooperative goals and rewards were found to be most appropriate when teachers seek to promote retention, application, and transfer of factual information, concepts, principles; mastery of concepts and principles; verbal abilities; problem-solving ability and success; cooperative skills; creative ability; divergent and risk-taking thinking and productive controversy; awareness and utilization of one's capabilities; and role-taking abilities. Competitive goals and rewards were found most effective when teachers sought to develop competitive skills and speed and quantity of work on simple drill activities; individualistic rewards and goal structures were most likely to enhance the acquisition of individualistic and simple mechanical skills and the learning of factual information.

Risk-taking is another variable that has been studied in foreign language learning. Beebe (7) contends that individuals with high motivation to achieve are moderate, not high, risk-takers, because in general they prefer to depend on skill and to exercise control. She stresses the importance of situational variables influencing this behavior: the degree of skill versus chance affecting outcomes, the influence of prior experience, the value of the reward, the degree of interest in the task. In her studies, skill contexts appeared to stimulate a moderate level of risk-taking, whereas a "chance" context seemed to induce extremely risky or conservative strategies; individuals took greater risks in group decisions than they did by themselves on the same task; the risk of looking foolish appeared to be greater in the presence of peers from the students' own country than in the presence of native speakers.

Ely (41) posits four dimensions to risk-taking behavior: lack of hesitancy about using a newly encountered linguistic element, willingness to use linguistic elements perceived to be complex or difficult, tolerance of possible incorrectness or inexactitude in using language, and an inclination to rehearse a new element silently before attempting to use it aloud. Thus, his categories make some assumptions about learners and language classroom experiences: (1) that learners have their own internalized systems for tolerance of error, regardless of classroom focus; and (2) that opportunities are provided in the classroom for silent rehearsal. He examined the effect of risk-taking and other situation-specific personality variables on attitudes toward different language-learning activities. While he had hypothesized that low risk-takers would enjoy the "safety" of controlled grammar exercises, his investigation showed the reverse effect. Ely concludes that these students may, in fact, be less comfortable during controlled practice than high risk-takers, since the correctness of their production is being closely monitored by the teacher and by other students and since low risk-takers are more concerned about making mistakes.

If fear of error is associated with low risk-taking, teachers may want to examine classroom activities in terms of their potential for error display—those exercises in which there is one right answer and only one right answer offer opportunities (perceived or real) for obvious error demonstration, monitoring, teacher correction, and judgment. Beebe (7) contends that, in risk situations, the cost of failure is a greater deterrent than the value of success is an incentive. Students will perhaps be more likely to take risks if they are invited to do so without penalty.

Research has yet to define the phenomenon of risk-taking clearly and capture it operationally as distinct from other traits. We require at this point a better sense of what *learners* perceive to be risk-taking situations, not just in oral performance, but in other facets of language use as well. We might examine further how this trait is related to such cultural factors as social distance and face-saving (Kramsch, 64), as well as to learner perceptions of power and control within the classroom.

People as Learners Think Differently

Regardless of elusive traits like intelligence or aptitude, every individual has a cognitive style or set of mental-processing preferences. A cognitive style is a set of traits that shapes *how* one perceives and organizes information and concepts. The styles that have received the most attention in foreign language research are degree of field independence, degree of tolerance of ambiguity, and degrees of reflectivity and flexibility.

As will be noted throughout this section, the research in this area is both puzzling and troublesome for reasons such as the following: (1) the "styles" selected for investigation are global, each encompassing several traits and behaviors; (2) the "styles" may not be directly observable in the classroom by the teacher but measured only by external instruments; (3) the attributes of the styles and their variability according to the nature of the task are only speculative at this point; (4) the interaction among the styles of members of a group remains to be examined. Readers will want to bear in mind that whatever the style, it does not exist separate from the act of measuring it or from the total person that each learner is. In addition, it is important to note that individuals rarely represent the extremes, but will exhibit tendencies toward one style or the other.

Degree of Field Independence.   Researchers contend that individuals differ in the extent to which they rely primarily on self or are influenced by the world outside, or the "field." Field *independence* refers to the facility with which an individual distinguishes relevant from less relevant information, sees patterns and subpatterns, and perceives analytically. Field *dependence* describes a global, rather than analytical, approach and a tendency to perceive the total picture, often affording equal weight to both salient and less relevant stimuli (less relevant, that is, for those who do not normally attend to them). Chapelle and Roberts (23) speculate that cultures with more elaborate social structures and pressure to conform tend to rear children who are more field dependent, whereas cultures in which there is comparatively less emphasis on interpersonal relationships and where technology plays an important role tend to produce more field-independent children. They add that, for Western societies, this trait follows a developmental curve, which displays children becoming increasingly field independent until the age of fifteen, then stabilizing until the age of thirty, when this trait begins to decrease. It is plausible, then, that this trait may be pedagogically induced, that is, as much an artifact of the priorities and style demands of teachers, materials, methods, and grading norms of the school system as of the home, society, or culture in general. Dunn and Dunn (32) caution that in interpreting cross-cultural studies one should bear in mind that there is as much variability within groups as between groups and even within a given family unit.

   Degree of field independence is often measured by an instrument called the Group Embedded Figures Test (Oltman et al., 74), which requires subjects to identify geometric shapes embedded in the distraction of a complex design. A number of studies during the 70s and 80s have shown positive correlations between field independence and various acts presumed to be associated with or indicative of foreign language proficiency, including sentence disambiguation (Seliger, 89), sentence repetition (Naiman, Frohlich, and Stern, 70), performance on cloze testing (Day, 29), and performance on standardized tests of spelling, listening comprehension, and vocabulary (Tucker et al., 97). In a study of the relationship between field independence and achievement in reading, listening, writing, and grammar, however, Bialystok and Frohlich (12) found that field independence added nothing to the prediction that could not be accounted for by other variables. In addition, they recommended examining the relationship of this and other cognitive traits to functional and productive tasks rather than formal comprehension tasks. They suggest that factors may be differentially related to success on language-learning tasks in different language-learning situations, a position taken by Birckbichler (13) and Omaggio (75) as well.

   While caution is advisable in extending or elaborating this trait into other trait clusters, Brown (18) notes that the field dependent/independent continuum appears to have an affective dimension as well: field-independent persons display more independence, competitiveness, and self-confidence, whereas field-dependent learners demonstrate more sociability, empathy, and sensitivity. The "ideal" language learner, then, would be one displaying "cognitive flexibility"—enjoying the advantages of both styles, depending on the task and situation.

Chapelle and Roberts (23) hypothesized that field-independent learners, because of their analytical and problem-solving approaches, would be good at learning rules, applying rules, and finding patterns; field-dependent learners, on the other hand, would be better at acquiring language through integrative language use, such as interaction with native speakers in social situations. In a study of ESL students, the researchers sought to determine whether field independence is a predictor of success (as measured by the TOEFL, a multiple-choice grammar test, a dictation task, and an oral speaking test of communicative competence). Their hypothesis that field dependence would be related to superior performance on the oral test of communicative competence was not supported; instead, field independence was found to be a significant predictor here as well. These results give rise to abundant speculation: Perhaps field-independent individuals are good at dealing with testing situations or perhaps the tests were not sufficiently interactive so that the "social dimension" of field dependence would come into play. The authors conclude, however, that generalizations drawn from this study are limited because the trait of field dependence is *not measurable in its own right* but is defined operationally only in terms of *lack* of field independence:

> Some subjects have a greater ability to use their FI style to perform this task; they get high scores on the test. However, they are never called upon to use a FD style and we do not have a measure of the extent to which they are FD. It is thus inappropriate to label a lack of FI as FD; consequently . . . we cannot make claims about the relationship between FD and L2 acquisition. (p. 42)

Since field (in)dependence refers to *how* people learn, it may be questioned, as well, whether relationships between this trait and test performance alone (how *well*) provide information regarding the differences the researches sought to find. Carter (20) questioned, for example, whether cognitive style and course approach affect learners' perceptions of the *process* of learning a foreign language, thus influencing their learning strategies and, ultimately, their degree of success. Her study examined whether field independence / dependence is differentially related to success on language tasks and to language-learning *programs* focusing on form or on functional language use. The hypothesis—that field-independent learners would attend more to structural elements of language (form), whereas field-dependent subjects would focus more on meaning—was not supported. In fact, field-dependent subjects attributed less importance to meaning. Field independence was found to be conducive to success on both formal achievement and functional proficiency tasks independently of the relatively formal or functional orientation of the course. While perceptions of the learning process were similar for all students, correlations between individual factors of the learning process and both proficiency and achievement tests showed that one factor, focus on meaning, accounted for over 18 percent of the variance in students' scores in the grammar-oriented course.

In the area of field independence / dependence, more research is needed to address issues such as the following:

1. What does this trait mean in terms of cognitive *style?* Field independence, described throughout the literature as an ability to distinguish relevant from irrelevant cues, self from "field," carries the connotation not of style, but rather of cognitive skill (field dependence being the absence of this skill). If both field dependence and independence are legitimate *ways* of conceptualizing and organizing one's world and one's learning, then we need to have better measures of the traits themselves, perhaps through instruments tapping different perceptual modalities through a variety of tasks.

2. What do field-independent and field-dependent individuals *do* to learn? *How* does each approach and carry out different language-learning and language-use tasks? Correlating field independence with performance on tests (the product) may tell us little about the process of learning and the strategies used by field-independent learners.

3. If, indeed, field-independent behaviors are found to contribute to more effective language learning, then ways of promoting these behaviors might be sought. Birckbichler and Omaggio (14) and Omaggio (75) suggest classroom activities designed to encourage more field independence in task performance. By the same token, if the field-dependent learner's supposed sociability, empathy, and interpersonal orientation do not exhibit themselves in increased attention to meaning in communicative acts, then in what ways do or can these field-dependent characteristics contribute to effective language learning and communication? Guiora et al. (49) note, for example, that the more sensitive individuals are to the feelings and behaviors of another person, the more likely they are to perceive and recognize subtleties and unique aspects of the second language and to incorporate them in speaking. Clearly, there are many aspects of proficiency development and assessment to which present instruments are not sensitive.

4. Much research has used measures of achievement and focused on receptive skills. More research is needed across skills, across learning tasks within skills, and across levels of proficiency. Carter (20) notes, for example, that field-dependent and field-independent styles may be related to proficiency in different ways at different levels.

Merely knowing that individuals approach learning differently from the standpoint of global or analytic processing indicates that both inductive and deductive approaches should be incorporated in the presentation of new concepts. Such presentations should consist of successive small steps leading to understanding as well as broad concepts followed by detailed focus. Additionally, knowing that not all learners easily separate salient from nonsalient data in learning should encourage teachers to examine instructional materials and classroom practices to make sure that what is emphasized and how it is presented respond to students' needs rather than to teacher preferences and preparation. As Combs (26) notes: "If I don't know what is important, then everything becomes important."

Tolerance of Ambiguity.   Another aspect of cognitive style that has been examined in terms of foreign language learning is the "ability to function rationally and calmly in a situation in which interpretation of all stimuli is not clear" (Chapelle and Roberts, 23, p. 30). Individuals who are highly tolerant of ambiguity have the ability to cope effectively and remain unthreatened by novelty, vagueness, uncertainty, or contradiction. While few studies support a relationship between this trait and foreign language learning, the relationship is generally assumed to exist, simply given the nature of foreign language study. Individuals who have a low tolerance of ambiguity tend to look for black-and-white solutions and jump to conclusions easily. Ausubel et al. (5) note the prevalence of certain general reductionistic trends found in the thinking of *most* persons within a given culture; for instance, conceptualizing problems in terms of single rather than multiple causality, the tendency to think in terms of dichotomous propositions, and the preference for conceiving of variability in categorical, as opposed to continuous, terms.

In a study of the learning strategies used by AT (ambiguity-tolerant) and AI (ambiguity-intolerant) students, Ely (41) hypothesized that relatively lower tolerance of ambiguity would lead to relatively greater reliance upon the L1 when using the language and a stronger tendency to relate L2 items to elements known in the L1. Indeed, AT was found to be a negative predictor of the following acts (as reported by, rather than observed in, students): looking for similarities between new words and L1 words, looking up words in the dictionary, planning what to say ahead of time, and thinking about grammar when writing. AT was found to be a positive predictor of looking for overall meaning in reading and guessing meaning from context. Ely notes, however, that because the amount of variance in dependent variables was modest, many other factors were also acting to influence use of strategies, including, perhaps, prior training and practice in strategy use, as well as other individual differences not measured in the study.

Chapelle and Roberts (23) found that AT was not related to ESL proficiency at entry time (as measured by TOEFL) but after one semester of L2 study, those who had higher levels of AT tended to attain higher levels of proficiency at the end of the semester. The researchers concluded that those students who were able to tolerate ambiguities present in the L2 environment apparently gained more from L2 study.

Several considerations for further attention to this area of learning style suggest themselves.

What does the *learner* consider ambiguous? Chapelle and Roberts (23) contend that there is less ambiguity in a formal language class in which individual elements of language are isolated for study than in an immersion situation in which the learner has to attend to multiple language cues simultaneously. Ely (41), however, has described the ambiguity present in structured classroom situations at the level of discrete learning tasks: knowing the precise meaning of a new lexical item, understanding the exact temporal reference of a second language verb form, or pronouncing a given sound with accuracy. An examination of his situation-specific scale for measurement of ambiguity identifies three broad categories of learner discomfort: frustration with one's own developmental level (which could be a result of the learner's own awareness of the incompleteness of his/her knowledge and ability or the perceived mismatch between this and teacher's demands); frustration due to the inexactitude of correspondence between the L1 and the L2; and frustration with the L2 system itself (or its classroom presentation). Intolerance of ambiguity might therefore be construed as a global manifestation of a host of factors, including an individual's persistence, need for structure, concrete/abstract orientation, perceived demands from the teacher or the program, degree and type of motivation and risk-taking tendencies, and one's *prior expectations and experiences*. Research in different skills—with different language-learning and language-using tasks, comparing different teaching and grading styles, comparing learners with different notions and prior experiences in different learning settings (e.g., immersion as well as formal classrooms)—may shed more light on the *learners'* varying concepts of ambiguity.

Naiman et al. (70) suggest that those learners who experience extreme difficulty coping with ambiguity may be among the early dropouts in language programs. If many of our students cannot tolerate ambiguity, three choices are available: dismiss the students; disambiguate the learning; or help students discover strategies for coping with ambiguity.

Immersion settings—with their cue bombardment, multiple stimuli, lack of imposed structure and unpredictability—may represent intolerable ambiguity to some learners. Many learners may, however, find their sense-making more severely challenged by grammar analysis—rules and exceptions, decontextualized practice of forms, contrastive paradigms, and random vocabulary items.

According to Ausubel et al. (5), vague, diffuse, ambiguous, or erroneous meanings may emerge from the very beginning of the learning process. Contributing factors are the unavailability of relevant anchoring ideas in one's cognitive structure, the unstable or unclear nature of these anchoring ideas, and the lack of discriminability between the learning material and the anchoring ideas themselves. This unfavorable outcome is particularly likely if the learner's need for, and self-critical attitude about, acquiring adequate meanings is deficient. Ausubel et al. contend that the meaningfulness of a word depends on whether it has a concretely identifiable referent and also on such factors as the *frequency and variety of the contexts in which it is encountered*.

It would seem that, in foreign language study, learners may be confronted with varying degrees of ambiguity of *two* types: (1) ambiguity of the *language itself* as an arbitrary system and (2) ambiguity in the classroom *presentation* of language for learning. Past attempts to simplify language and remove ambiguity have resulted, for example, in textbook materials that may be showing learners inappropriate systems for coping with the ambiguity present in the language itself: a focus on serial presentation of grammar points (abstract) has often resulted in a neglect of lexical learnings, which have more concrete referents; constant references and even translation to English have directed students to irreconcilable comparisons between L1 and L2; textbook compartmentalization through self-contained chapters, however instructionally or editorially efficient, has left to students the tasks of cross-referencing and transfer within the language. Ausubel et al. (5) note the consequences of this approach in learning in general: (1) multiple terms are used to represent concepts that are intrinsically equivalent except for contextual reference, thereby generating cognitive strain, confusion, and rote learning; (2) artificial barriers are erected between related topics, obscuring important common features, thus rendering impossible the acquisition of insights dependent upon recognition of these commonalities; (3) adequate use is not made of relevant, previously learned ideas as a basis for subsuming and incorporating related new information; and (4) since significant differences between apparently similar concepts are not made clear and explicit, these concepts are often perceived and retained as identical.

In terms of disambiguating the classroom, a further consideration might be that of establishing more real-world anchors. What languages and cultures have in common, to some extent, is *function;* where they will differ enormously is in *form.* Well-sequenced presentation and use of the language can build off the familiar language use *purposes* and familiar contexts. Bialystok (10) notes that "decontextualizing" the language has been assigned an important causal role in both the difficulty experienced by adults in learning a second language in an artificial environment and the difficulty experienced by some children in acquiring literacy skills or in coping with schooling in general.

It would be instructive, as well, to look at how learners tolerate ambiguity and discover ways to share their strategies with other students. The rote memorization, *one* right answer *only,* and fact orientation of much of schooling in general has served to sanitize course content, creating discrete pockets of knowledge composed of events, analyses, reasons, equations, and formulae, perhaps not preparing students as learners to experience, let alone cope with, the *right kinds* of ambiguity. Materials and practices can be deliberately designed to help students form hypotheses and analyze the apparent inconsistencies of surface-level cues in order to discover meaning and arrive at believability of the foreign language and culture in terms of its own framework.

Degree of Reflectivity. This continuum describes one's conceptual tempo (Kagan, 61), that is, the speed and accuracy with which an individual responds in situations posing some response uncertainty. Reflective learners tend to test their language mentally before verbalizing and therefore will be slow but accurate in responding. Impulsive students display more spontaneity in their responses, along with less accuracy. They will respond quickly with the first answer that occurs to them and thus may underuse their capabilities. In speaking tasks, reflective learners are likely to remain silent if unsure. In listening and reading tasks, Birckbichler (13) speculates that reflective students may overattend to detail to the detriment of comprehension; however, a study by Messer (69) found reflectives more systematic in searching for information with written texts—they gathered more information and spent more time evaluating it with respect to their hypothesis. Hewett's (52) study indicates that the stronger a subject's self-assessment on reflectivity was, the higher the score on a culturally weighted difficult reading test was likely to be, regardless of previous experience with language and culture, current proficiency level, language aptitude, or intelligence.

While schools attempt to train students to be lightning thinkers, the demands for both speed and accuracy may be realistic for only the most rote and manipulative of tasks. Rowe (87) found that teachers allow students approximately *one second* to answer questions. Shrum (90), investigating postsolicitation wait time, found that the mean length of time between teacher questions and student response was 1.91 seconds, which, she contends, allows merely for sensory storage and recognition of very simple solicitations. She points out that the nature of the activity (drills) allowed for quick answers and did not require extensive thought or attention to meaning. This practice may not be confined to oral skills, however. In observations of high school English classes, Applebee (3) found that the average preparation for writing in the classroom amounts to about three minutes: scant time for students to use their capacities to conduct memory searches, construct and reconstruct complex plans, or transform data. Yet if thoughtful communication rather than manipulation of grammar forms is our goal, perhaps longer periods of wait time are indicated and would benefit both reflective and impulsive learners.

Some researchers have experimented with a latency period under conditions in which the problem posed is within the learner's capabilities and requires thoughtful reasoning. Rowe (87) reports of training more impulsive students to use self-talk or verbal-control strategies. However, in a study designed to train impulsive students to become more reflective, Kagan (62) found that (1) the subjects' improvement was evidenced only when adults were present, and (2) although they learned to respond more reflectively, their accuracy on tasks decreased. Other researchers, rather than attempting to adjust the *learner*, have met some success by adjusting the pedagogical apparatus. Holley and King (55) permitted a latency period by withholding teacher intervention: teachers were counseled to wait five to ten seconds when students hesitated in responding. They found that this pause reduced by 50 percent the need for teacher correction. Teachers, using methods such as the Silent Way, self-impose wait-times of up to forty seconds before rephrasing or switching topics. Such practices may not only increase student confidence but also increase teacher respect for true learner answers.

Meredith (68) experimented with an *imposed,* rather than a permitted, latency period. He administered an oral sequence-construction test using word triplets to both reflective and impulsive responders under two treatments—free latency and imposed latency (a twenty-second pause was imposed between the administration of the task and the command to begin). When impulsive students were not merely permitted, but required, to delay their responses, gains, though not significant, were found in fluency, amount of relevant information conveyed, and linguistic quality. Performance of reflectives remained relatively stable with significant gains in levels of fluency under imposed latency.

In the area of reading, attempts to modify impulsive behavior have generally fallen into four categories: forced delay, reinforcement, modeling, and direct teaching of scanning strategies. Of these, Hewett (52) contends that the use of scanning strategies appears to be the most successful method of improving both accuracy and latency of response.

Further research may tell us whether the issue is one of time or *use* of time, by comparing a pure latency period with one in which students use mental imaging, conversational mapping, or other organizing strategies. Clearly, both reflective and impulsive learners have much to tell us about their strategies.

Degree of Flexibility. The flexible learner is one who perceives alternative solutions and engages in the variations necessary to the development of a generalization. Birckbichler (13) suggests that the flexible learner may be similar to Guilford's (48) divergent thinker, that is, an individual who thinks in many different directions, makes adjustments when solving problems, and provides a variety of answers to a particular problem or question. She emphasizes the relationship between linguistic flexibility and communication in both "produc- tive" and "receptive" use. Certainly, the need to move *within* the language, to adapt, to devise alternative forms of expression, and to cope with the unpredic- tability of real-life situations will place demands on language users that far exceed memorized expressions and pat forms of behavior. Speakers lacking in flexibility will likely place a burden on communicative partners: one-word utterances will be subject to varying interpretations; a patterned repertoire will result in the forced fit of message/intent. This flexibility trait, however, relates not merely to skills in paraphrasing, circumlocuting, and the way language is used, but to the way learning and performance in general are approached.

Rigidity refers to the tendency of a learner to resist a new activity in favor of repeating an old activity or doing the same thing in the same way over and over again. According to Birckbichler (13), the oral and written performance of this student will be characterized by brevity and terseness. The highly repetitive performance that characterizes rigidity will often lead to simplification of the task and to "splinter learning" (Kephart, 63): the student learns the specific actions necessary to success in the task but does not expand these learnings to include other activities associated with the task—only a collection of isolated unconnected data are available. As a result, transfer of learning from one type of task to another is limited. Kephart notes that rigidity reflects not the lack of awareness of the need to alter response, but rather the *difficulty* of altering it and the inability to conceive of options in problem solving. Thus, this student's use of the language may be best described as rehearsed to perfection, but rutted in selection.

Although no studies could be found that establish relationships between this trait continuum and foreign language learning, it might be speculated that the learner who lacks flexibility is similar to Ausubel et al.'s (5) description of the learner who develops a "rote learning set" in relation to potentially meaningful subject matter. As proposed by Ausubel et al., this behavior can be attributed to the sad circumstance that students know what substantively correct answers lacking in verbatim correspondence to what they have been taught receive no credit whatsoever from certain teachers and that pressures may lead them to "create a spurious impression of facile comprehension" (p. 43), rather than accept and remedy problems in understanding.

Perhaps then, rather than place students into categories of rigid and flexible, we need to examine and correct possible sources of problems, such as a preponderance of "one-right-answer" drills; correction and testing techniques that attend consistently to form over meaning; lack of deliberate, guided transfer in instructional progressions; instructional strategies that assume grasp of funda- mental concepts as evidence by mere manipulation of language; and extremely competitive environments that can produce learner "shutdown." In terms of linguistic flexibility, we certainly cannot assume that students enter foreign language classrooms either equipped with such oral skills as circumlocution and paraphrasing in a foreign language or trained in written reformulation of ideas in a foreign language or in possession of nonliteral interpretive abilities with a written foreign language text. Flexibility, if desired, must be both fostered by the classroom climate and instructional approach and supported through learner-centered techniques.

Conclusion

In reviewing the literature on learning styles, it becomes clear that our present knowledge base offers more questions than answers. This is not surprising, given the nature of what it is we are attempting to observe and measure and the exploratory status of this area of learner-focused research in foreign language education. For the moment, we are wise to interpret research results with caution and be wary of distorting their implications. The following are some of the perplexing issues in discussions of learner styles.

Learner Style or Learner Problem? We know less about the ways learners approach their individual acts of learning than we do about how we, as teachers, would like them to approach learning. We might like, for example, for every learner to be naturally field-independent; highly tolerant of ambiguity; a fast but accurate risk-taker; independent yet teacher-oriented; competitive, yet able to work cooperatively—in short, tolerant and responsive to any instructional system imposed. The problem is that, while we refer to these traits as "styles," we also too often define them as "absence of style." When learners are said to have a *"lack* of field independence" or "lack of tolerance of ambiguity" or "lack of flexibility," the words "foreign language learning problem" are read between the lines.

Much of the research to date has focused on the attempt to identify "predictors of success" in foreign language learning. This orientation conveys some rather insidious messages: (1) it carries the notion that we have identified *what language learning is* and that we are therefore prepared to identify those traits relevant to its pursuit; (2) it carries the notion that we can also predict lack of success and that we can, in advance, gauge our expectations accordingly; (3) it carries the notion of learner sameness rather than uniqueness; and (4) it places the onus on the learner, who, once labeled and classified, may cease to be a relevant consideration in planning and conducting teaching. These notions are not satisfying to us as educators. Predictors of success have no place in education when they explain away the learner. Absolute classifications have no value when applied to humans who embody scores of other traits, all of which interact.

Real or Reified Traits? Another problematic aspect of much of the research on learning styles lies in the nature of the measures and investigative techniques themselves. Particularly in relation to the identification of cognitive styles, there are both methodological and construct validity problems, some of which have been addressed in this section. In general, on the basis of correlational studies, labels have been coined and assigned that have no theoretical support other than the positive (and not necessarily high) correlations obtained. Although it may be argued that this is a necessary condition for identifying components or factors in any scientific endeavor, it does not follow that this is, in fact, sufficient to explain human behavior. In his powerful critique of the "mismeasure" of man, Gould (46) points out that in addition to detecting correlations between certain tests, it is also necessary to have "knowledge of the physical nature of the measures themselves" (p. 250). Thus, no matter how long, complex, innovative, or sophisticated the instruments and measures taken may be, there must be something else aside from mathematics alone that will allow us to assign labels to traits. Irrespective of their usefulness or explanatory potential, the results of statistical manipulations become, too often and too dangerously, labels—or are *reified* (that is, given pragmatic and theoretical value so that they become entities in and of themselves)—and are subsequently used to create even more reified labels.

The reification of certain cognitive styles dear to the cultures or groups who coined them may obscure our understanding of how learners—and even allegedly whole cultures—who lack such traits still manage to know and organize their worlds and find success in varied social, professional, and artistic settings.

Process or Product?   Another concern is that the instruments used to measure both style and language elicit *products* from individuals, and products of a task may tell us very little about "style"—the process by which different individuals achieve these products. Rarely do we get a glimpse of how, if at all, the protagonists oriented themselves or were oriented toward the task. For meaningful learning, the power of goal and objective generation by the testee is known to have a strong bearing on results. All too often, however, studies tend to gloss over the effects of instructions, the setting, and the perceived purpose on learner approach to the task. When surveys are used to assess trait ownership, confounding factors are likely to include a reactivity effect as well as variation in individuals' capacities to self-assess.

In terms of language-performance correlations with cognitive-style measures, Frawley and Lantolf (42) point out that tests based on performance or display of certain behaviors produce data that can be indicative of language development or of different degrees of student adjustment to the conditions of task performance itself. Furthermore, in the real world, proficiency and linguistic ability lie in the group—dyads, groups, linguistic communities—not in isolated persons. Mass testing, however, is by its very nature devoid of the natural uses of language in interaction and in extended discourse. Noninteractive tests, therefore, cannot tap the potential that lies in every speaker and thus cannot stretch the individual's competence and skills while working on a meaningful activity with others. Needed are more interactive tests that better respond to human tendencies to collaborate and interact when collaboration and interaction are naturally called for. True exploration of the nature of style awaits the development of more contextualized constructs that, in Hewett's (52) words, are able "to describe adequately a flexible, dynamic, adaptive process of interaction between the individual's preferred style and a changing environment" (p. 82).

Perhaps rather than focus on correlating traits to aspects of performance, we should look at how our teaching is responding to these traits. In other words, is our instruction biased toward those who already possess certain skills or tendencies as nurtured through other academic learnings? Is there anything we can do to unbias our teaching to the benefit of all learners? This is the topic of the next section.

The "Teaching/Learning" Process

Behind the words of any discussion of learner differences looms the ubiquitous and discomfiting notion of "individualized instruction." For many teachers trained in the 60s and 70s, this notion is securely anchored in and summarily dismissed by such practices as self-pacing, programmed instruction, and behavioral objectives. For others, "individualization" evokes the defeating image of one-on-one instruction guided by 150 variations on a lesson plan.

It would seem that "individualization" is a concept badly in need of reframing. If standard classroom fare is, itself, learner-resistant, it is likely that no amount of frenetic teacher activity will help, simply because the real learning problems and processes will not surface. The particularization of teaching acts conveyed by the notion of individualized instruction can only purposely emerge from the *person*alization and *human*ization of experiences that constitute individualized learning. The reframing of this concept must begin somewhere, with some thoughtful anchors derived from current thought, and must lead to the questioning of some long-held, but often unspoken, assumptions that underlie much of past and present classroom practice. Before we can begin to identify and meet the needs of *specific* learners, we must attend to some needs of *all* learners.

This section will touch on some issues of a complex question adapted from that proposed by Spolsky (91); that is, *who guides whom to learn under what conditions?* The various subquestions will be discussed in terms of insights derived primarily from learning theory and cognitive and educational psychology. The aim is not to review the various theories of cognitive processing and second language acquisition nor to distort blithely the applicability of these theories to matters of foreign language education. Rather, this section will explore some notions gleaned from the various perspectives that seem to hold promise for facilitating learning through teaching and materials that are first and foremost "learner friendly."

Who Guides

Different eras, different programs, different levels of instruction have defined different roles for the teacher: from depositor of knowledge and deficiency expert, to catalyst and counselor, to model and monitor. Yet, one of the most incomplete notions of the role of the teacher is also one of the most prevalent: the teacher as presenter/evaluator. Likewise, one of the most incomplete notions of teaching is the one heard most frequently: "covering" material. Langer and Applebee (66) note that we speak of cheating and grading rather than of helping and finding ways to solve a problem. All these notions are reflected in the common practice of "present, drill, test, move on." All these notions assume teaching expertise in the materials themselves, an assumption that, at least at present, is rarely justified (Kramsch, 65). Yet a common practice is to define a field of study or area of learning in terms of the materials that exist to organize it and to define teaching as the administration of this material and the measurement of its consumption. The common admonition to "test what is taught" has an equally relevant converse—"teach what is tested"—for classrooms can be lonely and confusing places if learners are expected to bridge on their own the gap between the teacher's or textbook's presentation of the language and their own performance in it.

None of the above definitions of the role of the teacher seems to include the purposeful sense of "teaching" conveyed by Ausubel et al. (5) and others concerned with cognitive processing—that is, the deliberate guidance of learning processes along lines suggested by relevant classroom learning theory. Parallel concepts emerging from recent learning theory and cognitive psychology are providing a foundation for what Jones (60) calls "cognitive instruction." Cognitive instruction refers to efforts to help students process information in meaningful ways and to become independent learners; to help students construct meaning, solve problems, develop and select effective strategies, transfer skills and concepts to new situations, and take responsibility for their own learning. According to Jones, such instruction has the potential to alter substantially the capability of the learner, especially the low-achieving learner. This type of instruction speaks to two crucial roles for the teacher: (1) that of the "architect," who, based on client needs and a rich repertoire of professional skills and knowledge, carefully plans the construction, connection, consolidation, and comfort of classroom experiences; and (2) that of the "mediator" (see Duffy and Roehler, 31), who guides students to observe, activate prior knowledge, represent information, select strategies, construct meaning, monitor understanding, assess strategy use, organize and relate ideas, and extend learning. Paramount to this view of teaching, as distinct from the well-worn present/test model, are the notions of "scaffolding" (providing purposeful structured guidance) and "fading" (gradually retreating and withdrawing support as students gain greater task autonomy). This expert guidance is more than simply providing practice opportunities, clear instructions, task guidance, and learner feedback; it is, rather, guiding learners in how to solve the task *strategically,* in how to *define the situation* or task for themselves. Expert guidance is also knowing *when* to remove the scaffolding, when to transfer control. As Langer and Applebee (66) note, when something works well, we tend to keep using it without being sensitive to whether students still need the kind of support that the activity was initially meant to provide.

Acceptance of this more "interactive" role requires, in Rivers's (85) assessment, "a high degree of indirect leadership, along with emotional maturity, perceptiveness, and sensitivity to the feelings of others" (p. 10). It requires, above all, the ability and willingness to exit center stage and work effectively behind the scenes, guiding learners to interact with the task and negotiate meanings with other members of the group. As Kramsch (64) states, "learning how to learn, or how to acquire control over the discourse of the classroom, is at least as important as what is said and learned" (p. 18). Teachers who are unaccustomed to this role frequently cite their fear of losing control of the classroom; the feeling of control experienced in teacher-centered classrooms, however, may be deceptive: in such classrooms teachers may perhaps be in control of *themselves,* in control of *equipment,* in control of the *information* to be imparted, in control of their *materials,* and often in control of the very *utterances of the learners.* But they may not be in control of what students are learning and learning to do. Teachers may, in fact, find that well-conceived and well-structured tasks that are both high-interest and purposeful from the learner's standpoint offer more real internal control, because the students are able to *take charge* of their learning. At least part of the art of interactive teaching involves a process of finding a balance between providing enough support but not imposing too much control.

Who Guides *Whom?*

Individuals do not enter the classroom as tabulae rasae, but rather with varied histories and identities that are profoundly meaningful and superbly complex. While the histories of individuals as classroom learners may include some shared knowledge and experiences, it is likely that their personal investment in, perspective on, and internalization of these experiences will differ vastly. Thus, where we find their commonalities, we also find their differences.

To illustrate, adult learners will have a first language. We usually assume that they will have a wide array of linguistic functions in this first language with which to express ideas, that they will have received some formal instruction in this language, and that they will have the ability to use knowledge of their first language to gain access to another (Birckbichler, 13). What we can no longer assume, however, is that this first language will be English. Nor can we make assumptions regarding the type and amount of formal instruction students have received in English and the degree to which this instruction has been accepted and internalized—this is especially true for recent immigrants and, perhaps, speakers of nonmainstream English dialects. Learners will also differ in *how* they use their first language as a tool in accessing the foreign language. The ability to perform a wide array of linguistic functions in one's first language says nothing about the awareness of the linguistic functions themselves, nor of the variety of ways in which a given function may be performed in the L1. It is plausible, in fact, that it is precisely this lack of awareness of function that results in the translated word strings so common a product in lower-level foreign language classrooms. While learners may share an ability to use a language to varying degrees of precision and effectiveness, they may not share the ability to describe, analyze, or talk about a language as an object. Because of these differences, we cannot assume that all learners are equally equipped to approach the study of a foreign language through grammar analysis, comparison and contrast with English, and metalanguage in English. Nor, as recent reports indicate (Rivers, 85; Applebee et al., 4), can we assume that students understand what it means to "write" or "listen" or "read" or "speak" for different communicative purposes in their own language. Most importantly, we must begin to rid ourselves of the notion that foreign language teaching can be reduced to a two-step process: (1) fill in gaps in students' knowledge about the L1; and then, (2) transfer that knowledge to a different—but parallel—system. Langer and Applebee (66) make this case quite clearly in referring to the development of writing skills:

> If writing is going to play a meaningful role in subjects other than English, then the teachers of those subjects will need to have a conception of writing specific to their disciplines, one that emphasizes *what is unique about writing (and thinking) in their subject,* rather than one that emphasizes ways in which such activities will foster the work of the English teacher (p. 150).

It is often assumed, as well, that adult learners will have a certain degree of cognitive maturity and well-developed conceptual categories in areas of interest, but these traits, as well, are a function of one's experiences (personal, academic, social) as well as one's degree of L1 verbal control. In addition, one's social and cultural background will influence the selection, interpretation, and integration of phenomena as well as their differential assignment of value and meaning.

Spolsky (91) cites the particular importance of three learner characteristics whose combination accounts for the use the learner makes, consciously or unconsciously, of the learning situation: previous knowledge (of the first or other languages), motivation, and learning aptitude (seen as an aptitude for language learning in a formal situation). Of these, motivation and aptitude are most commonly cited by teachers as the crucial differentiating elements; yet we know so very little about either of them.

Rivers (86) reminds us that every living being is motivated, albeit to different aims, and that it is the teacher's task to discover the "springs of motivation" in individual students and channel this motivation, through course content and classroom activities, in the direction of language acquisition. Whitehead (104) appeals for more *vitality* in the classroom context: "Pupils have got to be made to feel they are studying something and are not merely executing intellectual minuets" (p. 9). Lubasa (67) cites such driving elements as interest, freedom of choice, and confidence about being on the right route and contends, further, that motivation is goal-oriented and supported by perseverance. Among those factors that influence perseverance are the pleasure of being a member of a group, the satisfaction of group interaction, the pleasure of struggling with a task or problem, and the satisfaction resulting from solving it. The syllabus that will best account for the learner's motivation and perseverance will be one in which "the learner is told why and how to do what he is required to do, and encouraged to explain why and how he is doing what he is doing as well as to ask for reasons and purposes of what he is asked to do" (p. 110).

"Aptitude" is one of the most enigmatic and cumbersome constructs we have inflicted on ourselves. Although, in this standardized-test–crazed society, we have yet to measure satisfactorily one's aptitude for acquiring a foreign language, we are wont to use the term frequently. As teachers, we are surrounded by decision makers who claim they themselves have no "aptitude" for foreign language study and who seek instruments for measuring this trait in students for counseling, screening, or placement purposes. Egan (36), among others, contends that no one "has" *an* aptitude; "rather each person also 'has' an intelligence, a set of personal relationships with teachers and other students, varying distractions and fluctuating abilities to control them, desires, hopes, and the usual changing array of complicated things we imprecisely distinguish and crudely name" (p. 100).

The construct of "aptitude," as well as the constructs of "developmental level" and "cognitive maturity," are all too frequently measured on the basis of what learners can successfully do *alone,* and thus fail to consider the power of *expert guidance,* i.e., teaching. This thinking is reflected in the belief that if we simply give students a topic and tell them to write, for example, they will know how to do it; it is reflected as well in the assumption that every element of a new task must be taught from scratch. The most evident result of adherence to this thinking is the systematic *underestimation* of what people can learn and curricula and instructional practices that focus on "filling in" or "firming up" supposed gaps on learning (Egan, 36); in other words, education that focuses primarily on yesterday's knowledge and skills.

If one considers education as a purposeful activity, however, the power of expert guidance (teaching) is perhaps best reflected in Vygotsky's (98) critique:

> In studies of children's mental development it is generally assumed that only those things that children can do on their own are indicative of mental abilities. We give children a battery of tests or a variety of tasks of varying degrees of difficulty, and we judge the extent of their mental development on the basis of how they solve them and at what level of difficulty. On the other hand, if we offer leading questions or show how the problem is to be solved and the child then solves it, or if the teacher initiates the solution and the child completes it or solves it in collaboration with other children—in short, if the child barely misses an independent solution of the problem— the solution is not regarded as indicative of his mental development. (cited in Egan, 36, p. 100)

Vygotsky's theory, based on the premise that learning is a social activity, proposes for each learner a "zone of proximal development," which is the distance between actual developmental level as determined by independent problem solving and level of potential development as determined through problem solving under adult guidance or in collaboration with more capable peers. Exploration and exploitation of this zone of potential depends not only on what the learner brings to the situation but also on the nature and quality of the pedagogical skills the teacher applies. Egan (36) contends that the only real learning is that which occurs in the learner's zone of proximal development. Thus, precisely because there are thirty different students in a classroom, pedagogical practice should center on providing varied kinds of support (including peer support or activity-centered work grouping), rather than assuming that the same textbook drill will develop this potential equally in all learners. Instruction that stretches students' abilities into their areas of potential will include the provision of collaborative problem-solving activities, which incorporate the teacher's and/or the learners' varied skills, foci of interest, and strategies, as well as student feedback that takes into account the quality of the solution and the process through which it was accomplished rather than merely the accuracy of the language used in its reporting.

Compartmentalized views of the learner often ignore the global picture. We are dealing with individuals who have *personalities* they like to express; we are dealing with people who are *interesting* not just as academic learners. Materials and instructional practices that are based on restrictive—and often erroneous—assumptions about students' linguistic background not only offer fragile and tenuous hooks for accessing a new language, they ignore other types of background and experience and potential that learners bring to the language-learning situation. Needed are more personalized and flexible learning frameworks, with structured yet open-ended tasks that allow learners to share the new language tools to construct their *own* realities. Needed as well, perhaps, are higher expectations for all learners, gauged not in terms of what they have done, but of what, with guidance and valid incentive, they can do.

Who Guides Whom to Learn . . .

The old metaphor of the mind as a "tower of building blocks" has an extension in education: "and the students will supply their own mortar." While this analogue and its friend, the "empty vessel" will find few outspoken proponents today, much of educational practice continues to reflect the view of learning as an additive or incremental process. This assumption is evidenced in classroom materials that package and segregate elements of language within their respective chapters, as well as in pedagogical practices concerned with the mastery of self-contained units that presumably serve as the necessary "foundation" for mastery of subsequent units.

Peterson et al. (82), at the risk of posing an equally simplistic analogy, present the image of the mind as a construction of Tinker Toys to illustrate that learning, rather than the linear accumulation of impermeable chunks, is the making of connections between new information and the learner's existing *network* of knowledge. These are not simple bonds, however. Rather, acquiring the new involves an *interaction* with existing knowledge and results in a modification of both the new information and the existing aspect of cognitive structure to which the new is linked. Ausubel et al. (5) refer to this process as *subsumption*. Discussion of how theories of cognition and second language acquisition account for this phenomenon is beyond the scope of this chapter. To the educator concerned with providing expert guidance to learners, one of the most powerful implications, however, is the concept of *transfer;* namely, the mental process whereby information in short-term, or working, memory is stored (constructed and integrated) in long-term memory.

According to Perkins and Salomon (81), our assumption that transfer occurs naturally in learners in a classroom context reflects the "Bo-Peep Theory" of education: "Let them alone and they'll come home . . . ." These researchers contend that transfer must be planned and guided through materials and teaching practices—strategies for effective transfer must be taught. They define two types of transfer: low-road transfer and high-road transfer. Low-road transfer refers to the automatic triggering of well-practiced routines in circumstances where there is considerable perceptual similarity to the original learning context (e.g., from driving a car to learning to drive a truck). High-road transfer is the abstraction of skill or knowledge from one context for application in another. It may be forward-reaching (one learns something and abstracts it in preparation for application elsewhere) or backward-reaching (one reaches backward into one's experience for matches). Both involve reflective thought in making connections from one context to another.

For Ausubel et al. (5), in any new learning the first transfer individuals must be guided to make involves calling up existing knowledge: "If I had to reduce all of educational psychology to just one principle, I would say this: The most important single factor influencing learning is what the learner already knows. Ascertain this and teach him accordingly" (p. 1). We have in memory many types of knowledge, organized into networks of schemas and scripts. We have complex ideational and associational networks that combine cultural and idiosyncratic, concrete and abstract notions for people, objects, actions, places; scripts for events, routines, transactions, procedures, along with academic learnings and interest-specific learnings, and so on.

Meaningful learning, according to those concerned with cognitive processing, must somehow hook into relevant field or schemas of one's existing cognitive structure. In fact, if this does not occur, individuals will most likely experience cognitive dissonance resulting in the creation of what Nummela and Rosengren (73) call the critical/logical barrier to internal processing. He notes that new information not congruent with the individual's existing complex intellectual structures must be questioned or aborted. The learner will dwell on the conflict. Yet much of present textbook design not only bombards the learner with grammatical and lexical "newness" in each chapter while closing the door on previous chapter learnings but also makes selected technical aspects of the study of language by specialists the main focus of study by young, inexperienced nonspecialists who have very different goals and prior knowledge to attack the task.

Ausubel et al. (5) use the term *advance organizer* to refer to the pedagogical practice of helping learners activate an appropriate anchoring framework to aid the subsumption of new learning. An advance organizer is distinct from an overview or summary of new material to be learned in that it is presented at a higher level of abstraction, inclusiveness, and generality than the new material to be learned. Thus, guiding students to recollect a relevant everyday event sequence or to brainstorm the communicative functions involved in a common transaction, or to contribute their opinions on an issue, or to list the types of information normally included in particular genre of oral or written text, are all acts which, performed *prior* to the new learning task, can serve as broad anchoring devices for approaching the particulars of the task or making comparisons between existing notions and new notions. Writing tasks can serve as advance organizers to speaking tasks; reading tasks can serve as advance organizers to listening tasks; and so on. Advance organizers can help students call to the fore not only relevant topical or contextual frameworks, but communicative procedures and existing linguistic tools as well.

The notion of forward-reaching transfer implies that all real learning—that is, internalization, assimilation, integration—is preparation for new learning, offering potential for new connections. These connections may not occur, however, if ideas are too "local" or inert," merely "received into the mind without being utilized, or tested, or thrown into fresh combinations" (Whitehead, 104, p. 1). Instruction that does not include deliberate attention to the continued utilization of learned language as well as to its transfer into new and varied contexts during the performance of new and varied functions may result in "splinter learning" (Kephart, 63), performance learned in a specific manner to satisfy a specific need or demand. By extension, splinter performance, because it may be very rehearsed and precise, can be misleading, for while the end product may be judged excellent, the process by which this product was achieved may be very limited and specific. According to Kephart, "any alteration in the conditions surrounding the task or any shift which calls for the same task in a slightly different situation disrupts performance. The child is not dealing with the significant variables of the task, he is dealing with a series of specifics" (p. 61). The oft-discussed notion of "recycling" language in materials and teaching practices thus means more than "bringing it back for review"; rather, it involves constant, updated awareness of the learner's existing language repertoire and consistent attention to its reactivation, elaboration, and integration with new learning. The concept of *forward-reaching* transfer also conveys the notion of stretching or conceptual foreshadowing of the new language elements; that is, providing learners with a "feel" for what is to come. Listening and reading tasks can help students cast forward a familiarity net by which aspects of language prompt initial recognitions and are later, gradually, pulled into the learner's productive repertoire.

O'Malley et al. (76) contend that while current linguistic theories are limited in their attention to the role cognitive processes play in second language acquisition, cognitive theories also fail to account adequately for the integrative use of language in all four skills and the phenomenon of language acquisition from the earliest stages of second language learning to fully proficient use of the language. How does deliberate and conscious attention to how language is used lead to the ability to use the language with some automaticity? At present, the answer most commonly offered is: practice in transfer and transferred practice.

Perkins (80) discusses the need for teachers to help learners construct "thinking frames." A frame is a representation intended to guide the process of thought, supporting, organizing, and catalyzing that process. When we initially learn a frame, the frame itself takes up much of our working memory, so we cannot apply it to very complex problems, because we cannot hold them in mind. *Use* results in automatization of the frame, which drastically reduces its demand on working memory. Practice liberates one's working memory from the load of the frame itself and permits one to address complex problems with it. For Perkins, "The pitfall here is that many instructional efforts to develop students' thinking do not provide nearly enough practice to internalize frames. Others provide practice but escalate the difficulty of the problem too quickly" (p. 8). Since learning tends to become contextually welded to the learning situation, we must encourage students to seek applications of what they have learned in remote contexts.

Anderson (2) distinguishes between two types of information that is "stored": what we know *about,* or "declarative knowledge" and what we know *how to do,* or "procedural knowledge." The latter is the ability to perform mental procedures, such as understanding and generating language. According to Anderson, as we use the same knowledge over and over in a procedure, we can lose our access to the rules that originally generated or enabled the procedure and thus lose our ability to verbally report of declare these rules. Whereas declarative knowledge or factual information may be acquired quickly, procedural knowledge or ability to use the language is acquired gradually and only with extensive opportunities for practice. O'Malley et al. (76), in their discussion of Anderson's theory, contend that "knowing about language as a grammatical system, which involves knowing the rules . . . is not a sufficient condition for knowing how to use the language functionally. . . . In order to use a language for communicative purposes, procedural knowledge is required" (p. 295).

Thus, procedural knowledge must be stored in integrated fashion with declarative knowledge and must consist not merely of awareness of syntactical and morphological rules but of pragmatics, context-based communicative procedures, and protocols—knowledge of what, when, where, why, and with whom—and of the powerful influence of these factors on the hows of language use. This storage and transferral from knowledge to use will require practice. Practice is not to be confused with drill, however, in that drills, like rituals, says Stevick (94) consist of predetermined behaviors and socially programmed use of time and are "designed to get a group of individuals through the hour without anyone having to get close to anyone else" (p. 70). Whereas drill is the repeated rehearsal of a language element at the same level of depth, meaningful practice involves stretching learners from deliberate use of the new in the context of the old, scaffolding the task and gradually fading task support, to establish new zones of comfort through play, elaboration, variation, and transfer and reintegration with previous learning. Long-term storage and flexibility require use of the language in varied contexts at increasing levels of depth and complexity.

Who Guides Whom to Learn under What Conditions?

Of the many factors of schooling that are said to influence learning, researchers cite student engagement time as the major intervening variable between teacher instructional behavior and student achievement (Berliner, 8; Newmann, 71, 72). *Engagement* refers to more than such deceptive overt behaviors as cooperation, attentiveness, and participation; it also refers to more than motivation or general desire to achieve academically; rather, engagement may both activate and generate motivation. Newmann (72) defines engagement as "psychological investment," involving connection, attachment, and integration in particular settings with particular other people, tasks, and objects; conversely, disengagement is isolation, separation, detachment, and fragmentation (p. 34). The pervasiveness of disengagement, especially at the middle and high school levels, has led some recent observers to conclude that there is a universal treaty among teachers and students—teachers will demand only minimal engagement from students if the students are to behave themselves (Newmann, 72). In high school observations and interviews, Eisner (39) found that students drew clear demarcation between life-relevant and school-relevant learning; moreover, the students were remarkably unquestioning as they moved ineluctably from little box to little box and did not expect to encounter connections between one thing and another—"that's just the way school is." He concludes: "Public high school students are examples of resiliency and acceptance. They accept, they listen, they respond, they write, they daydream, they whisper, they worry—and then they move on" (p. 24). Rivers (85) echoes this assessment: while, in the real world, language use is as natural as breathing, in classrooms all over the world one still finds language learning that is "a tedious, dry-as-dust process" (p. 11). Language experiences, while anchored in the learner's world, must stretch students' sights into new worlds and connect them with others through communication. Conditions for learner engagement must meet the learner's criterion of authenticity—personal and social.

Personal Authenticity.   Langer and Applebee (66) express the students' need to feel "ownership" for their learning, to see the point of it beyond simple obedience to teachers and parents or compliance with curricular requirements and predetermined routines. This sense of ownership must begin with a realization that what is to be learned has *usefulness.* Brandt (15) tells of a visit to a seventh grade remedial English class taught by an excellent teacher. Unfortunately, he argues, the substance being taught was of questionable purpose and long-term utility:

> Do you remember the four types of sentences? I make my living occupied with language, but I hadn't thought about the four types of sentences since my own school days. Yet here was a class of slow learners trying to remember the terms declarative, interrogative, exclamatory, and—that's right—imperative. (p. 2)

Foreign language learners will require frequent opportunities to experience that language as more than grammatical nomenclature, lexical listings, sentence-level display, and fabricated dialog or "culture notes." For students to accept the personal usefulness of the language, they must first perceive it as *useful and real to others,* particularly to their teachers, and in general to those for whom it serves not only as a communicative and cognitive tool, but as a cultural identity.

Scripted dialogs and constructed reading passages may not convey what a language means to its users, nor the way the language is naturally used by its speakers. On the other hand, authentic texts, both oral and written, capture the language in use *as it is spoken* and *as it is written* by its people, for its people, for myriad aims both lofty and mundane. No textbook culture note on the Hispanic family, for example, can replace the study of authentic birth or christening, wedding and death announcements, where, under the observable linguistic conventions, lie the rituals of events, the connotations of rites of passage, the meaning of "family," and the dynamic nature of culture. Perhaps we would not be fighting so hard to fit culture back into language study if we had never decontextualized language study to begin with.

Not only must the language have perceived usefulness for the learner, it must also have *usability*. Experiences that students are asked to undergo and to which they are asked to relate must be interesting, meaningful, and real, just as they are in the many worlds outside the learner's classroom. Tasks students are asked to perform must also be authentic. Students know that in the real world not all questions have complete, right—or even good—answers; students know that in the real world they don't read merely to respond to "comprehension questions"; nor do they listen in order to recall structural or syntactic features; and only in classrooms is the writing process reduced to copying sentences substituting the correct form of the verb. The communicative tools and strategies we give students to access and construct meaning must be durable and versatile and must be put to work in purposeful activity. Usability also involves an understanding of task demands, that is, the knowledge of what is involved in accomplishing a task. According to Wenden (103), an appreciation of task demands requires the ability to interpret exactly what is intended by a particular assignment or group task: "it means being able to determine whether what one knows and how much one knows will be adequate to perform the task" (p. 646). The cause of inappropriate performance or off-task behavior may not be linguistic or motivational; it may be, rather, lack of task knowledge, the inability to determine precisely what is expected in a certain task. Usability also requires opportunity to maximize one's resources. If students are not provided numerous and varied opportunities to negotiate their own meanings in the language, the experience may not appear genuine; and the language and culture themselves may not be believable on the only plane that is relevant to the learner—the personal one.

Social Authenticity.   Kramsch (64) argues that the foreign language is not only a communicative tool for future encounters in the world outside the classroom; it creates and shapes social meaning in the classroom such that the group achieves a social identity through the language. Language learning is socially mediated.

How or how much does classroom activity promote the use of the language in the classroom in realistic ways and the value of social mediation in learning? Trosborg (96) contends that in traditional teacher-centered classroom settings, conversation sometimes resembles a fill-in-the-blanks test and risks exposing learners to discourse patterns that are highly unusual and deviant when compared to actual discourse as it takes place outside the classroom. She states, further, that it is often the teachers, not the students, who use the range of functions that form communicative competence:

> In traditional classroom interaction teachers have overwhelming communicative privileges. They are responsible for topic selection and development, and for effecting conversational closings. This means that it is the teacher who performs the necessary framing and focusing moves. It is also the teacher who structures the conversation and decides when a topic has been appropriately dealt with. The students are not allowed to self-select, as turns are allocated by the teacher. In order to be allowed to speak a student has to wait until he has been nominated by the teacher. Consequently, he may not get a turn when he has something interesting to say, but can be called upon when he does not want to speak. (p. 177)

In a comparison of the discourse competence of students in teacher-fronted settings and those in group-interaction settings, Trosborg found that the group interaction resulted not only in increased participation and motivation, but in frequency of other-repairs, more flexibility and complexity within exchange patterns, and peer cooperation to fill in each other's gaps.

The terms *interaction, cooperative learning,* and *collaboration* are not simply fancy words for peer grouping in the classroom. Rather, they refer to a sense of community in which students work together to solve problems, to rehearse, to counsel and support one another, and to negotiate meaning in the language through tasks that have interest, purpose, and consequence. Communication is a social activity and authentic language use, as most real-life activity has both purpose and consequence. In many classrooms, however, the "purpose" of an activity is often known only by the teacher and may not be otherwise transparent to learners in terms of their real-world anchors. In many classrooms, the consequence of an activity is teacher praise, or correction, or a test, or nothing. Kephart (63) distinguishes between valid and veridical learning, in which veridical learning has both logical purpose and contextual consequence. This distinction is powerfully captured in the following concrete example:

> Requiring the child to cut out a circle from colored paper is a valid task. The reward is the approbation of the teacher, 'This is a very nice circle, Billy.' This approbation sometimes comes when the circle is not too accurate. In like manner, it sometimes fails to come when, to Billy's eyes, the circle is very fine. He has difficulty identifying superior performance. If the task is redesigned so that the child is asked to cut out a circle which will later, along with circles from other children, be combined to form a caterpillar, the task becomes more veridical. Now Billy's circle is presented along with others in a veridical representation. If his circle is inaccurate, it is apparent both to Billy and others, since it shows up in the final product as different and destroys the overall effect. The teacher's approbation is not necessary since the laws of form present to the child the consequences of his performance. (p. 195)

Functionally and thematically focused tasks that promote cooperation, that distribute responsibilities and diffuse power normally, that have both purpose and consequence—and hence learner accountability—allow for a wider range of roles to be played by those involved, roles that more closely reflect those of people interacting in the real world.

Conclusion

This section has looked at the learner in terms of the learning process and has described a view of teaching as the provision of expert guidance, or scaffolding, that complements, facilitates, and mediates this process. Inherent in the notion of scaffolding is the function of a temporary access structure or support system, for as Greene (47) notes, real teaching occurs when learners begin to develop autonomy:

> It happens when (a) person freely chooses to extend himself in order to find answers to questions he poses for himself, when he acts to move beyond what he has learned by rote . . . when a student begins to understand what he is doing, when he becomes capable of giving reasons and seeing connections within his experience, when he recognizes the errors he or someone else is making and can propose what should be done to set things straight" (cited in Barell et al., 6, p. 15).

Our goals as teachers include not only helping students learn, but helping them learn *how to learn*—to acquire and develop effective strategies that will serve them in becoming increasingly powerful learners and communicators long after the prompts and proddings of the classroom have ended. The following presents an overview of some of the research on these learning strategies.

Learner Strategies

If one were to ask a student who is having difficulty in the classroom what he or she does in order to learn, say, vocabulary, one might hear the response "I study." Likewise, if one were to ask that same student what could be done to improve his or her performance, a common response might be "Study more?" These nonspecific descriptions may reveal a learner who has not developed the ability to use or identify effective and appropriate learner strategies. Learner strategies are task-specific tactics or techniques, observable or nonobservable, that an individual uses to comprehend, store, retrieve, and use information or to plan, regulate, or assess learning. We use strategies, for example, to store lexical information, to internalize grammatical concepts, to memorize, to create meaning from or through oral or written texts, to interpret cultural phenomena. We use strategies, as well, to provide ourselves the opportunity for rehearsal, to encourage and motivate ourselves, to examine the demands of a task and plan its undertaking.

The label is deceptive, for many researchers contend that strategies, far more than mere tricks or artifice, can determine the success or failure of an undertaking. To view the importance of strategies, it may be useful to analyze one's own approach to an independent problem-solving task. In keeping with the scholarly endeavors of our readership, we might select as a hypothetical example the task of professional writing. Depending on the individual nature and complexity of the task, one might employ the following types of strategies as part of the process of generating such a product:

> The writer might begin by deliberately *directing* her *attention* to the task by conscious decision to ignore distractors such as competing demands for time. The writer may engage in a variety of *planning* techniques—analyzing the nature and parameters of the task itself as well as the background and orientation of her readership. She may conduct a general *self-assessment*, pulling to the fore her own knowledge of the topic in the form of *list making*, and follow this by *self-prescription*, identifying areas in need of further development. Long-term and short-term *goal establishment* may lead to the development of an *outline*, which will guide the preliminary writing efforts. The writer may choose to *monitor* her approach through *peer cooperation*, sharing information with others, seeking feedback or *verification* of her perception of the task. At this point, she may wish to use *resourcing strategies*, consulting reference materials to add to her knowledge base. In doing this, she may decide to exercise *selective attention*, and her use of *advance organizers* will guide her in this endeavor. She may encounter unfamiliar or confusing material, in which case she may rely on *clarification* strategies, *inferencing* or informed guessing techniques, which may lead her to further resourcing. Surely the writer will use *note taking* or *summarizing* to retain information, *highlighting* to extract salient points, or *grouping* to classify information received. Her use of *elaboration* strategies will help her link new knowledge to that which already lies within her repertoire. At this point, she may require affective strategies to reduce anxiety and keep her on task, and these might involve *positive self-talk, relaxation techniques,* or *self-monitoring* to review progress to date and recommit to her goals.

Though her task is not yet complete, this individual has used many strategies thus far. Are there other strategies and strategy combinations she could have used to carry out this task? Certainly. Are there more effective strategies she could have used? Perhaps. Are there things she could have done that would have been less effective? Undoubtedly.

Thus, strategies may be simple or complex, appropriate or inappropriate, precise or vague, intelligent or unwise. Chamot and Kupper (22), among others, contend that although students of all ability levels use learning strategies, many language learners are low achievers simply because they rely on infrequent or inappropriate use of a narrow, limited repertoire of strategies such as rote memorization, translation, repetition, and deduction. Such tactics, often promoted by certain instructional approaches to surmount short-term obstacles such as tests, may not lead to more long-term internalization of language. According to Stern (92): "The poor learner's language does not develop into a well-ordered system or network. It remains an untidy assemblage of separate items. He makes no attempt to relate items to each other. Because his approach is passive, unsystematic, and fragmented, he will complain that he has no memory for language" (p. 314).

One's use of learning strategies will vary according to preference, perception of how language works, teacher demands, nature and difficulty of task, prior knowledge and experience, course objectives, context, age, stage of learning, perceived purpose, and degree of self-investment. Research indicates that strategy selection and use may also be influenced by sex (Ehrman and Oxford, 38), learning style (Ehrman and Oxford, 37), cultural conditioning (Politzer and McGroarty, 83), and communicative modality. Bialystok (9) contends that because the modality in which language is expressed results in different language forms and cognitive operations, strategies suitable for language learning in one modality may facilitate language learning of that type only.

Learning strategies may include the use of communication strategies when the latter are used to contribute to learning. Bialystok (11) notes that while communication strategies may be revealed through linguistic analysis of learners' interlanguage, learning strategies are often revealed only by learners themselves. For this reason, research aimed at identifying learning strategies has depended on verbal reporting systems, which Cohen (24) classifies as being of three types: (1) *self-reporting,* or collection of learners' generalized statements about their behavior, including characteristics they attach to themselves; (2) *self-observation* of specific learning tasks, either through introspection or retrospection; and (3) *self-revelation,* or think-aloud techniques in which learners disclose their thoughts during a task in stream-of-consciousness fashion (Hosenfeld, 56). Because research data have relied on the ability or willingness of learners to describe the inner working of their minds, they are admittedly speculative, open to question on issues such as the following (Cohen, 24; Harlow, 50):

1. Much of learning may be unconscious and therefore inaccessible to mental probes.
2. The combination of performing and attending to process or strategies may produce cognitive overload in learners and may alter performance, or process, or both.
3. Learners may forget their distinct combination of strategies once their learning goal or task is accomplished.
4. Learners may misclaim strategies or describe what the interviewer wants to hear.
5. Verbalizing may have an intrusive effect on the development of mental activity.
6. It is difficult to ascertain from self-reports which strategies contributed significantly to the process and which had only marginal effect.

Chamot and Kupper (22), in longitudinal data on learner strategy use, however, conclude that all students, regardless of their language-learning success, have some cognitive control over their efforts and are able to describe their own mental processes. Observation and elicitation of learning strategies may, at present, be a rather cumbersome and inconclusive process; nonetheless, it may represent a more satisfying and informative investigative focus than that offered by cognitive style mapping or description alone, for several reasons. First, however incomplete the information, it is derived from the source—the individual learners themselves in learning contexts—rather than assumed through imposed instruments. Second, strategies are task-specific and process-oriented and may therefore respond more directly to our research questions regarding *how* people learn. They are also amenable to change—in Wenden's (101) words, they are part of our mental software, not hardware. And third, through self-reports, learners may develop more self-awareness of their procedures and improve their use of latent strategies. Learners' effective use of strategies may be their key to autonomy and self-directed learning, releasing them from excessive dependence on a teacher or materials whose "styles" may not be compatible with their own.

Research efforts in the area of learner strategies have been principally directed to identifying those strategies and combinations of strategies used by "effective" language learners in various contexts in the performance of various language tasks and have explored, as well, the extent to which these strategies may be taught. While inventories and taxonomies are exhaustive and will often vary in nomenclature, definition, and degree of overlap according to discipline and investigator, most researchers refer to three types of strategies: (1) *metacognitive* strategies for directing the learning process; (2) *cognitive* strategies for accomplishing particular learning tasks; and (3) *social and affective* strategies for enjoying and maximizing the learning experience. This section will look first at how some of these strategies are manifested and then at what role expert guidance, or teaching, might play in their fostering and development.

Metacognitive Strategies for Directing the Learning Process

According to Holec (54), it is the use of metacognitive strategies that distinguishes a *program,* or a collection of language drills and activities, from a learning *process,* which involves active learner responsibility in decision making, self-investment, and management of operations. Likewise, students who have not yet learned how to learn—how to plan, direct, and assess their learning—often equate programs with instructional materials and the process of learning with "being taught"—that is, doing what the teacher and teaching materials say to do.

Metacognitive strategies are those procedures used by students to *think about their learning* in general, to plan their approach and strategy use, to monitor their performance, and to evaluate their progress. They may involve a range of behaviors, such as setting up frames of reference or opening mental files (advance organizers); adjusting to the physical environment; analyzing a task; deciding in advance to ignore distractors or attend to specific input; surveying and reviewing in preparation for an upcoming task; consciously postponing speaking until sufficient confidence is gained; checking or correcting one's own comprehension, production, or impression of the language; identifying language functions necessary to an upcoming task and assessing relevant linguistic resources; judging one's own progress by comparing present status with earlier stages of learning; identifying problems and strengths and setting new goals.

All these behaviors involve an awareness of self as learner—of one's patterns, needs, approaches, and goals—as well as some personal philosophy of what language is, how it works, and how it is learned. These implicit beliefs influence both the variety of strategies learners use and their ability to use them flexibly (Abraham and Vann, 1). In studies of learner strategy use, Chamot and Kupper (22) found that intermediate students used metacognitive strategies more frequently than beginners, and further, that the type of strategies varied: while beginners relied on focusing attention and delaying production, intermediate students incorporated advance preparation and self-monitoring. The use of metacognitive strategies to plan and reflect on the learning process appears to be crucial to maintaining and transferring cognitive strategies. According to O'Malley et al. (77): "Students without metacognitive approaches are essentially learners without direction and ability to review progress, accomplishments and future learning directions" (p. 24). However, while these strategies are the backbone of the learning process, their effectiveness is limited without a repertoire of appropriate *cognitive* strategies.

Cognitive Strategies for Accomplishing Particular Learning Tasks

All teachers have, to some extent, witnessed student use of strategies to undertake classroom tasks. We observe students taking notes, asking questions for clarification and verification, preparing flashcards, and repeating models orally. Students' written products often bear traces of effective or ineffective strategy use—verb conjugation charts scribbled in margins of test papers, reading passages displaying results of (often unsuccessful) attempts at literal translation and ample dictionary use, and used textbooks, as Harlow (50) notes, bearing copious applications of yellow highlighter pens.

Learners apply strategies *directly* to the learning task itself as they seek to store or retrieve relevant information or create meaning through receptive and productive channels. The most comprehensive inventory of such strategies is that developed by Oxford-Carpenter (79), who lists over forty distinct tactic types grouped as *memory strategies* (including grouping, association, imaging, physical response, keyword, elaboration); *cognitive strategies* (including repetition, recombination, reasoning and analysis, translation, summarizing, and note taking); and *compensation strategies* (including guessing, approximation, word coinage, circumlocution, and topic avoidance). For the sake of simplicity and space, we refer to all these as *cognitive* strategies and select for description a few of the more interesting and significant ones identified to date (Chamot and Kupper, 22; Oxford-Carpenter, 79). What all the following cognitive strategies have in common is (1) the active mental engagement of the learner in the purposeful establishment of new functional knowledge through contextualized practice, and (2) the formation of stable and meaningful connections between prior knowledge and new information.

Memory Strategies.   Learners may set up mental and/or written clusters, networks, and categories in order to store and retrieve lexical information. Grouping and associational schemes may be based on classifying or reclassifying material by common attributes or opposition—contextual, functional, semantic, auditory—or by establishing linkages through visual or mental imaging, physical response, or sensation. Thought groups or mappings (such as semantic maps) may be devised in preparation for speaking, writing, reading, or listening tasks. Learners may also break down tasks into sequential steps or groups of steps in order to retain information.

Emphasis and Summarizing Strategies.   These strategies are used to analyze or synthesize information, to separate salient from nonsalient material, or to group main or related points. They may consist of such techniques as note taking, outlining, summarizing, or using text organizers to identify key points.

Inferencing Strategies.   Learners use available information—linguistic, pictorial, topical, or situational—to guess unfamiliar meanings, to form hypotheses or predictions, and to fill in information gaps. Harlow (50) notes that inferencing strategies, including informed guessing, have been shown to improve achievement significantly on reading, writing, and speaking tasks.

Elaboration and Transfer.   To *elaborate* is to add a symbolic construction to the learning task in order to make it more personally meaningful or to relate the new to the known or one new item to another in meaningful associations. The existing framework may be background knowledge or experience gained from everyday life or academic contexts. Strategies of this type might include creating analogies; paraphrasing or summarizing; transforming information into chart, graph, or diagram; using comparison and contrast; verbalizing or acting out mental scenarios; or teaching what is being learned to someone else. *Transfer* is the application of linguistic or conceptual knowledge to the accomplishment of a new language-learning task and may include a variety of strategies: recognizing cognates, anticipating linguistic functions required in certain common transactions, or brainstorming words or questions related to a given topic or context in preparation for listening, reading, speaking, writing, or interpretation of cross-cultural phenomena.

Functional Practice.   Learners may engage in strategies for using the language in communicative contexts where the focus is on creating or constructing meaning. These tactics may involve contextualization, recombination, and naturalistic practice—using the foreign language in natural settings with native speakers, viewing foreign films, and so on. Derry (30) observes, as well, the use of what she terms "part practice"—students attempt to improve complex performance by perfecting and automating an important subcomponent of that performance. In a study of the effects of formal *versus* functional practice, Bialystok (9) found that the strategy most responsible for achievement on all tasks was *functional* practice. Formal practice was effective only to a limited extent and, after a particular point, no longer facilitated performance.

Cognitive strategies such as these provide learners the benefits of deep processing, meaningful associations, and ordered retrieval of complex information. Combined with metacognitive awareness, they hold great potential for maximizing the learning or internalization process. Their combination with affective and social strategies enhances this potential by allowing more learner control of input and personalization of the learning experience.

Social-Affective Strategies for Enjoying and Maximizing the Learning Experience

Included in this category are strategies individuals use to motivate, encourage, and reward themselves; to generate energy or tolerance; to reduce or counter anxiety, frustration, or fatigue; to benefit from learning as a social activity through interaction and cooperation with others. These affective-social strategies might involve asking for assistance, explanation, examples, clarification, or rephrasing; identifying questions or problem areas; and working with peers for rehearsal, feedback, practice, counsel, joint problem-solving, and pooling of information. They might also be manifested in learner efforts to seek or derive input or interaction opportunities from teachers, peers, native speakers, and media resources for personal enrichment of practice opportunities.

In observations of Hispanic and Asian ESL learners, Politzer and McGroarty (83) noticed the influence of cultural background and previous academic training on the use of social strategies. Classroom behaviors such as correcting fellow students, asking for clarification, volunteering, seeking help or confirmation, or requesting repetition were more part of the Western than the Asian learning behavior repertoire.

As to which of these strategies and combinations of strategies seem to work best, research results are rather tentative at this point, given the variety of factors that influence strategy use and the lack of investigative techniques that can tap the significance of a given strategy or combination of strategies for an individual learner approaching an individual task. Harlow (50) provides a synthesis of seven studies that reported levels of significance for particular strategy use according to task or modality and level of language study. What stands out in all these studies is the value of functional or naturalistic practice in listening comprehension, speaking, reading comprehension, and oral and written grammar tasks. Other tactics related to effective achievement are the social/affective strategies of clarification and verification, creating opportunities for functional or a naturalistic practice, self-talk, and attention and silent response to fellow students; the metacognitive strategies of self-monitoring and functional planning; and the cognitive strategies of inferencing for reading and writing tasks and grouping and association for written or spoken vocabulary use.

Implications for Expert Guidance in Strategy Development

The notions of cognitive instruction and learner accountability discussed in the previous section speak to a role for educators and materials designers in helping students learn how to develop and steadily assume responsibility and control in their learning process. Provision of expert guidance in learning-strategy development will involve considerations in three areas: expectations for learners, conditions for learning, and mediation of learning.

Wenden (102) notes that we expect people to learn, yet seldom teach them how to learn. We expect students to memorize often large quantities of material without teaching them the art of memory: the discovery of effective, appropriate, and satisfying options for long-term storage, integration, and retrieval. We expect adult learners, perhaps, to have acquired study skills and learning strategies in other academic contexts and to be able to apply this procedural knowledge in the foreign language learning context. Studies have repeatedly shown, however, that many foreign language learners, especially novice learners, tend to rely heavily, even exclusively, on repetition, rote memorization, and translation. Chamot (21) found, for example, that of all strategies, repetition was used most frequently by learners. She notes, further, that this strategy requires significantly less mental engagement than other strategy options. Weinstein et al. (100) include mnemonic devices as a popular strategy among learners, yet conclude that some types merely afford artificial memory support—they may be helpful for remembering isolated bits of information, but are less useful for meaningful long-term knowledge acquisition and transfer. Cohen (25) adds that mnemonic devices are simply concerned with bolstering memory strategies for retrieving a word and one of its meanings, not with developing semantic understanding. He expresses the concern that retrieval cues used to prompt item recall in mnemonic systems are so different from those used in natural communication that carryover to such situations might be negligible.

As teachers, we often expose students to a very narrow set of strategies, often taking for granted their effectiveness, without analyzing *how* or *if* they are working with students. The use of flashcards, for example, is a popular classroom device in all subjects at all levels. It is *what students do* with these flashcards, however, not the flashcards themselves, that constitutes strategy: students may use them for grouping and association; for self-monitoring; for separating known from unknown; for activating imaging or physical response; and so on. Evidence suggests, as well, that strategies learned or applied in one academic context are not necessarily transferred to others. Just as learners must be taught to use reading strategies in their first language, for example, they must be taught to read in the foreign language—to activate schemas, to focus on the known, to predict, to search for clues to meaning, to separate salient from nonsalient information. Teachers may notice, moreover, that students do not necessarily recognize cognates unless this transfer strategy is called to their attention and directed under guidance.

We assume as well, perhaps, that learners have some conscious system for learning that enables them to plan tasks, to monitor task performance and overall progress, to identify learning problems and request assistance, and to critically assess their abilities. Yet, at least one study (Davidson and Henning, 28) provides counter-evidence of the validity of learners' self-ratings. Oxford-Carpenter (79) found that learner self-assessment was more accurate for specific language situations such as grammar learnings than for global skills, such as oral production. And while we might assume that learners have some concept of what language learning entails, we are unaware of what idiosyncratic and distorted notions learners have of what language is and how these underlie and feed their efforts to perform.

In interviews with ESL instructors, Chamot (21) discovered that some of the teachers had never stopped to consider what might be going on in their students' minds as they were learning the language. They tended to confuse learning strategies with teaching strategies, describing in detail how they taught, but in most cases uncertain about how students actually went about learning.

Perhaps a first step in providing expert guidance to learners, then, involves an adjustment in these assumptions derived from a greater awareness of how students are learning and why. According to Hosenfeld (56), the first teaching act in the learning-teaching process consists of receiving information from students rather than sending information to them. Reading instruction, for example, is incomplete if we discover only *what* students comprehend in a given text without also discovering *how* they arrived at their meanings, what processes they used, and what clues were salient in their comprehension. Think-aloud techniques using peer interaction can be incorporated into classroom activities by having students take turns verbalizing their thoughts as they actually perform the task. Chamot and Kupper (22) contend that such procedures not only afford teachers more awareness, but contribute to students' metacognitive strategies as they describe their own thinking processes and discover those of their classmates.

Real learning, however, requires interaction between the learner and his or her environment. In order for learners to engage in the use of learning strategies, they must be afforded conditions for real learning and interaction—opportunities to work with others to negotiate meaning, exchange unpredictable information, attend, respond to, and elaborate on one another's thoughts and utterances in sustained fashion. Evidence suggests that curricular goals, instructional priorities and practices, and the nature of classroom tasks all influence learners' selection and use of strategies. In one study of language learners' strategy use, Chamot (21) found that classroom observations yielded limited information about learning strategies because classes tended to be teacher-directed and students had few opportunities to engage in active learning. Teachers tended to focus on correct answers rather than the process by which answers were obtained. Langer and Applebee (66) conclude, as well, that contemporary approaches to schooling continue to emphasize testing over learning, students as recipients rather than active agents, declarative knowledge over procedural knowledge, and accuracy of recitations over adequacy of thinking.

Helping students develop effective strategies for language learning will also require time and tolerance for error. Students will require time for self-monitoring, time for silent rehearsal, time for planning, and time for processing problem-solving tasks. As teachers, our concept of time must be measured less by quantity—chapter increments and coverage—than by quality of investment. Time must be viewed not as that temporary stay in a particular classroom but as a period in the long-term development of the student as autonomous learner and language user.

Creating conditions for the development of effective approaches to internalizing and using language may also require attention to discriminating between students' use of profitable learning strategies and students' use of *coping* strategies—those strategies applied merely to surmount obstacles created by the materials or tasks themselves. Careless presentation of the language through lists of random vocabulary items, nonauthentic models of written or spoken text, and focus on manipulation of discrete elements without attention to transfer and integration may all be sending learners the wrong signals of what language and language learning are about and may be directing learners' energies to ineffective, stop-gap measures. Oxford (78) obtained retrospective data from foreign language teachers about their experiences as foreign language learners. The data indicate that negative situations stunted strategy use, restricting it mainly to indirect strategies that allowed these learners to cope with their day-to-day struggle with a dysfunctional environment. Hillocks (53), in a review of research on L1 English teaching, concludes, for example, that the study of traditional school grammar has no effect on raising the quality of student writing, since such grammar does not adequately describe language. A heavy emphasis on mechanics and usage, in fact, results in significant losses in overall performance. On the other hand, process-oriented approaches that include prewriting components, conscious planning, and self-assessment result in longer compositions of higher quality.

Materials themselves can begin to afford learners better models of thinking and language use by attention to the integration of effective strategies in the design of tasks, as well as to deliberate transfer of learnings to new situations. Such materials may help in weaning students away from excessive and exclusive dependence on "old reliables" to experience new options for approaching tasks. Jarvis (58) contends that more variety in problem-solving tasks is needed as well: "Competent instruction will continually confront learners with carefully structured problems that extend their ability without repeating problems and without including any that are nonsolvable" (p. 399). Teaching and testing that focus on what learners can do in the language, rather than on what items they can recall about the language, may not only provide the foundation for new levels of cognitive and social strategy use, but may help learners gain a better sense of what a language is and possibly improve their abilities to monitor and assess their performance in terms of meaningful real-life criteria.

Incorporating more attention to *process* through materials that model effective task approaches may help to improve learner performance on the tasks themselves. However, strategy use alone may not further our educational goal of learner autonomy unless it is accompanied by learner opportunities to reflect on these strategies, to examine their effectiveness and applicability, and to work toward improvement. As Wenden (102) notes, "blind training" will not necessarily result in the learner's independent use of the strategy through transfer and experimentation in similar or novel contexts. Scaffolding learners' acquisition of effective cognitive strategies may, in fact, require direct training—helping learners acquire metacognitive awareness, not only through demonstration, modeling of appropriate use, and practice, but even discussion and labeling of the strategy to bring about learner consciousness. Chamot, an advocate of this strategy mediation, describes a procedure for direct instruction within the context of the language-learning classroom and provides sample teacher scripts for facilitating the training process in specific modalities (Interstate Research Associates, 57):

- Identify students' current strategies
- Assess students' strategy needs in conjunction with general course objectives and demands of the learning tasks
- Model new, more effective strategies through a think-aloud procedure, demonstrating the steps involved in approaching and completing the language task
- Label the strategies used so students each will have an identity
- Provide guided practice in use of the strategies, followed by discussion
- Gradually reduce the reminders to use the strategies on similar language tasks
- Provide varied practice on appropriate use of these strategies with other tasks

This training does not constitute a separate component of instruction; rather, modeling and practice of effective strategy use must be integrated into language-learning experiences. The aim of such training is not to direct all students to use the same set of strategies or to prescribe a right way to plan, manage, and assess performance. Learning is, above all, a personal affair, and should remain a personal affair. The aim of strategy training is, rather, to help each learner to explore consciously the wealth of effective options available; to consolidate and systematize those strategies that best fit his or her learning style and the task at hand; to experiment within his or her stretching zone, moving from deliberateness and discomfort to ease and automaticity with some new strategies; to reject others with wisdom and self-awareness.

Guiding students to explore effective options for learning the language, using the language, and enjoying the language will demand that as teachers we are first and foremost aware not just of ways to present and test materials, but of ways to learn. This knowledge must *begin* by suspending our views of ourselves as teachers to reflect critically on ourselves as *learners,* for if we have no notion of the strategies we ourselves use and therefore no notion of the true complexity of a task, it will be difficult for us to construct tasks for learners, much less teach them the strategies they may use to plan and conduct these tasks. But while our efforts must begin with self-awareness, they must not end there. Our ways are not the only ways. All of us think we have a clear notion of *the* right way to think—and all of us are wrong.

Conclusion

This chapter has been about "individualization." Yet, had this word appeared in the title, we would perhaps have risked extensive loss of readership. Because the topic is old. Old notions often surface from memory entangled in, or even replaced by, the artifacts with which they were stored. We recall past answers to individualization—differentiated staffing, modular scheduling, terminal objectives, mastery learning packets, IEPs, and minicourses—often with much greater clarity than the questions that spawned them. Yet these questions have only deepened in importance and complexity. The past two decades have brought us closer to the real issues behind learners and learning, beyond the external indicators of difference such as speed, interest, motivation, and the amorphous quality we call ability—to begin to examine the internal nature of these differences in terms other than aptitude, attitude, or intelligence.

Philosophers have battled for centuries with the notion of intelligence and, as Perkins (80) notes, have defined it in various ways: as the neurological efficiency of one's original equipment, or *power;* as the possession of a rich knowledge base, or *content;* and as the possession of a repertoire of strategies or *tactics* for using the mind. To view intelligence as merely one's original equipment is to reject education and the notions of teaching and learning. To view intelligence as merely a rich knowledge base is to ignore the acquisition and use of this knowledge base. In resolving this dilemma, Perkins suggests that we recognize the multiple nature of intelligence through a metaphorical equation:

$$\text{intelligence} = \text{power} + \text{tactics} + \text{content}$$

While we can recognize the power of the original equipment, we cannot change it. While we can recognize the power of a rich knowledge base, we have had dissatisfying results in the teaching of the considerable content of current school curricula. It is the focus on tactics or strategic knowledge that allows the window of opportunity, or "zone of development." According to Perkins, we might represent this as a continuum:

general approach ⟶ content-specific tactics ⟶ content
TACTICS   **CONTENT**

This chapter has viewed the learner and learning in terms of such a continuum. We began by looking at learners in terms of their general approaches or "styles"— those sets of developmental or biological frameworks that dispose or influence or orient individuals to sense, act, interact, and think in certain ways. Although we sense that such styles exist, our research efforts have yet to capture and explore their nature. It may well be that one's style, neither good nor bad, is simply one's own very individual zone of preference, comfort, and priority in perceiving, acting, and interacting in one's own very personal world. One's learning style, then, can be viewed as a problem only when it is categorized and judged in response to rigid learning conditions. Neutral labels, such as "field-dependent learner" are too often equated with negative labels, such as "distractible," assignations based on hidden criteria on how people should think rather than knowledge of how people do think.

The second section has focused on the content end of Perkins's continuum, in the broadest sense, including how we, as teachers, perceive, organize, represent, and structure the experience of foreign language learning. Content is viewed not as "things to learn" through the accumulation of discrete bits of information, but as the stable internalization of highly complex communication equipment. Providing expert guidance in the development of this equipment, that is, teaching for "proficiency," requires a general awareness of the two entities that our scaffolding will connect—the language and the learner. If our concept of language is merely that of boxes of rules, if our concept of the learner is merely that of someone who, somehow, can give us back these rules when we ask for them, then our concept of teaching is a simple one, indeed. Our charge is rather to provide materials, instruction, and classroom conditions that encourage, rather than dare, individuals to learn.

The final section of this chapter has explored the middle section of Perkins's continuum, that is, the development of tactics or strategies for language learning, not as tricks or artifice but as the glue that holds it all together. In considering the development of strategies, we must take a look at both ends of the continuum—*general approach,* or learner styles that may predispose learners to rely on certain types of strategies, and *content,* or the way we have represented this learning experience. The idea of "scaffolding and fading" discussed in this chapter speaks to the purposeful attention to learner stretching. The stretching process begins with deliberateness. Ehrman and Oxford (37) observed, for example, that while personality characteristics or learner styles may initially set preference or comfort parameters for certain strategies, learners independently and effectively apply other learned strategies, in more deliberate and conscious fashion. Repertoires can expand purposefully, with guidance, if the nature of the learning is true and clear. And it is this repertoire and its appropriate use that not only distinguishes the effective from the ineffective learner but will help to carry all learners beyond our classrooms.

According to Goodlad and Oakes (45), we must rid ourselves of the dangerous notion that individual differences call for substantially differentiated curricula. The curriculum best suited to providing all students with access to knowledge is organized around central concepts and grounded in real-life experiences; the knowledge offered is important and rich with meaning, stretching the sense-making of all learners through inquiring, questioning, probing, hypothesizing intellectual endeavor. Providing expert guidance to all learners in acquiring the knowledge and skills of language learning will require that, as architects, we systematically construct frameworks for learning within the experience of the learner and in keeping with learning processes. And it will require that, as mediators, we help students to use their minds.

As the image of the classroom comes increasingly into focus, we are presented not with a collection of uniform cardboard silhouettes, but with a lively and varied composite of histories, faces, and feelings—with learners who are as different inside as they look outside. What we do with this image will reflect our concept of teaching purpose and affect our concept of learning potential. The words of the philosopher Giovanni Gentile acquire new significance at the present junction of decades:

The teacher must not stop at the classification of the pupil or at the external observation of his face or behavior. He must enter into the very mind of the child where his life is gathered and centered. (43, p. 191)

Thinking of students as *learners* is not only an interesting perspective, it is our primary responsibility and challenge as teachers.

References, From Student to Learner: Style, Process, and Strategy

1. Abraham, Roberta G., and Roberta J. Vann. "Strategies of Two Language Learners: A Case Study." pp. 85–102 in Anita Wenden and Joan Rubin, eds., *Learner Strategies in Language Learning.* Englewood Cliffs, NJ: Prentice-Hall, 1987.
2. Anderson, John R. *The Architecture of Cognition.* Cambridge, MA: Harvard Univ. Press, 1983.
3. Applebee, Arthur N. "Writing in the Secondary School: English and the Content Areas." NCTE Research Report No. 21. Urbana, IL: NCTE, 1981.
4. _____, Judith A. Langer, and Ina V. S. Mullis. *The Writing Report Card.* Princeton, NJ: National Assessment of Educational Progress at ETS, 1986.
5. Ausubel, David P., Joseph D. Novak, and Helen Hanesian. *Educational Psychology: A Cognitive View.* New York: Holt, Rinehart and Winston, 1968.
6. Barell, John, Rosemarie Liebman, and Irving Sigel. "Fostering Thoughtful Self-Direction in Students." *Educational Leadership* 45 (April 1988): 14–17.
7. Beebe, Leslie M. "Risk Taking and the Language Learner," pp. 36–66 in Herbert W. Seliger and Michael H. Long, eds., *Classroom Oriented Research in Second Language Acquisition.* Rowley, MA: Newbury, 1983.
8. Berliner, David C. "Contemporary Teacher Education: Timidity, Lack of Vision and Ignorance." Paper presented at the meetings of the National Academy of Education, Berkeley, CA, October 1984.
9. Bialystok, Ellen. "The Role of Conscious Strategies in Second Language Proficiency." *Modern Language Journal* 65 (1981): 24–35.
10. _____. "Inferencing: Testing the 'Hypothesis Testing' Hypothesis," pp. 104–23 in Herbert W. Seliger and Michael H. Long, eds., *Classroom Oriented Research in Second Language Acquisition.* Rowley, MA: Newbury, 1983.
11. _____. "Some Factors in the Selection and Implementation of Communication Strategies," pp. 100–118 in Claus Faerch and Gabriele Kaspar, eds., *Strategies in Interlanguage Communication.* London: Longman, 1983.
12. _____, and Maria Frohlich. "Variables of Classroom Achievement in Second Language Learning." *Modern Language Journal* 62 (1978): 327–36.
13. Birckbichler, Diane W. "The Challenge of Proficiency: Student Characteristics," pp. 47–78 in Gilbert A. Jarvis, ed., *The Challenge for Excellence in Foreign Language Education.* Report of the Northeast Conference on the Teaching of Foreign Languages. Middlebury, VT: The Northeast Conference, 1984.
14. _____, and Alice C. Omaggio. "Diagnosing and Responding to Individual Learner Needs." *Modern Language Journal* 62 (1978): 336–45.
15. Brandt, Ron. "What We Need to Know." *Educational Leadership* 46 (September 1988): 1.
16. Brooks, Nelson. *Language and Language Learning: Theory and Practice.* New York: Harcourt, 1960.
17. Brophy, Jere E., and Thomas L. Good. "Teaching Behavior and Student Achievement," in Merlin C. Wittrock, ed., *Handbook of Research on Teaching.* 3rd ed. New York: Macmillan, 1986.
18. Brown, H. D. *Principles of Language Learning and Teaching.* Englewood Cliffs, NJ: Prentice-Hall, 1980.

19. Cafferty, Elsie. "An Analysis of Student Performance Based upon the Degree of Match between the Educational Cognitive Style of the Teacher and the Educational Cognitive Style of the Students." Ph.D. diss., University of Nebraska, 1980.

20. Carter, Elaine Fuller. "The Relationship of Field Dependent/Independent Cognitive Style to Spanish Language Achievement and Proficiency: A Preliminary Report." *Modern Language Journal* 72 (Spring 1988): 21–27.

21. Chamot, Anna Uhl. "The Learning Strategies of ESL Students," pp. 71–83 in Anita Wenden and Joan Rubin, eds., *Learner Strategies in Language Learning*. Englewood Cliffs, NJ: Prentice-Hall, 1987.

22. _____, and Lisa Kupper. "Learning Strategies in Foreign Language Instruction." *Foreign Language Annals* 22 (1989): 13–28.

23. Chapelle, Carol, and Cheryl Roberts. "Ambiguity Tolerance and Field Independence as Predictors of Proficiency in English as a Second Language." *Language Learning* 36 (March 1986): 27–45.

24. Cohen, Andrew D. "Studying Learner Strategies: How We Get the Information," pp. 31–42 in Anita Wenden and Joan Rubin, eds., *Learner Strategies in Language Learning*. Englewood Cliffs, NJ: Prentice-Hall, 1987.

25. _____. "Use of Verbal and Imagery Mnemonics." *Studies in Second Language Acquisition* 9 (February 1987): 43–61.

26. Combs, Arthur W. "New Assumptions for Educational Reform." *Educational Leadership* 45 (1988): 38–40.

27. Conrad, Brenda Dorn. "Cooperative Learning and Prejudice Reduction." *Social Education* 50 (April/May 1986): 283–86.

28. Davidson, F., and Grant Henning. "A Self Rating Scale of English Difficulty: Rasch Scaler Analysis of Items and Rating Categories." *Language Testing* 2 (1985): 164–79.

29. Day, R. "Student Participation in the ESL Classroom or Some Imperfections in Practice." *Language Learning* 34 (1984): 69–102.

30. Derry, Sharon J. "Putting Learning Strategies to Work." *Educational Leadership* 46 (December 1988–January 1989): 4–10.

31. Duffy, Gerald G., and Laura R. Roehler. "The Subtleties of Instructional Mediation." *Educational Leadership* 43 (April 1986): 23–27.

32. Dunn, Kenneth, and Rita Dunn. "Dispelling Outmoded Beliefs about Student Learning." *Educational Leadership* 44 (March 1987): 55–62.

33. Dunn, Rita, J. Beaudry, and Angela Klavas. "Survey of Research on Learning Styles." *Educational Leadership* 46 (March 1989): 50–58.

34. Dunn, Rita, and Shirley A. Griggs. *Learning Styles: Quiet Revolution in American Secondary Schools*. Reston, VA: NASSP, 1988.

35. Edmonds, R. R. "Effective Schools for the Urban Poor." *Educational Leadership* 37 (1979): 15–24.

36. Egan, Kieran. *Education and Psychology: Plato, Piaget, and Scientific Psychology*. New York: Columbia University, 1983.

37. Ehrman, Madeline, and Rebecca Oxford. "Ants, Grasshoppers, Badgers and Butterflies: Qualitative Exploration of Adult Language Learning Styles and Strategies." Paper presented at Ohio State University Research and Perspectives on Adult Language Learning Symposium, October 1988.

38. _____. "Effects of Sex Differences, Career Choice, and Psychological Type on Adult Language Learning Strategies." *Modern Language Journal* 72 (1988): 253–64.

39. Eisner, Elliot W. "The Ecology of School Improvement." *Educational Leadership* 45, 5 (1988): 24–29.

40. Ely, Christopher M. "An Analysis of Discomfort, Risktaking, Sociability and Motivation in the L2 Classroom." *Language Learning* 36 (March 1986): 1–25.

41. _____. "Tolerance of Ambiguity and Use of Second Language Strategies." *Foreign Language Annals* 22 (1989): 437–45.

42. Frawley, William, and James P. Lantolf. "Second Language Discourse: A Vygotskyan Perspective." *Applied Linguistics* 6 (1984): 19–44.

43. Gentile, Giovanni, as cited in J. Donald Butler, *Four Philosophies and Their Practice in Education and Religion.* New York: Harper and Row, 1968.

44. Goodlad, John I. "A Study of Schooling: Some Implications for School Improvement." *Kappan,* April 1983, pp. 552–58.

45. _____, and Jeannie Oakes. "We Must Offer Equal Access to Knowledge." *Educational Leadership* 45 (February 1988): 16–19.

46. Gould, Steven Jay. *The Mismeasure of Man.* New York: Norton, 1981.

47. Greene, M. *Teacher as Stranger.* Belmont, CA: Wadsworth, 1973.

48. Guilford, J. P. *The Nature of Human Intelligence.* New York: McGraw-Hill, 1976.

49. Guiora, Alexander Z., Robert C. L. Brannon, and Cecilia Y. Dull. "Empathy and Second Language Learning." *Language Learning* 22 (1972): 111–30.

50. Harlow, Linda L. "The Effects of the Yellow Highlighter—Second-Language Learner Strategies and Their Effectiveness: A Research Update." *The Canadian Modern Language Review* 45 (1988): 91–102.

51. Hawley, Willis D., Susan Rosenholtz, Henry Goodstein, and Ted Hasselbring. "Effective Teaching." *Peabody Journal of Education* 61, 4 (Summer 1984): 15–52.

52. Hewett, Nancy Maisto. "Reading, Cognitive Style, and Culture: A Look at Some Relationships in Second-Language Acquisition," pp. 62–87 in Angela Labarca and Leslie Bailey, eds., *Issues in L2: Theory as Practice / Practice as Theory.* Norwood, NJ: ABLEX, 1989.

53. Hillocks, George, Jr. "Synthesis of Research on Teaching Writing." *Educational Leadership* 44 (May 1987): 71–81.

54. Holec, Henri. "The Learner as Manager: Managing Learning or Managing to Learn?" pp. 145–57 in Anita Wenden and Joan Rubin, eds., *Learner Strategies in Language Learning.* Englewood Cliffs, NJ: Prentice-Hall, 1987.

55. Holley, Freda M., and Janet K. King. "Imitation and Correction in Foreign Language Learning." *Modern Language Journal* 55 (1971): 494–98.

56. Hosenfeld, Carol. "A Learning Teaching View of Second Language Instruction." *Foreign Language Annals* 12 (1979): 51–56.

57. Interstate Research Associates. *Learning Strategy Instruction for Writing in French: A Possible Script.* McLean, VA: Interstate Research Associates, 1988.

58. Jarvis, Gilbert A. "The Psychology of Second Language Learning: A Declaration of Independence." *Modern Language Journal* 67 (1983): 393–402.

59. Johnson, David, and Roger Johnson. *Learning Together and Alone.* Englewood Cliffs, NJ: Prentice-Hall, 1975.

60. Jones, Beau Fly. "Quality and Equality through Cognitive Instruction." *Educational Leadership* 43 (April 1986): 4–11.

61. Kagan, Jerome. "Reflection-Impulsivity: The Generality and Dynamics of Conceptual Tempo." *Journal of Abnormal Psychology* 71 (1966): 17–24.

62. Kagan, Spencer. *Cooperative Learning Resources for Teachers.* Riverside, CA: Univ. of California Riverside Press, 1985.

63. Kephart, Newell. *The Slow Learner in the Classroom.* Columbus, OH: Charles E. Merrill, 1971.

64. Kramsch, Claire J. "Interactive Discourse in Small and Large Groups," pp. 17–32 in Wilga M. Rivers, ed., *Interactive Language Teaching.* Cambridge, MA: Cambridge Univ. Press, 1987.

65. _____. "The Cultural Discourse, " pp. 63–88 in Alan J. Singerman, ed., *Toward a New Integration of Language and Culture.* Report of the Northeast Conference on the Teaching of Foreign Languages. Middlebury, VT: The Northeast Conference, 1988.

66. Langer, Judith, and Arthur Applebee. *How Writing Shapes Thinking: A Study of Teaching and Learning.* NCTE Report No. 22. Urbana, IL: NCTE, 1982.

67. Lubasa, N'ti Nseendi. "Motivation and Perseverance in Foreign Language Learning," pp. 101–13 in D. M. Singleton and D. G. Little, *Language Learning in Formal and Informal Contexts.* Dublin, Ireland: Irish Association for Applied Linguistics, 1984.

68. Meredith, Alan R. "Improved Oral Test Scores through Delayed Response." *Modern Language Journal* 62 (1978): 321–26.
69. Messer, S. B. "Reflection-Impulsivity: A Review." *Psychological Bulletin* 83 (1976): 1026–52.
70. Naiman, N., Maria Frohlich, and H. H. Stern. *The Good Language Learner.* Toronto Ontario Institute for Studies in Education, 1975.
71. Newmann, Fred M. "Priorities for the Future: Toward a Common Agenda." *Social Education* 50, 4 (April/May 1986): 240–50.
72. _____. "Student Engagement and High School Reform." *Educational Leadership* 46 (February 1989): 34–36.
73. Nummela, Renate M., and Tennes Rosengren. "What's Happening in Students' Brains May Redefine Teaching." *Educational Leadership* 43 (May 1986): 49–53.
74. Oltman, Philip K., Evelyn Raskin, and Herman A. Witkin. Group Embedded Figures Test. Palo Alto, CA: Consulting Psychologists Press, 1971.
75. Omaggio, Alice C. *Helping Learners Succeed: Activities for the Foreign Language Classroom.* Washington, DC: Center for Applied Linguistics, 1981.
76. O'Malley, J. Michael, Anna Uhl Chamot, and Carol Walker. "Some Applications of Cognitive Theory to Second Language Acquisition." *Studies in Second Language Acquisition* 9 (1987): 287–306.
77. O'Malley, J. Michael, Anna Uhl Chamot, Gloria Stewner-Manzanares, Lisa Kupper, and Rocco P. Russo. "Learner Strategies Used by Beginning and Intermediate ESL Students." *Language Learning* 35 (March 1985): 21–45.
78. Oxford, Rebecca L. "The Best and the Worst: An Exercise to Tap Perceptions of Language-Learning Experiences and Strategies." *Foreign Language Annals* 22 (1989): 447–54.
79. Oxford-Carpenter, Rebecca. "Taxonomy of Second Language Learner Strategies." Washington, DC: ERIC Clearinghouse on Languages and Linguistics, n.d.
80. Perkins, D. N. "Thinking Frames." *Educational Leadership* 43 (May 1986): 4–10.
81. _____, and Gabriel Salomon. "Teaching for Transfer." *Educational Leadership* 46 (September 1988): 22–32.
82. Peterson, Penelope, Elizabeth Fennema, and Thomas Carpenter. "Using Knowledge of How Students Think about Mathematics." *Educational Leadership* 46 (December 1988–January 1989): 42–46.
83. Politzer, Robert, and Mary McGroarty. "An Exploratory Study of Learning Behaviors and Their Relationship to Gains in Linguistic and Communicative Competence." *TESOL Quarterly* 19 (March 1985): 103–23.
84. Price, Gary E. "Which Learning Style Events Are Stable and Which Tend to Change?" *Learning Styles Network Newsletter* 1 (Autumn 1980).
85. Rivers, Wilga M. "Interaction as the Key to Teaching Language for Communication," pp. 3–16 in Wilga M. Rivers, ed., *Interactive Language Teaching.* Cambridge, MA: Cambridge Univ. Press, 1987.
86. _____. *Ten Principles of Interactive Language Learning and Teaching.* Baltimore: Johns Hopkins University, The National Foreign Language Center, 1989.
87. Rowe, M. B. "Wait-Time and Rewards as Instructional Variables, Their Influence on Language, Logic, and Fate Control." *Journal of Research in Science Teaching* 11 (1974): 81–94.
88. Scott, Mary E. "Learning Strategies Can Help." *Teaching Exceptional Children* 20 (Spring 1988): 30–33.
89. Seliger, Herbert W. "Does Practice Make Perfect?: A Study of Interaction Patterns and L2 Competence." *Language Learning* 27 (1977): 236–78.
90. Shrum, Judith L. "Wait Time and the Use of Target or Native Languages. *Foreign Language Annals* 18 (1985): 305–13.
91. Spolsky, Bernard. "Formulating a Theory of Second Language Learning." *Studies in Second Language Acquisition* 7 (1985): 269–88.

92. Stern, H. H. "What Can We Learn from the Good Language Learner?" *The Canadian Modern Language Review* 31 (1975): 304–18.

93. Stern, Mark J. "The Welfare of Families." *Educational Leadership* 44 (March 1987): 82–87.

94. Stevick, Earl W. *Memory, Meaning and Method: Some Psychological Perspectives on Language Learning.* Rowley, MA: Newbury, 1976.

95. Strong, Larry A. Opening editorial, *Educational Leadership* 46 (February 1989): 1.

96. Trosborg, Anna. "Stimulating Interaction in the Foreign Language Classroom through Conversation in Small Groups of Learners," pp. 177–90 in D. M. Singleton and D. G. Little, eds., *Language Learning in Formal and Informal Contexts.* Dublin, Ireland: Irish Association for Applied Linguistics, 1984.

97. Tucker, G. Richard, Else Hamayan, and Fred H. Genessee. "Affective, Cognitive and Social Factors in Second Language Acquisition." *The Canadian Modern Language Review* 32 (1976): 214–26.

98. Vygotsky, Lev S. *Mind in Society: The Development of Higher Psychological Processes.* Cambridge, MA: Harvard Univ. Press, 1978.

99. Walsh, Debbie. "Critical Thinking to Reduce Prejudice." *Social Education* 52 (1988): 280–82.

100. Weinstein, Claire E., D. Scott Ridley, Tove Dahl, and E. Sue Weber. "Helping Students Develop Strategies for Effective Learning." *Educational Leadership* 46 (December 1988–January 1989): 17–19.

101. Wenden, Anita. "Background and Utility," pp. 3–13 in Anita Wenden and Joan Rubin, eds., *Learner Strategies in Language Learning.* Englewood Cliffs, NJ: Prentice-Hall, 1987.

102. _____. "Incorporating Learner Training in the Classroom," pp. 159–68 in Anita Wenden and Joan Rubin, eds., *Learner Strategies in Language Learning.* Englewood Cliffs, NJ: Prentice-Hall, 1987.

103. _____. "A Curricular Framework for Promoting Learner Autonomy." *The Canadian Modern Language Review* 44 (May 1988): 639–52.

104. Whitehead, Alfred North. *The Aims of Education.* New York: The Free Press, 1920.

5

Reforming Foreign and Second Language Teacher Education

Gilbert A. Jarvis
Sheryl V. Taylor
The Ohio State University

Introduction

It was a half century ago that Freeman (18) premised his analysis of what constitutes a well-trained language teacher by asserting the importance of teacher education:

> More cogent and far-reaching than curricula or methods or even than content, the formation of the teacher is the key to the success of an educational program. A poor teacher will impart but little to his pupils in spite of the best possible program; while a superior teacher will transcend a poor subject or faulty organization, and with a method all his own, will compel the intellectual development of his pupils (p. 293).

Gilbert A. Jarvis (Ph.D., Purdue University) is Professor of Foreign and Second Language Education and Chair of the Department of Educational Studies: Humanities, Science, Technological and Vocational at The Ohio State University. He has edited several foreign language education publications, including volumes 5 through 8 of the ACTFL Foreign Language Education Series, and is a coauthor of many language textbooks. He has made more than a hundred presentations to language educators and has contributed to many major journals and volumes. He has served as a consultant to numerous agencies and institutions and recently has been particularly active in efforts to establish an agenda for teacher-education reform.

Sheryl V. Taylor (M.A., Colorado State University) is currently a doctoral candidate in Foreign Language Education at The Ohio State University. She has supervised student teachers, advised undergraduate language education majors, and given a methods course. She has taught at the elementary level in a bilingual-bicultural program and has taught English as a second language at the secondary and university levels. Her undergraduate degree is from Western Illinois University in Spanish and bilingual-bicultural education.

Today most of the general public and many educators would still feel comfortable with this view. It captures what seems to be a commonsense view of education. Its inadequacy for others is not in its being erroneous but in its failure to capture the complexity and greater precision with which we are now beginning to understand education and therefore teacher education.

Today multiple factors propel teacher education to special attention and to a special status:

> Teacher education is at a threshold. Never before has the profession received more attention than that of the past four years. . . .Teacher educators must respond by exerting vigorous leadership and envisioning the needs of teachers now being prepared to educate children in the twenty-first century (Quisenberry, 33, p. 246).

In addition to such assertions and the remarkable political attention directed toward teacher education, the most powerful factor that must ultimately transform teacher education and the quality of teachers in our schools is the changing knowledge base dealing with teaching. We have learned just enough about teaching and learning to recognize that we are on the brink of dramatic progress. A new conceptualization of teaching and how to become a teacher is emerging, and the next several years will undoubtedly see elaboration of this conceptualization. It is for this reason that this chapter will not rehearse many topics that have dominated the literature in recent years—topics such as language proficiency, competency tests, and legislative initiatives such as alternative certification. It will instead look to the future.

The future of foreign and second language teacher education is increasingly dependent on our connection with inquiry being done outside our field and on our ability to use that knowledge to conduct our own inquiry. Change will not come quickly, however. Lack of adequate funds, faculty who do not keep up with the changing knowledge base, strongly entrenched traditions, uninformed legislative decisions, and attitudes that reinforce past realities all assure that change will come slowly. The challenge in such a context will be to have sufficient patience and yet maintain momentum through multiple decades of what can become the most important educational reform effort in history.

Any analysis of foreign language teacher education and its potential reform must begin with an acknowledgment that thus far little new teacher-education knowledge is being generated in foreign language education. Teacher education for other subject areas could probably be similarly indicted. Most of the current research is being done by scholars who study teacher education in general. Thus, the perennial tension between generic teacher education and its realization in a specific field such as foreign language education is inevitably underscored. This dichotomy is strongly entrenched in tradition, and the current issues of reform vivify the need for defining an appropriate relationship among all participants and activities in teacher education.

Researchers in general teacher education do not represent the sum or synthesis of knowledge from the specific fields of teacher education. By and large, scholars in this field see their role as one of studying teacher education, rather than "doing" teacher education. Increasingly, the "doing" is the responsibility of specialists in the subject areas. During the past two decades, this slowly developing trend has led to many advantages, particularly in terms of student satisfaction with their teacher-education programs. The risk is, however, an absence of communication—and even familiarity—with those who conduct the inquiry in teacher education. That absence is readily apparent when one examines the citations in our own literature.

New knowledge, new roles for all participants in teacher education, these appear to be at one and the same time powerful slogans and realistic predications for the next decade. Foreign language teacher educators, the primary "doers" of our teacher education, must see their roles changing by the end of the century. Proposals for change already define major new roles for school faculty. They entail major revision of the teacher-education curriculum. They raise questions about relationships among domains of knowledge. Are procedures and models developed in mathematics education instructive in foreign and second language education? They force confrontation with major issues such as how the knowledge generated in generic teacher education becomes transformed so that it has an impact on the preparation of foreign language teachers. The intent of this chapter is to begin exploring such matters and the many issues imbedded in them.

The Context in Which We Work

Commission and panel reports have had significant impact on education during the 1980s. Most directly relevant to teacher education were the Holmes and Carnegie reports. The Holmes consortium was formed by deans of colleges of education at major research universities. Their widely quoted report, entitled *Tomorrow's Teachers,* has become the focal point for planning program revision in the 97 original member institutions (and 10 others added in early 1989). In short, the goals of the effort are to improve the education of teachers, both in academic content and teaching skills; to recognize differences in teachers' knowledge and skill; to create defensible standards for entry to the profession; to connect the teacher-education institutions with schools; and to make schools better places for teachers to work and learn. These goals, which are intended to—in a word—*professionalize* the teacher role, would involve moving certification to the postbaccalaureate level. Thus, in the heat of discussions about how best to structure teacher education, it must be remembered that postbaccalaureate programing is not an end in itself but a means to achieve fundamental restructuring of all of education.

The evolution of the Holmes Group principles became evident in early 1989 as evidenced by a Holmes Group update of activities:

> The Holmes Group does not advocate any particular program structure, nor does a particular change, such as elimination of the undergraduate degree, bespeak fealty to Holmes goals. Rather, the 1988 reports [from Holmes

institutions] suggest that the Holmes Group claim for more time to prepare a teacher is being staked out in the form of "integrated, extended" programs—usually five (or more) years in duration, including an internship that is both intensively supervised and formally reflected upon. In these programs, a prescribed, coherent course of education studies begins in the undergraduate years, alongside work in a liberal arts major (*Work in Progress,* 40, p. 7).

Thus, the cardinal principle of Holmes reform becomes one of increasing the available time in order to have greater impact on the prospective teacher. "In the twentieth century, professional education in all fields *except education* has been extended, partly in response to the rapid growth of knowledge underlying practice. The reform of teacher education, then, requires more of that most precious resource—time" (*Work in Progress,* 40, p. 6).

It is also interesting to note that it is these same Holmes institutions, the major research institutions, that prepare at the doctoral level a large number of teacher educators who work in small-college baccalaureate programs. Thus, in reducing their involvement with undergraduate programs, these institutions reduce their identity with the activity as well as their potential for providing practicum experiences for doctoral students. Their Holmes activity does not appear in this sense to be motivated by self-interest. It is predictable, however, that their directions are opposed by organizations representing colleges with large undergraduate programs.

In an example of one of the strongest reactions, King (25) has argued:

> The Holmes Reform Program is both dangerous and formidable. It is *dangerous* because it would injure and hamper rather than support and assist the public and private colleges now producing 80 percent of the teachers for the country. It is dangerous because it offers simplistic answers to many serious, complex questions faced by teacher-educating institutions. It is dangerous because it would place control of teacher education in the hands of the very universities that have shown the least support and concern for it during the past twenty-five years (p. 34).

Another major document, *A Nation Prepared* (Carnegie Forum, 10), the report of the Carnegie Task Force on Teaching as a Profession, was written in 1985 and 1986 by a group of professionals from education, business, journalism, public service, and science. The group had been charged to draw America's attention to the link between economic growth and the skills and abilities of the people who contribute to that growth, and to help develop education policies to meet the economic challenges ahead. The recommendations parallel those of the Holmes Group but in some ways are more specific. In their briefest form, the goals are to create a national board for teaching standards and to certify teachers who meet the standards, to create a professional environment for teachers, to create leadership roles and designations among teachers, to require a bachelor's degree in arts and sciences as a prerequisite to the study of teaching, to develop graduate

programs based on the systematic study of teaching, to attract minority youngsters into teaching and prepare them, to relate teacher incentives to student
performance, and to make teacher salaries competitive with those of other
professions.

Juxtaposed with these goals are sobering realities now so familiar that they can
be evoked by their labels alone: underpaid and besieged teachers; incoherent
curricula; dangerous schools; low standards; unsatisfactory student achievement,
particularly among the urban poor; impending shortages of teachers, especially
minority teachers; the spread of drugs in schools; increasing numbers of at-risk
students and dropout rates; and tremendous fiscal and social burdens placed on
schools. The challenge is unprecedented. Moreover, the past must not be an
indicator of the future. There has been "no fundamental reform in teacher
education during the past 50 years. . . . The improvements made—and there
have been some—have been gradual, slow, and in small and halting steps" (Bush,
9, p. 13).

At this point, progress depends upon moving beyond the rhetoric to action, to
where teachers are actually prepared. The appropriateness of the report goals
must be interpreted for language teachers as well as for teachers of other subject
areas. A review of teacher-education documentation at any institution reveals that
everyone wants foreign language teachers to be renaissance persons. They should
have consummate professional skills and a comprehensive understanding of the
foreign language teaching-learning process. They should be masters of the
content and skills that they teach. They should be splendid communicators whose
interpersonal skills evoke admiration in all who interact with them. As role
models for the students that they teach, they should be broadly informed about
all domains of human knowledge and have skills that lead them to remain current
in these domains. Their value systems, moreover, should be sophisticated and
lead to sensitivity in relating to others.

The rhetoric and the reality have not converged very frequently in language
education. It is now time to attend to the reality; continuing energy devoted to the
rhetorical ideals may be collective avoidance behavior of the formidable work that
lies ahead.

The Context within Language Education

The evolution in foreign language teacher education mirrors the development of
the knowledge base underlying language teaching. One can readily trace a slowly
increasing level of differentiation, detail, and sophistication over recent decades.
Pedagogical knowledge prior to the late 1960s or early 1970s was primarily craft
knowledge that was developed by practitioners who reflected upon their practice
and disseminated their interpretations. Near the mid-century, for example,
Freeman (18) exhorted foreign language teachers:

So we conclude that we need a generous dose of that same medicine which
we prescribe for our pupils—drill, repetition, and more drill. How many of

us practice reading French *aloud* at home, as a part of our daily preparation? . . . If we plan a dictation for class, we should read that passage aloud, at home twenty-five times, to perfect a clear distinct articulation as well as correct pronunciation. The best of it is that such drill requires no expensive apparatus, and it will bring surprising results (p. 298).

Already, in the mid-1950s, one can see greater specificity in, for example, the "Qualifications for Secondary School Teachers of Modern Foreign Languages" (32). Minimal, good, and superior levels of competence are defined in areas such as language skills and professional preparation. These statements were ultimately translated into classroom prescriptions in "Guidelines for Teacher Education Programs in Modern Foreign Languages" (20). The basis for the Guidelines, according to Paquette (30), who directed the study that generated them, was general belief.

In the mid-1960s classroom prescriptions were no less authoritarian than they had been earlier, but they were promulgated as reflecting the results of scientific inquiry.

Pronounce a whole sentence or full utterance four or five times, walking around the room so that all students can hear and see you easily. . . . Repeat the model sentence loudly, clearly, and at normal speed. Indicate by a gesture that the whole class is to repeat it, imitating as accurately as possible. This process should be repeated with full-choral response eight to ten times. The teacher should not repeat with the class (Modern Language Materials Center, 29).

Unfortunately, the scientific base was wrong.

By the early 1980s one can identify examples of considerably greater precision in our conceptualizations. Wing (39), for example, provides a model for classroom target language competence in which communicative language competencies are differentiated from cognitive/academic language competencies. In the late 1980s Phillips (31) provides a detailed analysis of current issues that range from methods courses to political action.

This gradually increasing ideational sophistication is paralleled by evolution in the personnel within teacher education. The backgrounds of teacher educators are now different from those of a few decades ago. As will be discussed later, many now have advanced degrees in language education and specific preparation for the field in which they work. A few decades ago, especially in small colleges, they were more likely to be professors of literature by preparation and teacher educators by avocation. In many institutions, much of teacher education was accomplished by generalist educators whose backgrounds usually included school experience in one subject (rarely a foreign language, it appears). This pattern persists in many smaller and medium-sized institutions.

In terms of generating a knowledge base specifically in foreign language education, we have primarily generated craft knowledge and proposed conceptualizations. Bernhardt and Hammadou (3) found only 78 articles dealing with foreign language teacher education in the decade from 1977 to 1987, only 8 of which reported the results of research. Their answer to the question of what comprises the research base in our field is "the perceptions of experienced foreign language educators" (p. 293). The major disadvantage of such a fact is the tendency for a literature of perceptions, assertions, and not a small amount of "show and tell" to have a high susceptibility to error. We have not had the benefit of the safeguards built into research to minimize the possibility of bias or error.

Thus, what we believe that we know about effective teacher education is codified in a literature of impressions, experiences retold, and extrapolations from research in generic teacher education. We may have acculturated ourselves into seeing this status as "normal," and we may thereby perpetuate it. In many ways, we have arrived at a state that can legitimately be labeled anti-intellectual. Clearly, we can envision alternative versions of our profession that could have been created or that can still be created.

Modern Conceptions of Teaching

This state of affairs in foreign and second language education must be reconciled with an evolving conceptualization of teaching as a complex intellectual activity. Teaching is increasingly understood as an activity in which the teacher's role is one of intense hour-after-hour immersion in a constant flux of thousands of factors requiring sound pedagogical reasoning and decision making. The constellation of concepts and skills necessary for the teacher is far more complex than any list of discrete competencies or any delineation of technical skills; moreover, it must at the same time be blended with a commitment to basic human values and the interests of the students. Metaphorically, one can imagine a teacher as controlling an enormous panel with a thousand fluctuating meters, oscillating gauges, flashing warning lights, each with several adjustments, and all interconnected so that a change in any one influences all the others.

The very definition of expertise is at issue. Scardamalia (34) and her colleagues in the Centre for Applied Cognitive Science at the Ontario Institute for Studies in Education have concluded from their work with teachers and students that inquiry at the limits of one's knowledge is where teachers must "live."

> There's a huge social-emotional factor in understanding that expertise is more a matter of working at the limits of your competence than it is spouting well-learned information. . . . [T]hese students get a sense of "Well, I don't understand that," but that's not at all a defeating notion any more. It's very much "So! I'm working at the limits of my competence. And that's where experts are forever moving, and that's how they gain new knowledge." We're letting these students know that that's a really good place to be. We all have our limits of understanding, and working at the edge of understanding is what very knowledgeable and expert people do. And that's an idea that's very powerful (p. 5).

Research supporting the dynamic complexity of teaching is represented by that of Berliner (2), who has demonstrated that expert teachers possess insight into the significance of carefully selected information. They know what to abstract from the flux as the critical attributes of the particular situation. What is pedagogically significant is separated from what is not. Experience takes on a very different function from that which is usually assumed: Teacher candidates do not, in a sense, learn *from* experiences, but learn *to* experience more fully, to conceptualize such that teaching is viewed differently.

Berliner also contrasts the relationship between semantic and procedural knowledge in teachers with that in other fields:

> Other fields seem to take greater pains to relate semantic knowledge to the procedural knowledge needed to perform on the job. For example, every medical doctor learns that concussion and pupil dilation are related; they also learn how to check for it. Every engineer learns about metal fatigue and stress, and learns how to check for it. Each of those engineers is capable of computing Ohm's law or deducing velocity and force, not merely knowing about them. Every dentist learns about plaque and gum disease and learns, also, how to check for it. The elementary, most basic, findings of a scientific field are not just known by the practitioner in those fields. The findings become part of his or her behavior repertoire (p. 7).

Although the rhetoric may have been different and now appears anachronistic, the foreign language education literature is replete with parallel references to "theory and practice" dichotomies.

Shulman (36), who has probably conducted the greatest quantity of research in this domain, has argued that the foundation for teacher-education reform is a conceptualization of teaching that emphasizes comprehension and reasoning, transformation, and reflection. His conceptualization does not accommodate well a distinction such as theory versus practice. "Technique" becomes much less important than why a teacher chooses to act in a particular way. Historically, discussions of teacher effectiveness have focused on the management of the classroom rather than the management of ideas. Shulman utilizes powerful case studies to vivify the conceptual frameworks, decision making, and versatility of successful teachers. His research approach, through several years of inquiry, has been to observe the development of teacher candidates

> from a state of expertise as learners through a novitiate as teachers. . . . The result is that error, success, and refinement—in a word, teacher-knowledge growth—are seen in high profile and in slow motion. The neophyte's stumble becomes the scholar's window. (p. 4)

While acknowledging that the current "blueprint" for the knowledge base of teaching has many cells with only the most rudimentary placeholders, "much like the chemist's periodic table of a century ago" (p. 12), Shulman has hypothesized a six-stage model of pedagogical reasoning: comprehension, transformation, instruction, evaluation, reflection, and new comprehensions.

Briefly described (and with a risk of distortion through brevity), *comprehension* involves more than understanding the subject matter. It involves an understanding of purposes and contexts. (Understanding a text, for example, may not be an end in itself but a vehicle for achieving other educational ends.) It may also involve understanding ideas outside the discipline.

Transformation may be the function that is most critical to educational success. It involves critical interpretation and analysis of ideas and texts, structuring and segmenting, development of a curricular repertoire, and clarification of purposes. It requires use of the teacher's repertoire of alternative ways of representing the content, which include analogies, metaphors, examples, demonstrations, and explanations. It further involves choices of modes of teaching, organizing, managing, and arranging as well as adaptation to student characteristics, which requires consideration of conceptions, preconceptions, misconceptions, difficulties, language, culture, motivations, social class, gender, age, ability, aptitude, interests, learning styles, strategies, self-concepts, and attention.

Instruction involves management, presentations, interactions, group work, discipline, humor, questioning, and other aspects of active teaching, discovery or inquiry instruction, and the observable forms of classroom teaching.

Evaluation entails checking for students' understanding during interactive teaching, testing student understanding at the end of segments of instruction, and evaluating and adjusting one's own performance.

Reflection involves reviewing, reconstructing, reenacting and critically analyzing one's own and the class's performance, and grounding explanations in evidence.

New comprehensions revisit the purposes, subject matter, students, teaching, and the self. They involve consolidations of new insights with previous experience.

Especially within the transformation stage, Shulman (35) places considerable significance on the concept of pedagogical content knowledge or subject-matter-specific pedagogical knowledge. It is "the particular form of content knowledge that embodies the aspects of content most germane to its teachability" (p. 9). It therefore includes the ways of representing and formulating the subject that make it comprehensible to others. "Since there are no single most powerful forms of representation, the teacher must have at hand a veritable armamentarium of alternative forms of representation, some of which derive from research whereas others originate in the wisdom of practice" (p. 9). Pedagogical content knowledge also must incorporate knowledge of the preconceptions (often misconceptions) that students of different ages and backgrounds bring to the situation. "The teacher not only understands the content to be learned and understands it deeply, but comprehends which aspects of the content are crucial for *future* understanding of the subject and which are more peripheral and are less likely to impede future learning if not fully grasped" (Shulman, 37, p. 37). Thus, Shulman's apt aphorism becomes: "Those who can, do. Those who understand, teach" (35, p. 14).

Pedagogical content knowledge must not be confused with knowledge of the subject matter. In light of today's understanding, knowledge of the subject matter could be viewed as a prerequisite to acquiring pedagogical content knowledge, though in the future it is clear that we shall come to understand more about the efficacy of various "knowledges of subject matter." What we now unitarily view as knowledge of the subject is merely one version—one selection and organization—of it. Other organizations of it are certainly possible, and some are likely more amenable to helping a learner come to comprehend and develop proficiency than others. Indeed, in an ideal world the content portion of the teacher-education curriculum would be organized in the manner that best facilitates or enhances the prospective teacher's pedagogical content knowledge.

Research in the domain of teacher effectiveness may be identifying the same phenomenon that has been here called pedagogical content knowledge. Although still plagued by definitional problems, research on what has been called "teacher clarity" has focused on operational characteristics of teacher behavior such as organization, making the organization of a presentation explicit to students, and use of questions and examples (Cruickshank and Kennedy, 13). Clarity has been shown to be related consistently to student achievement.

Research on the impact of teachers' content knowledge is just beginning to shed light on the important role of this knowledge. The U.S. General Accounting Office (19), for example, concluded that there is no evidence of a consistent relationship between the teacher's subject knowledge and student achievement. Blank (6), utilizing research by Hanushek (22) and Druva and Anderson (15), concluded that general measures of teacher knowledge of subject matter do not show a strong relationship to teaching effectiveness. Evertson, Hawley, and Zlotnik (16) conclude: "Knowing one's subject does not necessarily make one a good teacher of that subject" (p. 30). Berliner (2) concluded that "hopes that an increased level of subject matter competency on the part of the teachers will result in increased student achievement seem naive, except, of course, for the most advanced courses in an area" (p. 2).

Three observations must be made about these findings. First, good data have not been collected on foreign language teachers, and this issue may be one in which the characteristics of language teaching and learning come into play. Second, most of the studies incorporated what can be broadly defined as a correlational approach: Is more subject matter associated with more effectiveness or student learning? This approach may well be inappropriate because we may be dealing with a "threshold" phenomenon, rather than one of simple correlation. There may be a particular level of knowledge and skills below which it is difficult or impossible to be effective and above which one has the potential for effectiveness, rather than equal benefit from each additional unit of expertise that one possesses. Third, measures used in this type of inquiry are often not very precise. Possessing a bachelor's degree versus a master's degree is sometimes used to differentiate subject-matter knowledge; at other times, assumptions are made about greater language content in programs in colleges of arts and sciences than in colleges of education. In fact, in some institutions education degrees require more language content than do the counterpart degrees in arts and sciences.

Before asking what a reformed conceptualization of teaching in foreign language education might entail, or how one might effect a transformation of language-teacher education, it seems appropriate to review who is now doing the language-teacher education. Such questions entail implications for how change can occur. The existence, for example, of a body of scholars who contribute to and partake of an identifiable knowledge base would argue for an approach that is very different from that which is needed for a disparate collection of teacher educators who come from diverse backgrounds and who are substantially unconnected to each other.

What Do We Know about Foreign Language Teacher Educators?

Good demographic data describing those who are responsible for foreign language teacher education are not available. Across all fields, "teachers of teachers—what they are like, what they do, what they think—are typically overlooked in studies of teacher education. Even researchers are not exactly sure of who they are" (Lanier and Little, 26, p. 528). This description certainly applies to foreign language education. First, we have to acknowledge that in any institution many faculty are involved in teacher education (though the teacher-education faculty may range from only 1 or 2 to 200 in different institutions). The professor of Spanish literature, the professor of educational philosophy, and school administrators are in fact teacher educators, though in the same institution or the same small city they may never have met one another, and they may never have entertained a thought of themselves as teacher educators. If we restrict our definition to the faculty who have expertise and responsibility in foreign language teacher education, we still find diversity. In many institutions there is no such person; the prospective teacher may never interact with a person who has done advanced study or inquiry in foreign language teacher education. In others, the responsibility is delegated to a local teacher. In still others, it is a language-department faculty member who has interest in teacher education and who therefore takes responsibility. In many major research universities faculty members with doctorates in language education may have the responsibility, though much of the instruction may be delegated to graduate teaching assistants. Clearly, in whatever way that we define relevant expertise, all levels from zero to the best possible in light of current knowledge are represented in the United States in the late 1980s.

One historical factor that has to be considered in foreign language education is the very large number of teacher educators who entered the profession at an atypical time, the 1960s, when audiolingualism permeated the profession. Although the prescriptions and assumptions about teaching and learning of that era have since been rejected, the metalearning of these teacher educators is unknown. We do not know, for example, the consequences of having entered the profession when successful teaching was comfortably defined as knowing a litany of teaching prescriptions and during one's career having seen successful teaching evolve to something more like "developing comfort with the fluid nature of most knowledge" (Shulman et al., 38, p. 3).

A proposed set of guidelines for foreign language teacher education programs (ACTFL, 1) addresses the background of teacher educators. If adopted, these guidelines are intended to fill for NCATE the "learned society" guidelines for foreign language teacher-education programs. The draft guideline on faculty states:

> The faculty responsible for the foreign language education component of the candidate's professional development will:
> 1. be proficient in a foreign language;
> 2. have preparation and expertise in foreign language pedagogy;
> 3. have a record of excellence in language teaching;
> 4. maintain clear relationships with foreign language and education faculty and with school administrators and teachers. (p. 79)

The guidelines address some of the problems of past teacher education practices, such as the lack of any expertise related to foreign language education. It does not specify detailed expertise, and it accommodates many different administrative arrangements for teacher-education institutions. One might raise a question whether expertise in foreign language *teacher education* should be specified. Success as a language teacher and knowledge of pedagogy (even if broadly defined) does not entail knowledge of teacher-education. Such knowledge becomes even more important as the teacher-education knowledge base becomes more sophisticated.

New Roles for All Personnel

One of the major emphases in Holmesian reform is the strengthening of the practice component. Quite apart from the Holmes agenda, there seems widespread support of a goal

> to strengthen the practice dimension by bringing practitioners onto the education school faculty, creating authentic, dynamic field experiences interspersed and aligned with all of students' course work, so that the prospective teacher can engage in a dialectic between theory and practice. This effort requires collaboration with expert practitioners—finding representative but hospitable schools for placements, accomplished teachers to place them with, and more accomplished teachers to join the faculty as clinical professors (*Work in Progress*, 40, p. 24).

In addition to a better integration of procedural and semantic knowledge, such strengthening should favorably influence the nature of inquiry on teaching by bringing together university faculty and experienced teachers who can articulate their craft knowledge. Most new arrangements are also sensitive to the sociological aspects of induction to teaching. Instead of student teaching being an individual school experience connected only to a university supervisor and a cooperating teacher (a term that must be replaced by one implying more status and dignity), programs now involve more frequently the concept of cohorts of students who proceed together through a program and who are sometimes supervised by a team of professionals (*Work in Progress,* 40). One of the earliest Holmes-type programs in foreign languages, that at the University of Minnesota, does utilize the concept of cohorts (Mellgren et al., 27). Use of cohorts is an innocent-appearing arrangement that seems to enhance greatly the sense of community and the professional dialog in which the prospective teacher participates.

> Teacher education needs to develop teachers who know how to create a community of learners. To be able to create a community of learners, teacher candidates must first be a part of a community of learners. Students progressing though a teacher education program as a cohort is one way to contribute to this (Curriculum Committee, 14, p. 2).

Community implies a sense of collegiality that has not been characteristic of earlier teacher education. The participants must have equal status. "The traditional hierarchical relationships between university professors and K–12 classroom teachers must be eliminated" (Binko and Neubert, 5, p. 16). The traditional model in which universities and school districts established working agreements that permitted the universities to place student observers, student tutors, and student teachers in field settings seem to be increasingly supplemented by research and exchange models. In the research model, individual teachers and researchers work collaboratively in developing and carrying out research. There is considerable built-in professional development for the participants; however, it usually does not address the curriculum of learning to teach (Clift and Say, 11). In the exchange model, school-district personnel are granted clinical faculty status to work in the college or university teacher-education program. In its most interactive form this model seems synonymous with the Holmes concept of the professional development school.

Mentoring relationships have become an area of active inquiry. Zimpher and Rieger (41) have synthesized current knowledge about mentor arrangements. They review the many synonyms that reflect the various ways in which the role is conceptualized: coach, positive role model, developer of talent, opener of doors, protector, sponsor, successful leader, colleague teacher, helping teacher, peer teacher, and support teacher. What the role seems to demand is intense interaction—not of the sort where the more experienced person critiques and prescribes to the student but rather where together they inquire and reflect so that the mentor's experience and the student's fresh perspectives become resources on which they both draw.

Reforming Foreign Language Teacher Education

Are the general directions of teacher education compatible with the characteristics of language teaching? If not, what alternatives should be explored? Such questions are particularly important at a time of major reform and at a time when foreign language educators may be reaching a point of professional maturity that would justify their becoming masters of their own future.

Organization

One of the major dilemmas in contemporary foreign language teacher education has been the incompatible desires to provide meaningful field experience at the earliest possible time and the need for students to have good language proficiency in order to maximize the meaningfulness and overall quality of that field experience. One cannot overlook, moreover, the serious ethical problems that result from asking elementary and secondary school students to be the victims of a prospective teacher's language errors during an experience that is professionally helpful but linguistically premature. In the most extreme example, one can provide good arguments for first-year undergraduates having experienced in schools (especially in terms of its effect on their making wise career decisions), but in some cases these students at that point are scarcely beginning their own language study. This dilemma is especially acute in a subject matter like foreign languages because of the cumulative nature of language learning. The prospective history teacher who is asked to lead a discussion about the battle of Gettysburg can compensate for a lack of background by preparation the evening before; in vivid contrast, however, the prospective Spanish teacher in a similar situation cannot significantly overcome inaccurate pronunciation or halting fluency by preparation for tomorrow's class.

Arrangements such as postbaccalaureate professional preparation would seem to be a good match with foreign language teacher preparation. They permit "front-loading" the student's academic career with language study. Field experience would be delayed until the junior or senior years in integrated five- or six-year programs or until the fifth year in "add-on" programs. A new problem inheres, however, in this latter arrangement. It is the problem of reconciling the developmental nature of professional learning with the telescoped time that such arrangements provide. In the most extreme example, a single-year add-on program, the need to understand teaching in its full complexity within one year's time seems inconceivable to most serious scholars in teacher education. Each cycle of experience leads to greater understanding of the experience. The complexity is itself an argument for more time. The interaction between semantic knowledge and procedural knowledge requires time if it is to be consolidated. Teacher education does not exist, however, in an apolitical world where the only quest is for doing it better. It exists in an environment with teacher shortages and firmly held beliefs that anyone can teach, even without professional preparation.

The consequences of reduced time in professional preparation compound themselves: They do not simply result in a less thorough understanding, a less well prepared teacher. Reduction of the time becomes a *de facto* reduction in the conceptualization of teaching to a listing of concepts, procedures, techniques, or prescriptions. The teacher's understanding of his or her own profession becomes erroneous; it resembles the layperson's simplistic sense of education. (This same misunderstanding has unfortunately been fostered in foreign language education by the linking of teaching-assistant training to teacher education as if they should be two versions of the same process. The result, particulary when juxtaposed with a vision of tomorrow's professional teacher, is a reduction of the teacher's role and professionalism.)

Organizationally, the best arrangement in terms of use of time in language teacher education would seem to be an accommodation of both the need to front-load language and the need to provide adequate time for developmental understanding of teaching. This accommodation occurs in postbaccalaureate certification where initial work in education (either as a minor area in the baccalaureate program or as part of an integrated program where education and content extend throughout five or six years) begins about the junior year. In undergraduate programs (nominally, four years in duration but rarely so at most institutions) the sequence may well require intensifying the language study in the first two years so that as much as two-thirds of the major is accomplished during this time. Strong secondary school language programs also enhance this potential. Inevitably, other baccalaureate study—such as general education requirements—would be slightly decreased early and slightly increased in the last two years. Education field experience and associated coursework would begin by the beginning of the junior year. (Field experience that is primarily designed to foster career evaluation could occur earlier.)

On-campus laboratory settings offer another alternative for providing very early study of the teaching-learning process. Technology is beginning to offer considerable potential to create controlled and secure confrontations with dimensions of teaching without the risks of exposing school students to poor language proficiency and without the risks of overwhelming the teacher candidate with the complexity of the real classroom. Progress has been slow, however, in integrating technology into existing programs (Bruder, 8).

Relevant Knowledge Bases

Cost effectiveness and high-quality education have not been easily reconciled in teacher education. The practical problem of sorting what part of the professional knowledge base can be taught in a generic way across all disciplines from what is specific to each discipline has never been addressed in a systematic way. Almost invariably, only what was understood as fitting under a rubric of "special methods" was viewed as specific to the discipline, and occasionally, supervision of practicum experiences incorporated discipline-specific knowledge.

One of the important variables that must be taken into account in attempting to identify wisely the domains of knowledge is the user of the knowledge. A person with a sophisticated background in a domain can handle content that is far more abstract than can a neophyte in the domain. Such a person can benefit from instruction that addresses broad issues that relate to multiple disciplines and can see their realizations in his or her classroom. A simple principle about variety in students' encounters with language forms or patterns may have a wealth of meaning for the well-prepared, experienced teacher but will be virtually devoid of meaning for the teacher candidate. Without specialized applications and experience, the concept of variety has little meaning in that future teacher's cognitive structure beyond its lay sense or its apparent meaning inferred from the future teacher's own 15,000 hours of school experience as a student. Thus, much of what could become generic knowledge at an advanced level must be treated as special knowledge and concretized for the preservice teacher candidate. The "error" that we seem to have so often made is to raise specific knowledge to a higher level of abstraction in order to save resources by eliminating the need for foreign language teachers to be instructed alone.

A realistic view would seem to argue that there appears to be (1) some knowledge that all teachers should know, (2) some that is relevant to certain fields, (3) some that is relevant to one field but that has implications for one or more others, and (4) some that is important for only one. We would make a giant step forward if we were to begin designing programs by thoughtfully matching knowledge to such a scheme of categories. Surely, all teachers, for example, should have an understanding of legal matters that have impact on schools and on their roles as teachers. They need to understand the role of schools in today's society and how curricula are determined. Unfortunately, they even need to know how to deal with a student who comes to school armed with a weapon. Teachers whose fields involve laboratories where equipment is used must know about safety and health issues. Those in fields such as first languages, foreign languages, and speech need to know a great deal about the communication process. Thus, the knowledge needed by all teachers and the knowledge for confederations of disciplines that share affinities do not appear difficult to delineate. It is the other two categories that are more challenging.

Importance in one subject area with implications for another usually leads to the generation of research questions in the second area rather than clear guidance for teacher-education curricula. For example, science educators have long been concerned with the counterintuitive nature of science. The science teacher must convince students that what appears as if it cannot possibly be true is indeed true. The desks in front of them are not solid but are composed of tiny particles with space between them. A star that shines brightly in the nighttime sky may have burned out thousands of years ago (Howe, 23). A body of literature dealing with counterintuition in science may have implications for the foreign language teacher. Foreign language student reactions to newly encountered alphabets, syntax, and cultural patterns appear very similar: "How could they say it that way? It's so weird." Such a reaction is probably akin to the child's first reaction to a round rather than flat earth. The knowledge base in science education should at least help us to generate hypotheses to test if not to provide guidance for instruction.

Pedagogical subject-matter knowledge for the neophyte foreign language teacher appears considerably more substantial than its traditional role in the curriculum would indicate. Greater concern is evident for the interactions between what is being taught and how it is best taught. The argument is not that foreign language education is different from all other areas; rather, each area is unique. The meaning and the role of an educational concept like practice will be different in each area, as will the more (or less) desirable ways to make it occur. Knowledge of the role of practice in mathematics teaching may not be instructive to the foreign language educator, nor will generic knowledge about practice help the neophyte who cannot translate that knowledge into applications. A principle such as moving from simple to complex makes eminent sense in the abstract, but applying it wisely in instruction requires enormous pedagogical content knowledge. Indeed, what was complex at 10:00 A.M. in a particular class may be simple at 10:30, and what was simple at 10:00 may have become complex because of the interaction of new subject-matter structures.

At a relatively specific level, one could easily overwhelm the point with examples, for nearly every decision that a teacher makes is intimately connected with knowledge that appears to be best developed in the teacher in a subject-matter-specific way. At a somewhat broader level, there are powerful factors that impinge only upon foreign language teachers. Bernhardt and Hammadou (4) have delineated several of these factors:

1. The foreign language teacher works in a situation whereby the means of instruction is also the subject of instruction (p. 301).
2. The traditional classroom interactions between teacher and students that are acceptable and normal for the science or the music teacher are too limiting for the foreign language teacher . . . since conversation is a process of negotiation whereby conversational partners have fairly equal status and opportunity to interact (p. 301).
3. Teachers in other subject areas have the luxury of going to museums and libraries, watching television specials, and so forth to gain new knowledge. [Foreign language teachers] do not have spoken foreign language resources readily available. . . . Furthermore, since language is developmental, dynamic, and interactive, maintaining subject matter knowledge is extremely difficult (p. 302).
4. A foreign language teacher is charged with the awesome task of providing a unique environment for learning to occur . . . in as natural a setting as possible (p. 302).

Each of these factors is a powerful force shaping pedagogical content knowledge for the language teacher.

The pedagogical content knowledge literature consistently emphasizes teacher skill in using demonstrations, analogies, metaphors, paraphrases, examples, and effective explanations. These items link directly to ideational content being taught. Because of the process nature of language education where the means of instruction is the subject of instruction, one must ask what the process analogues of these ideational mechanisms might be. What, for example, is the analogue in the foreign language classroom to what has been called in other subject areas "demonstration?" Or should we assume that pedagogical content knowledge is so different in our area that we should not seek such analogues? That would be an extreme view. A reasonable view would suggest that the existing definition of pedagogical content knowledge provides a wise point of departure. We know that there is a factor that has not yet been adequately described that permits reliable identification of effective teaching; skilled use of pedagogical content knowledge could be that factor. Observers of a large number of teachers are highly reliable in differentiating those whom they call effective from those they see as ineffective. Explanations about the bases for the differentiation, however, resemble lay explanations: "The teacher was 'energetic,' 'enthusiastic,' 'caring,' etc." We must conjecture at this point about what creates the holistic impression of effectiveness in some teachers. It is plausible to conjecture that behaviors that conform well to the pedagogical content knowledge construct may be involved. An effective "demonstration," for example, of a new language form (e.g., a new word, pattern, or function) will involve wise choices about when it is introduced; its relationship to what the students know already; the kinds of application that can be made of it at that time; its connection to the other language and the contexts in which it can be used; how vivid its meaning will be in the uses that can be made initially; how much "connectedness" it has to realia, visualizations, cultural phenomena, and students' lives; how inherently complex it is (how many moving parts it has); etc.

One striking conclusion that such conjecture must lead to is the inextricable link between reforming teacher education and a very extensive research agenda. We seem to have arrived at the brink of new insights, but considerable research is going to be necessary to move into significantly different teacher-preparation behavior. This statement is not, however, the perennial exhortation for research so that *then* we shall know better how to prepare teachers. It is instead an assertion that teacher-education and research activity must be commingled at all times. Teacher education must be the vehicle for research, and research must be synonymous with teacher education. They are not separate activities. They are rather a collaborative inquiry by several individuals who are at different points on the career-long path of professional development. Thus, radically different roles are required. In foreign and second language education, how prepared are we for these roles?

Personnel in Reformed Teacher Education

One of the most disconcerting aspects of reforming a large and complex enterprise like teacher education is the enormous compounded inertia that must be overcome. The considerable impact of school personnel compared to that of university personnel upon prospective teachers is well documented. Thus, change in the next generation of teachers is dependent upon change in today's school personnel—and teacher educators in higher education have little direct influence on them. Teacher educators have been relatively impotent in evoking such change. Thus, questions can be raised about the aegis for change.

The nature of the school foreign language teacher population is not better known than that of the teacher educators in higher education. In the few published efforts to describe this population most samples have, by and large, been biased, and they have focused on varying characteristics of the population.

In 1982, for example, Brickel and Paul (7) surveyed the opinions of teachers about their preparation, professional growth, and workloads. Approximately half of the teachers had studied abroad while in college. Their foreign language curricula were typically apportioned to 45 percent literature, 35 percent language and linguistics, and 15 percent culture and civilization. They expressed concern about the periodically recurring phenomenon of states certifying liberal arts graduates without professional training. It is clear that the sample was not representative of the profession. They report, for example, that 20 percent of teachers attended national foreign language conferences, and approximately half attended state or regional meetings annually. The actual attendance at such meetings does not reflect this reported level of participation.

FitzPatrick and Liuzzo (17) described characteristics and career satisfaction of a sample of members of the American Council on the Teaching of Foreign Languages. Although they express confidence that "the responses were representative of the foreign language teaching profession" (p. 61), all but 7 of the 412 respondents were members of ACTFL, 40 percent were employed at postsecondary institutions, and respondents were self-selected. Thus, no claim can be made beyond members of ACTFL who elect to respond to questionnaires published in *Foreign Language Annals*. The sample, three-quarters female and one-quarter male, was highly experienced. More than three-quarters had more than ten years of experience, and 40 percent of the survey participants had at least twenty years of experience. Yet 71 percent indicated that it was not likely that they would leave the profession within five years. More than 80 percent indicated satisfaction with their careers. French, Spanish, and German accounted for more than 90 percent of the language distribution (43 percent in French and 35 percent in Spanish). A full 45 percent taught two or more languages.

In an effort to provide another perspective on the characteristics of school foreign language teachers, the entire population of foreign language teachers in the state of Ohio was examined (Jarvis and Taylor, 24). Data available was limited to variables included in Ohio Department of Education statistics. Ohio does not, of course, represent a random sample of all United States foreign language teachers. It does, however, include a broad range of school-related variables (urban, suburban, rural districts; schools of varying sizes; etc.), and many areas of Ohio are often used as test markets because of their representativeness nationally. The reader must therefore judge the applicability of these data to any other context.

Demographically, the 2696 Ohio teachers were 78.4 percent female and 21.6 percent male. Minorities composed just under 8 percent of the population with approximately equal distribution across blacks, Spanish-Americans, and native Americans. (Nationally, 11 percent of all teachers are black or Hispanic [Metropolitan Life, 27].) The mean age of Ohio teachers is 42.5, but the mean number of years of experience is only 12.4. (The oldest active teacher is 82.) A full 40 percent of the teachers work in more than one certification area; of these multiarea teachers, 70 percent of them teach a subject other than a language. Nearly 8 percent teach in three or more subject areas. Note that a teacher may additionally have multiple preparations within each subject area. Highest-degree information was not available for a large portion of the sample, and thus one must be very cautious with interpretations. It is nevertheless surprising to note that, among teachers for whom degree information was provided, 21 percent were designated as not holding a degree.

If the density of foreign language teachers in the total population of the state of Ohio is reflective of the density of foreign language teachers in the total United States population, the estimated school foreign language teacher population in the country is 60,500.

These data tell relatively little about language teachers. They do reinforce in concrete terms the magnitude of any reform task. The sheer numbers are intimidating, and one must remember that these numbers are spread across a vast nation—with as few as one teacher in some communities to many hundreds in large cities. It is clear that they are—as they have always been—very busy people.

One might ask whether teacher education should become the sole province of the schools without the involvement of higher education. The school data do not argue for doing so; school personnel are already overburdened, and there is no evidence of capacity to take on such a task. Particularly at this moment in history, such a decision would seem inconsistent with the new directions and future that we can now envision for teacher education. University and college personnel must continue to have a role in teacher education, especially because the largest pool of personnel who possess advanced inquiry skills is in higher education. As indicated earlier, their current roles, however, must change. Such change requires resolution of some fundamental tensions and solutions to existing problems. The genuinely collaborative partnership that is required in the new directions for teacher education draws attention to one of the major dilemmas that university teacher-education faculty face: Are they academic or professional? The university culture demands, on the one hand, a high level of productivity in what amounts to a relatively narrow type of scholarly activity. It is, moreover, activity that requires enormous time commitments. The collaborative inquiry, on the other hand, often leads to scholarship that appears unconventional to the academic community and that is itself tremendously labor-intensive. Ethnographic inquiry, for example, does not even appear to be scholarship to researchers in science, engineering, medicine, or psychology. The tension is a broader version of the tension sometimes experienced by teacher educators in language departments where research traditions are strictly literary. Many teacher educators have also weakened their status by arguing that service activities such as teacher workshops and how-to articles should count as research. The new types of research risk being seen as service activity and therefore dismissed.

The difference in levels of prestige and status that are accorded by society in general to the future participants in the teacher-education process is also an issue in school–higher education collaboration. Higher-education faculty usually hold doctorates and have been enculturated into a set of expectations that ascribe to them a learned status. Unfortunately, in this late twentieth century, school personnel are usually not viewed in this way, and they differentiate themselves from academics, frequently asserting that they have "practical" knowledge. Practicality, however, is rarely associated with high status.

A third issue related to personnel is cost. Reformed teacher education incorporating continuing dialog about the educational phenomena that the participants experience is inevitably expensive. It cannot be intellectually intensive without being labor-intensive. It cannot be labor-intensive without being more costly. Clearly, that fact entails a host of funding issues, both in schools and in higher education.

Conclusion

The reform that is just beginning in teacher education is far more important and more fundamental than any experienced previously in any current teacher educator's career. It is likely that the one opportunity for significant reform during this generation is before us. Foreign language education can be on the leading edge of the change. The history of language education shows a slow evolution toward what most would consider growing sophistication. Current reform efforts seem solidly compatible with the nature of language education.

The issues that must be analyzed and confronted are really twofold. They involve, on the one hand, the generation of new knowledge and, on the other hand, finding ways of utilizing that knowledge in reformed teacher education. The new teacher education emphasizes teacher cognitive processes as the heart of successful teaching. Such an approach is radically different from conceptualizations such as identification and development of teacher competencies or the development of a repertoire of teaching behaviors. It is radically different from the "Sit-next-to-Nellie" apprenticeship approach (Haberman, 21) that seems to have been transported to education from training in fields as unrelated as the textile industry a century ago.

Although much is unclear, tomorrow's teacher education will likely, in a phrase, resemble today's reflective teaching (Cruickshank, 12) carried to the ultimate. Thus, activities involved in teacher education are going to be more individualized. Educational phenomena will not be able to be decontextualized as we have so often done in the past. The prospective teacher will spend considerable time coming to understand the educational phenomena in which he or she is immersed and in which he or she is at the same time an important variable. The understanding will grow incrementally through such teacher-education experiences. Certainly, some teacher education will involve large-group instruction. Much, however, will be characterized by dialog about what has been observed, what has been experienced, and "what could have been."

How will we develop the needed mentoring skills in these teacher educators—those collaborators who are farther along the career-long continuum of professional development? The issue is fundamentally one of developing analytical and communicative skills. These are skills that are developed by practice. Thus, the opportunity to practice must be created.

In the future, sessions at national, regional, and local conferences would seem better spent by conversation about a videotape of a language classroom than in hearing a paper about someone's analysis of instruction or certainly than in hearing about yet another administrative organization of a program. Even within a single institution, discussion among colleagues, especially about concrete representations of teaching, would seem a ready contributor to one's insight. Professional-development seminars have never before seemed to have a more fitting application.

In many different ways, technology can have an impact on tomorrow's teacher education. Assuredly, two of the crucial needs will be accessible and accurate renditions of teachers and learners in action as well as communication links. Increasingly sophisticated videotaping capacity is readily available. Cameras have become more portable and produce better images and sound than ever before. Computers not only connect participants via electronic mail but can store data about the process in unobtrusive ways. Data banks of teaching solutions, alternative arrangements of content, and results of new research can be readily accessible to all participants in teacher education.

Research of many different types is needed. Substantively, the type of research being done by Shulman at Stanford must be done in foreign and second language education. Many advantages—both in terms of the knowledge generated and the benefits for our profession—would result. One of the ways in which language education is unlike other areas is the vivid way in which one can see learning in process. Much curricular content in social studies, biology, physics, physical education, and many other areas is learned outside of schools. This learning is confounded with that which occurs in the classroom. Foreign language proficiency, however, is a function of what occurs in the instructional setting; it is usually not a function of television, family activities, or other "living." Thus, the window on classroom learning presents very vivid images.

Methodologically, we must acknowledge the need for pluralistic approaches to knowledge generation. Qualitative approaches, including ethnography, must have equal status with quantitative methods, and the two must be integrated to address the complex issues of teaching and learning. The sharing of data among researchers must be facilitated. Traditional journal publications are no longer sufficient. Even computer-network bulletin boards for the dissemination of results and a complete record available of all other scholars who choose to comment on the research would be a major step in today's technological world.

The massiveness of the issues must not intimidate us, and patience must not elude us. Skilled elementary and secondary school language teachers who have thorough control of the knowledge available are within the realm of the possible. No insurmountable barrier exists.

References, Reforming Foreign and Second Language Teacher Education

1. "ACTFL Provisional Program Guidelines for Foreign Language Teacher Education." *Foreign Language Annals* 21 (1988): 71–82.
2. Berliner, David C. "Laboratory Settings and the Study of Teacher Education." *Journal of Teacher Education* 36, 6 (1985): 2–8.
3. Bernhardt, Elizabeth, and JoAnn Hammadou. "A Decade of Research in Foreign Language Teacher Education." *Modern Language Journal* 71 (1987): 289–99.

4. _____. "On Being and Becoming a Foreign Language Teacher." *Theory into Practice* 26 (1987): 301-6.

5. Binko, James B., and Gloria A. Neubert. "An Inservice Education Model: Teachers and Professors as Coequals." *Journal of Teacher Education* 35, 6 (1984): 15-17.

6. Blank, Rolf K. "Improving Research on Teacher Quality in Science and Mathematics: Report of a Symposium of Scientists, Educators and Researchers." *Journal of Research in Science Teaching* 25 (1988): 217-24.

7. Brickel, Henry M., and Regina H. Paul. "Ready for the '80s? A Look at Foreign Language Teachers and Teaching at the Start of the Decade." *Foreign Language Annals* 15 (1982): 169-87.

8. Bruder, Isabelle. "Future Teachers: Are They Prepared?" *Electronic Learning* 8, 4 (1989): 32-39.

9. Bush, Robert N. "Teacher Education Reform: Lessons from the Past Half Century." *The Journal of Teacher Education* 38, 3 (1987): 13-18.

10. Carnegie Forum on Education and the Economy. *A Nation Prepared: Teachers for the Twenty-First Century.* New York: Carnegie Forum, 1986.

11. Clift, Renee T., and Michael Say. "Teacher Education: Collaboration or Conflict?" *Journal of Teacher Education* 39, 3 (1988): 2-7.

12. Cruickshank, Donald R. *Reflective Thinking, Reflective Teaching: The Preparation of Students of Teaching.* Reston, VA: Association of Teacher Educators, 1987.

13. _____, and John J. Kennedy. "Teacher Clarity." *Teaching and Teacher Education* 2, 1 (1986): 43-67.

14. "Curriculum Committee's Beliefs about Schooling Generate Principles for Teacher Ed Curriculum." *The Holmes Group Form* 3, 2 (1989): 1-2.

15. Druva, Cynthia Ann, and Ronald D. Anderson. "Science Teacher Characteristics by Teacher Behavior and Student Outcome: A Meta-Analysis of Research." *Journal of Research in Science Teaching* 20 (1983): 467-79.

16. Evertson, C., W. Hawley, and M. Zlotnik. *The Characteristics of Effective Teacher Preparation Programs: A Review of Research.* Nashville, TN: Peabody College, Vanderbilt University, 1984.

17. FitzPatrick, Richard C., and Anthony L. Liuzzo. "Demographics and Assessments of Career Satisfaction of Foreign Language Teaching Professionals." *Foreign Language Annals* 22 (1989): 61-66.

18. Freeman, Stephen A. "What Constitutes a Well-Trained Modern Language Teacher?" *Modern Language Journal* 25 (1941): 293-305.

19. General Accounting Office. *New Directions for Federal Programs to Aid Mathematics and Science Teaching.* Washington, DC: General Accounting Office, 1984.

20. "Guidelines for Teacher Education Programs in Modern Foreign Languages." *Modern Language Journal* 50 (1966): 20-22.

21. Haberman, Martin. "Teacher Education." Lecture at The Ohio State University, Spring 1988.

22. Hanushek, Eric A. "Throwing Money at Schools." *Journal of Policy Analysis and Management* 1, 1 (1981): 19-41.

23. Howe, Ann C. "Current Issues in Science Teacher Education." *The Clearing House* 61, 7 (1988): 309-11.

24. Jarvis, Gilbert A., and Sheryl V. Taylor. "Selected Demographics of Ohio Foreign Language Teachers." Columbus, OH: Department of Educational Studies, The Ohio State University, 1989. [unpublished manuscript]

25. King, John E. "Should We Abolish the Bachelors Degree in Education: Absolutely Not." *Change* 18, 5 (1986): 31-36.

26. Lanier, Judith E., and Judith W. Little. "Research on Teacher Education," pp. 527-69 in Merlin C. Wittrock, ed., *Handbook of Research on Teaching.* 3rd ed. New York: Collier-Macmillan, 1986.

27. Mellgren, Millie Park, Constance L. Walker, and Dale L. Lange. "The Preparation of Second Language Teachers through Post-Baccalaureate Education." *Foreign Language Annals* 21 (1988): 121–30.

28. "Metropolitan Life Survey of the American Teacher 1988, The." New York: Louis Harris and Associates, 1988.

29. Modern Language Materials Development Center. *Teachers Manual: A-LM French.* Level 1. New York: Harcourt, 1961.

30. Paquette, F. André "Modern Foreign Language Teacher Preparation: A Quarter Century of Growth." *Modern Language Journal* 50 (1966): 7–20.

31. Phillips, June K. "Teacher Education: Target of Reform," pp. 11–40 in Helen S. Lepke, ed. *Shaping the Future: Challenges and Opportunities.* Report of the Northeast Conference on the Teaching of Foreign Languages. Middlebury, VT: The Northeast Conference, 1989.

32. "Qualifications for Secondary School Teachers of Modern Foreign Languages." *The Bulletin of the National Association of Secondary School Principals* 39 (1955): 30–33.

33. Quisenberry, Nancy L. "Teacher Education: Challenge for the Future." *Childhood Education* 63 (1987): 243–46.

34. Scardamalia, Marlene. "Cognition Research Drives Development of Collaborative, Intentional, Computer-Linked Learning." *The Holmes Group Forum* 3, 1 (1988): 5–7.

35. Shulman, Lee S. "Those Who Understand: Knowledge Growth in Teaching." *Educational Researcher* 15, 3 (1986): 4–14.

36. _____. "Knowledge and Teaching: Foundations of the New Reform." *Harvard Educational Review* 57 (1987): 1–22.

37. _____. "A Union of Insufficiencies: Strategies for Teacher Assessment in a Period of Educational Reform." *Educational Leadership* 46 (1988): 36–39.

38. _____, et al. "First Seminar on 'Tomorrow's Schools' Rejects Traditional Precepts for Learning." *The Holmes Group Forum* 3, 1 (1988): 1–4.

39. Wing, Barbara H. "For Teachers: A Challenge of Competence," pp. 11–45 in Gilbert A. Jarvis, ed. *The Challenge for Excellence in Foreign Language Education.* Report of the Northeast Conference on the Teaching of Foreign Languages. Middlebury, VT: The Northeast Conference, 1984.

40. *Work in Progress: The Holmes Group One Year On.* Unpublished manuscript distributed at The Holmes Group Meeting, Atlanta, January 1989.

41. Zimpher, Nancy L., and Susan R. Rieger. "Mentoring Teachers: What Are the Issues?" *Theory into Practice* 27 (1988): 175–82.

Index to Authors Cited

Index to Major Topics Cited

NTC PROFESSIONAL MATERIALS

ACTFL Review

Published annually in conjunction with the American Council on the Teaching of Foreign Languages

NEW PERSPECTIVES, NEW DIRECTIONS IN FOREIGN LANGUAGE EDUCATION, ed. Birckbichler, Vol. 20 (1990)

MODERN TECHNOLOGY IN FOREIGN LANGUAGE EDUCATION: APPLICATIONS AND PROJECTS, ed. Smith, Vol. 19 (1989)

MODERN MEDIA IN FOREIGN LANGUAGE EDUCATION: THEORY AND IMPLEMENTATION, ed. Smith, Vol. 18 (1987)

DEFINING AND DEVELOPING PROFICIENCY: GUIDELINES, IMPLEMENTATIONS, AND CONCEPTS, ed. Byrnes, Vol. 17 (1986)

FOREIGN LANGUAGE PROFICIENCY IN THE CLASSROOM AND BEYOND, ed. James, Vol. 16 (1984)

TEACHING FOR PROFICIENCY, THE ORGANIZING PRINCIPLE, ed. Higgs, Vol. 15 (1983)

PRACTICAL APPLICATIONS OF RESEARCH IN FOREIGN LANGUAGE TEACHING, ed. James, Vol. 14 (1982)

CURRICULUM, COMPETENCE, AND THE FOREIGN LANGUAGE TEACHER, ed. Higgs, Vol. 13 (1981)

ACTION FOR THE '80s: A POLITICAL, PROFESSIONAL, AND PUBLIC PROGRAM FOR FOREIGN LANGUAGE EDUCATION, ed. Phillips, Vol. 12 (1980)

THE NEW IMPERATIVE: EXPANDING THE HORIZONS OF FOREIGN LANGUAGE EDUCATION, ed. Phillips, Vol. 11 (1979)

BUILDING ON EXPERIENCE—BUILDING FOR SUCCESS, ed. Phillips, Vol. 10 (1978)

THE LANGUAGE CONNECTION: FROM THE CLASSROOM TO THE WORLD, ed. Phillips, Vol. 9 (1977)

AN INTEGRATIVE APPROACH TO FOREIGN LANGUAGE TEACHING: CHOOSING AMONG THE OPTIONS, eds. Jarvis and Omaggio, Vol. 8 (1976)

PERSPECTIVE: A NEW FREEDOM, ed. Jarvis, Vol. 7 (1975)

THE CHALLENGE OF COMMUNICATION, ed. Jarvis, Vol. 6 (1974)

FOREIGN LANGUAGE EDUCATION: A REAPPRAISAL, eds. Lange and James, Vol. 4 (1972)

Professional Resources

A TESOL PROFESSIONAL ANTHOLOGY: CULTURE

A TESOL PROFESSIONAL ANTHOLOGY: GRAMMAR AND COMPOSITION

A TESOL PROFESSIONAL ANTHOLOGY: LISTENING, SPEAKING, AND READING

THE COMPLETE ESL/EFL RESOURCE BOOK, Scheraga

ABC'S OF LANGUAGES AND LINGUISTICS, Hayes, et al.

AWARD-WINNING FOREIGN LANGUAGE PROGRAMS: PRESCRIPTIONS FOR SUCCESS, Sims and Hamm

PUZZLES AND GAMES IN LANGUAGE TEACHING, Danesi

COMPLETE GUIDE TO EXPLORATORY FOREIGN LANGUAGE PROGRAMS, Kennedy and DeLorenzo

INDIVIDUALIZED FOREIGN LANGUAGE INSTRUCTION, Grittner and LaLeike

LIVING IN LATIN AMERICA: A CASE STUDY IN CROSS-CULTURAL COMMUNICATION, Gorden

ORAL COMMUNICATION TESTING, Linder

PRACTICAL HANDBOOK TO ELEMENTARY FOREIGN LANGUAGE PROGRAMS, Lipton

SPEAK WITH A PURPOSE! Urzua, et al.

TEACHING CULTURE: STRATEGIES FOR INTERCULTURAL COMMUNICATION, Seelye

TEACHING FRENCH: A PRACTICE GUIDE, Rivers

TEACHING GERMAN: A PRACTICAL GUIDE, Rivers, et al.

TEACHING SPANISH: A PRACTICAL GUIDE, Rivers, et al.

TRANSCRIPTION AND TRANSLITERATION, Wellisch

YES! YOU CAN LEARN A FOREIGN LANGUAGE, Goldin, et al.

For further information or a current catalog, write:
National Textbook Company
a division of *NTC Publishing Group*
4255 West Touhy Avenue
Lincolnwood, Illinois 60646-1975 U.S.A.